CW00472710

JEWEL
INTERNATIONAL ANNUAL OF CONTEMPORARY JEWEL ART
BOOK
12|13

GLOBAL TACTILE PIECES II TOKYO AMSTERDAM ERENHOT
NECKLACE MADE FROM CERAMIC SCULPTURE, CUT INTO SLICES, GOLD

TED NOTEN THE NETHERLANDS

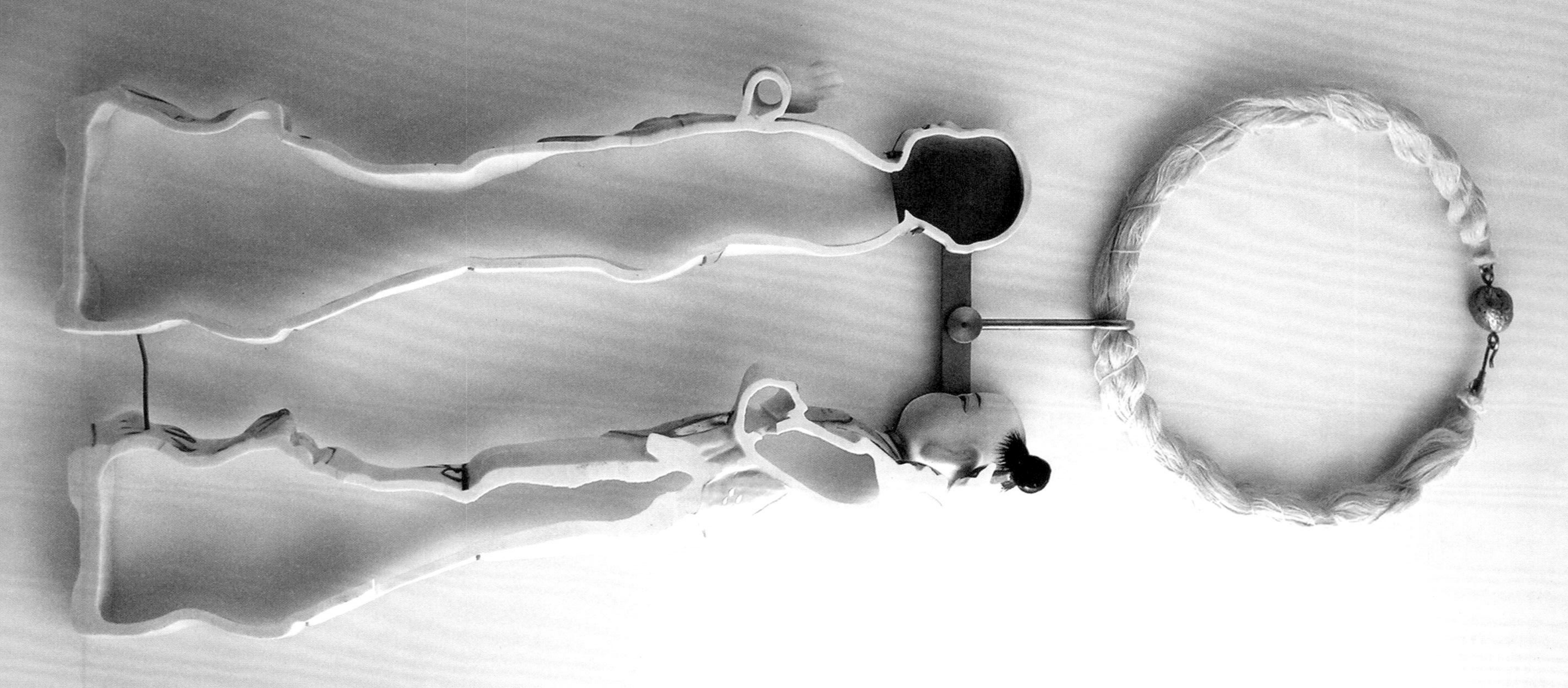

JEWEL BOOK

INTERNATIONAL ANNUAL OF CONTEMPORARY JEWEL ART

12|13

stichting kunstboek

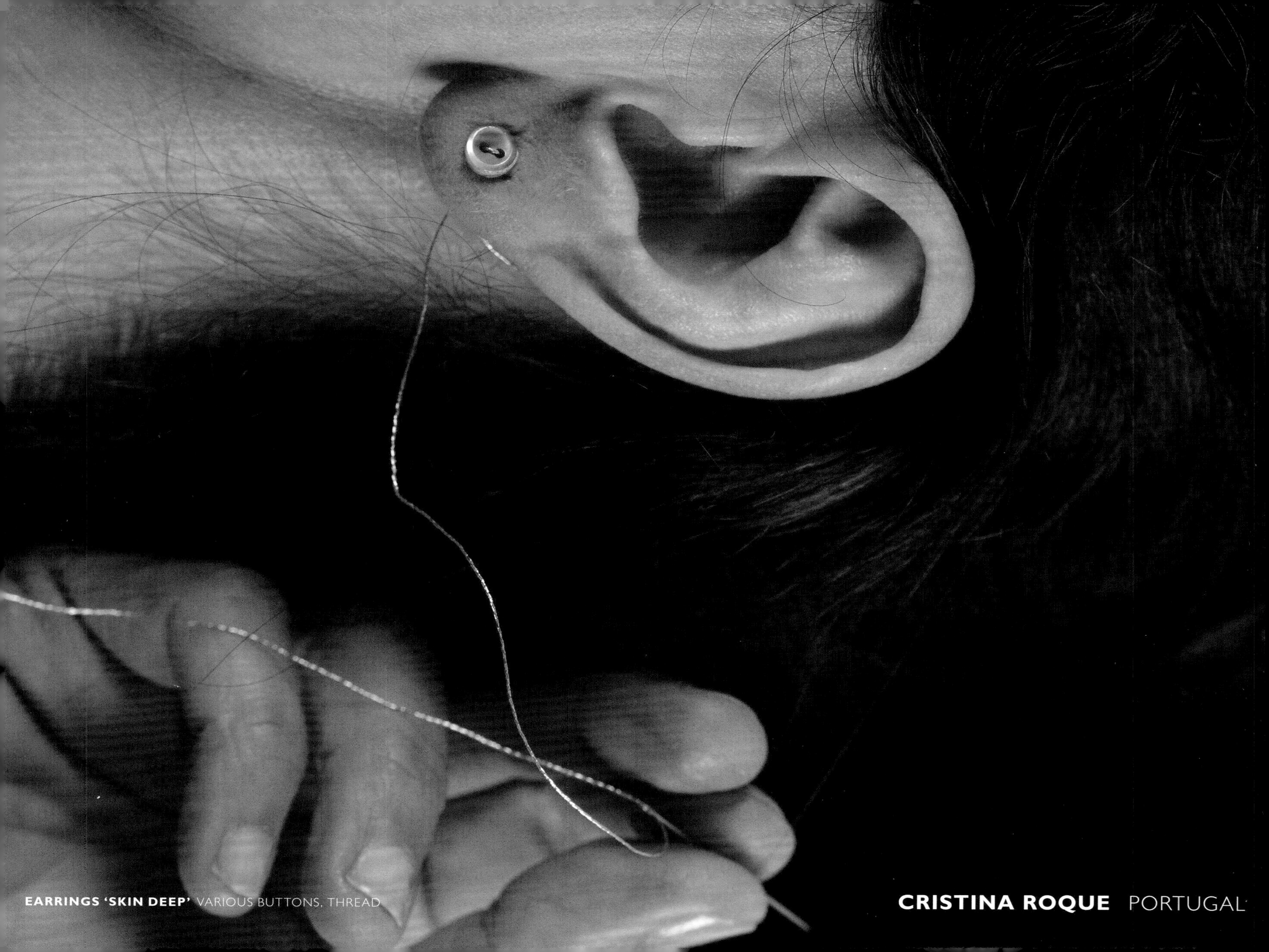

EARRINGS 'SKIN DEEP' VARIOUS BUTTONS, THREAD

CRISTINA ROQUE PORTUGAL

PREFACE

Dear Jewel World,

In the beginning there was The Plan. An ambitious and audacious plan; a mission to create a book that would give a voice to all creative people in the field of contemporary jewelry art and that would become a global platform for innovation and discussion among jewel artists. Achieving this ambitious goal needed careful planning and a thoroughly thought out strategy. A first step was communicating the plan to the world. The idea was launched in as many countries as possible and while we were immersing ourselves in this noble form of art, learning its specificities and its diversity, positive and enthusiastic reactions from all around the globe started to roll in. We had struck gold.

Jewel design is a very particular art form with a great cultural diversity and a large variety in techniques and materials. Jewel art stands out, not in the least because of its small dimensions, but at the same time jewel design testifies of the same essential characteristics as seen in any other applied art. A great deal of technical knowledge, tradition, imagination, freedom and discipline, and above all dedication and passion are necessities to achieve an end result that is esthetical, functional and precious.

The interest and the number of positive reactions to our plan were beyond expectations. Therefore, it is with great pleasure and pride that we present you this first edition of Jewelbook. A gem in itself and the impressive end result of a year's hard work and an international collaboration. Selecting the best designs out of a total of over 2000 entries was a dainty task and it is only with the help of a panel of international authorities in this field of art that we could bring this mission to a successful end. We are thankful for the specialist help and knowledge of Ana Campos (Portugal), Martina Dempf (Germany), Dorothy Hogg (United Kingdom) and Anne Leclerq (Belgium).

Quality and originality were important criteria for selection, but at the same time Jewelbook also aims to show as much as possible of the great variety in styles in contemporary jewel design. In the end 276 artists of 35 nationalities and 540 jewel designs made the final book selection. Three exceptional personalities, whose work was outstanding on many levels, received a special mention and an 'Oyster Award'.

Stichting Kunstboek Publishers have a strong reputation when it comes to pioneering book projects and starting successful initiatives. The company can already look back on 20 years of experience in publishing books on design and art, both the fine and the applied arts. With Jewelbook, Stichting Kunstboek adds another extraordinary art discipline to its fields of interest. Stichting Kunstboek's worldwide book distribution network guarantees this book the largest audience of readers as possible. Only when this book has become a tool to make jewellers more aware of what happens on an international level and encourages the exchange of ideas, we consider our mission accomplished.

With this first edition of Jewelbook we hope to establish a long-term relationship with all enthusiasts of jewel design, in the first place all artists who have chosen jewel art as their preferred form of expression, and secondly all likeminded people passionate about contemporary jewelry.
In the name of Stichting Kunstboek Publishers, I would like to wholeheartedly thank all jewel designers for their enthusiastic collaboration and I'd like to congratulate all designers in this book with their brilliant creative work.

Nika Leys
Assistant - Publisher

ANA CAMPOS
NIKA LEYS
DOROTHY HOGG
MARTINE DEMPF
ANNE LECLERCQ
JAAK VAN DAMME

THE JURY

ANA CAMPOS was born in Porto, Portugal, 1953. She is a jewellery designer, lecturer and coordinator of the jewellery BA course and of the Postgraduation course at ESAD – Superior School of Art and Design, in Matosinhos, Portugal. She graduated in Comunication Design at Fine Arte School, Porto. She studied jewellery design at Ar.Co in Lisbon, and later at the Massana School in Barcelona, with a scholarship from the Calouste Gulbenkian Foundation. Her post-graduate study in Intercultural Relations at the Open University in Porto led to a Masters Degree in Visual Anthropology. Her dissertation is entitled Sky and Sea: Ramón Puig, actor in the new jewellery scenario. Currently, she is following PhD studies in philosophy at UAB, Barcelona Autonomous University, directed by Gerard Vilar. This thesis is entitled Jewellery: art and reflection.

DOROTHY HOGG is a graduate of Glasgow School of Art and a silver medalist of the Royal College of Art in London. She set up her studio in Edinburgh in the 1970s and has exhibited her work internationally ever since. Appointed Professor by Edinburgh College of Art where she was in charge of the award winning Jewellery and Silversmithing department for 23 years. In 2001 she was awarded an MBE by the Queen for services to Jewellery and Silversmithing and in 2010 a lifetime achievement award by the Goldsmiths Craft and Design Council London. She was appointed the Victoria and Albert Museum's first Craft Resident in 2008. Her work can be found in many international collections.

MARTINA DEMPF is a jewellery designer, social anthropologist and philosopher, and there is a strong relation between her scientific work and her creative work. Her cross-over jewellery is a result of research into jewellery concepts, styles, materials and intercultural exchange. She aims at keeping the natural character of the material and simultaneously creating a piece of wearable art. Martina Dempf regards jewellery as a medium for communication within a group of people, within a culture, or as a universal language between cultures. A design consultant and lecturer, she works with students and craftsmen in Africa and Asia as a facilitator and translator between different cultures. She conducts lectures and workshops on design and craft promotion in co-operation with GIZ , Chambers of commerce, the World Craft Council, the German Goethe Institute and various international universities.

ANNE LECLERCQ Educated as a ceramicists and having been a teacher of ceramics for more than 20 years, Anne Leclercq is also the Director of the World Crafts Council-Belgium francophone (www.wcc-bf.org). She is also: Expert in European Applied Arts, especially ceramics and Jewellery. The curator of several Applied Arts exhibitions, in Belgium and abroad. The creator and organiser of the European Triennial for Contemporary Jewellery, the European Triennial for Ceramics and Glass and the European Prize for Applied Arts, which take place at the "Anciens Abattoirs" of Mons (Belgium).

OYSTER AWARDS

TED NOTEN THE NETHERLANDS

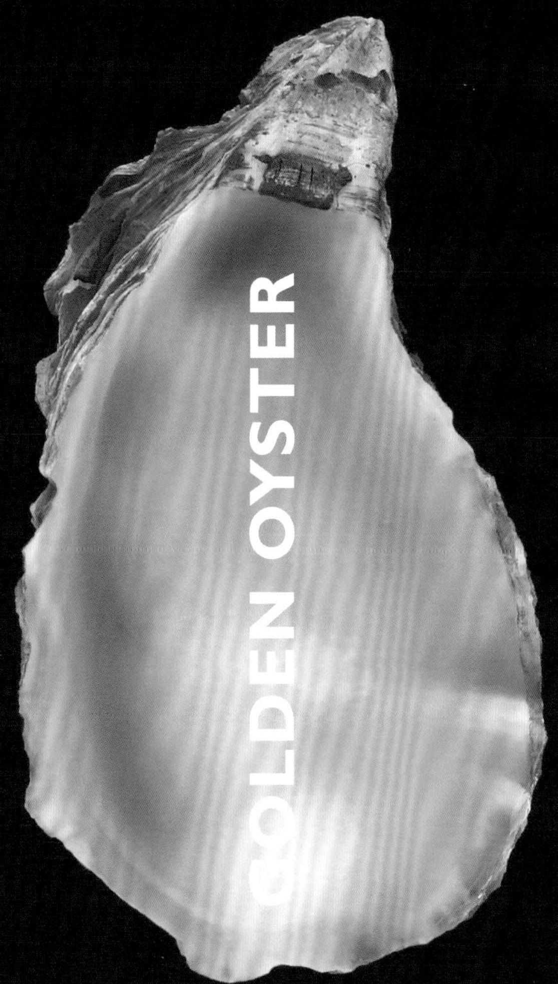
GOLDEN OYSTER

TED NOTEN THE NETHERLANDS

'GLOBAL TACTILE PIECES II TOKYO AMSTERDAM KYOTO'
SILVER NECKLACE, PAINTED WHITE, WITH ANTIQUE KIMONO STRING
AND READY-MADE MERMAID DOLL.

'FREDJES' (WITH PEARL) NECKLACE IN ACRYLIC

TED NOTEN THE NETHERLANDS

'THE HAUNTED BY 36 WOMAN AVONDVLINDER BRACELET'
NYLON WITH GLASS FIBRE

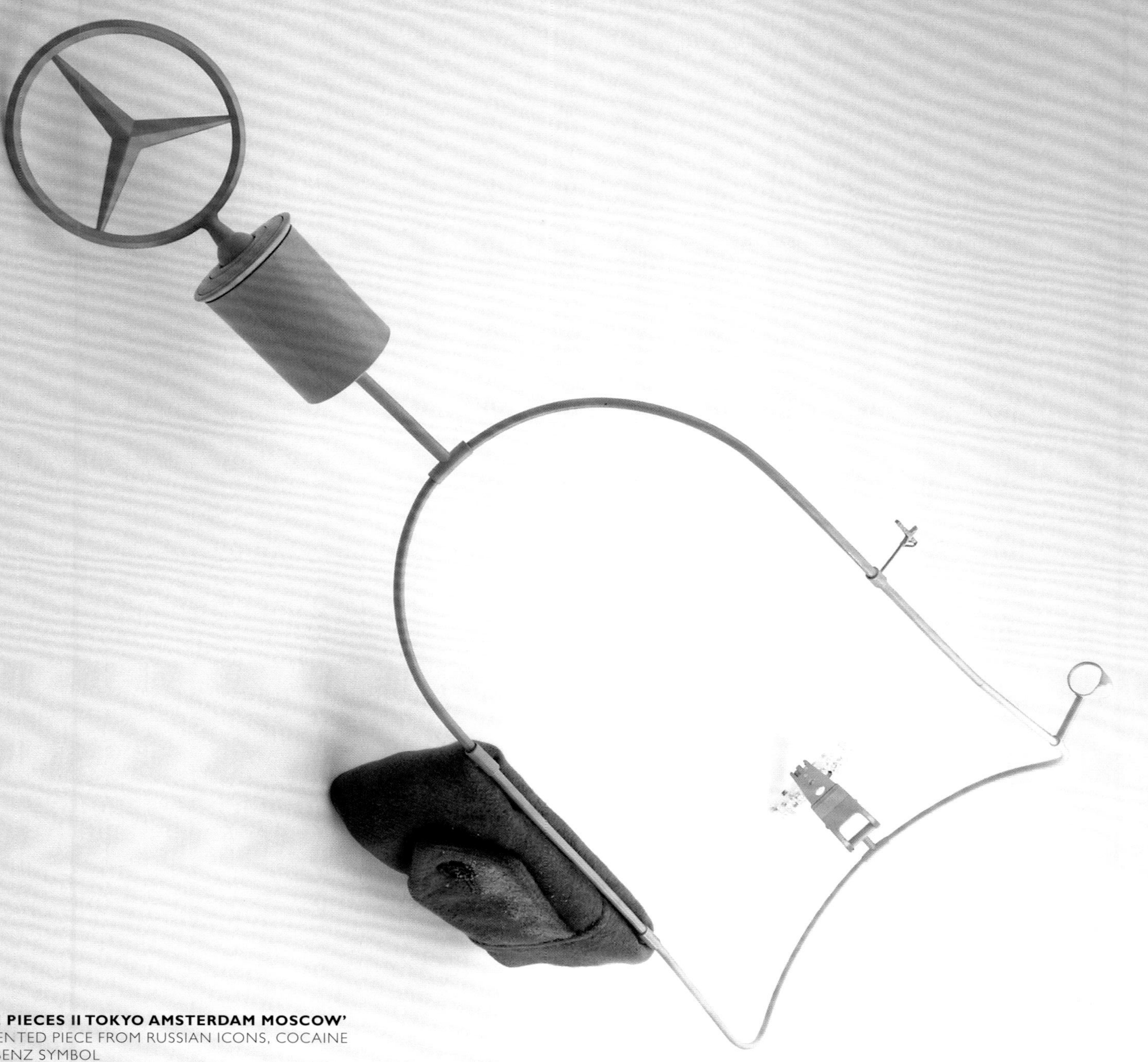

‘GLOBAL TACTILE PIECES II TOKYO AMSTERDAM MOSCOW’
NECKLACE, FRAGMENTED PIECE FROM RUSSIAN ICONS, COCAINE
AND A MERCEDES BENZ SYMBOL

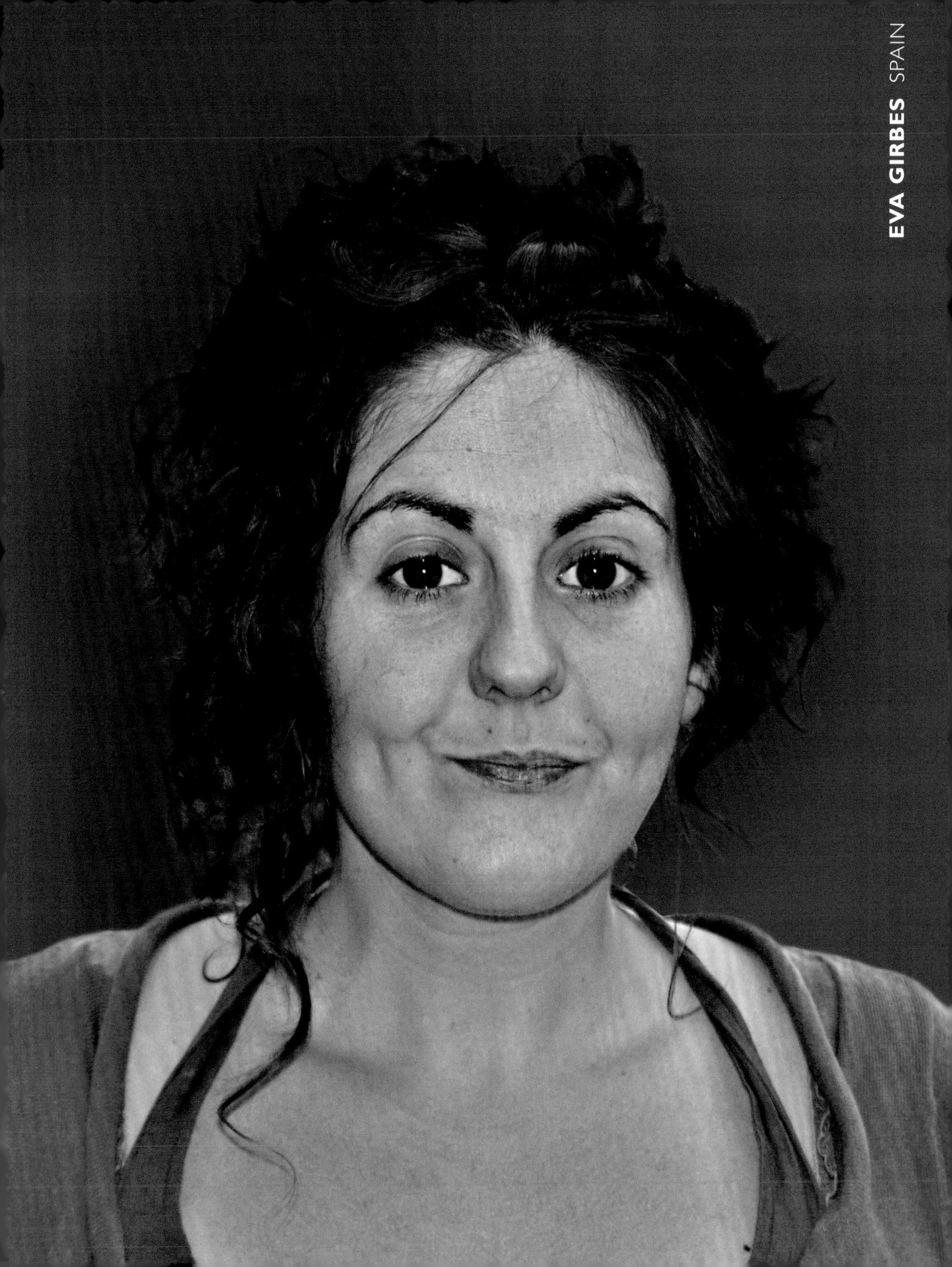

EVA GIRBES SPAIN

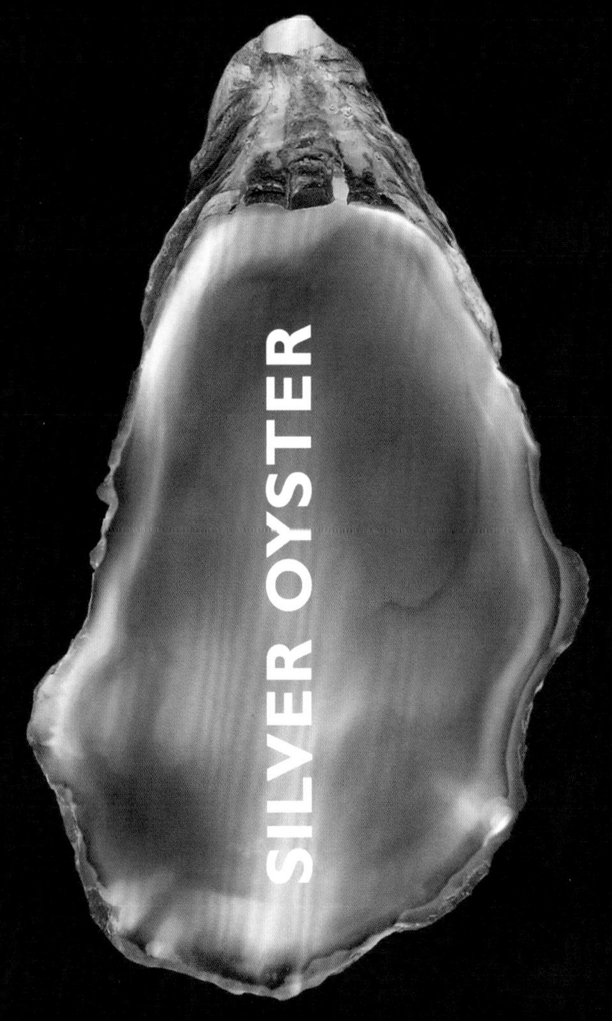
SILVER OYSTER

EVA GIRBES SPAIN

'PRIMITIVE AWAKE' A DIALOGUE BETWEEN WHAT IS AND WHAT MAY BE. BROOCH 06.012 ALPACA, WOOD TURNING

'PRIMITIVE AWAKE' A DIALOGUE BETWEEN WHAT IS AND WHAT MAY BE. BROOCH 11.012 ALPACA, WOOD TURNING

EVA GIRBES SPAIN

'PRIMITIVE AWAKE' A DIALOGUE BETWEEN WHAT IS AND WHAT MAY BE. BROOCH 08.012 ALPACA, WOOD TURNING

'PRIMITIVE AWAKE' A DIALOGUE BETWEEN WHAT IS AND WHAT MAY BE. BROOCH 03.012 ALPACA, WOOD TURNING

HANNA HEDMAN SWEDEN

BRONZE OYSTER

HANNA HEDMAN SWEDEN

NECKLACE 'PERCINA REX' OXIDIZED SILVER, POWDER-COATED COPPER AND PAINT

NECKLACE 'SYMPLOCOS SHILANENSIS' SILVER, OXIDIZED SILVER, POWDER-COATED COPPER AND PAINT

HANNA HEDMAN SWEDEN

BROOCH 'MANIS TRICUSPIS' OXIDIZED SILVER, POWDER-COATED COPPER AND PAINT

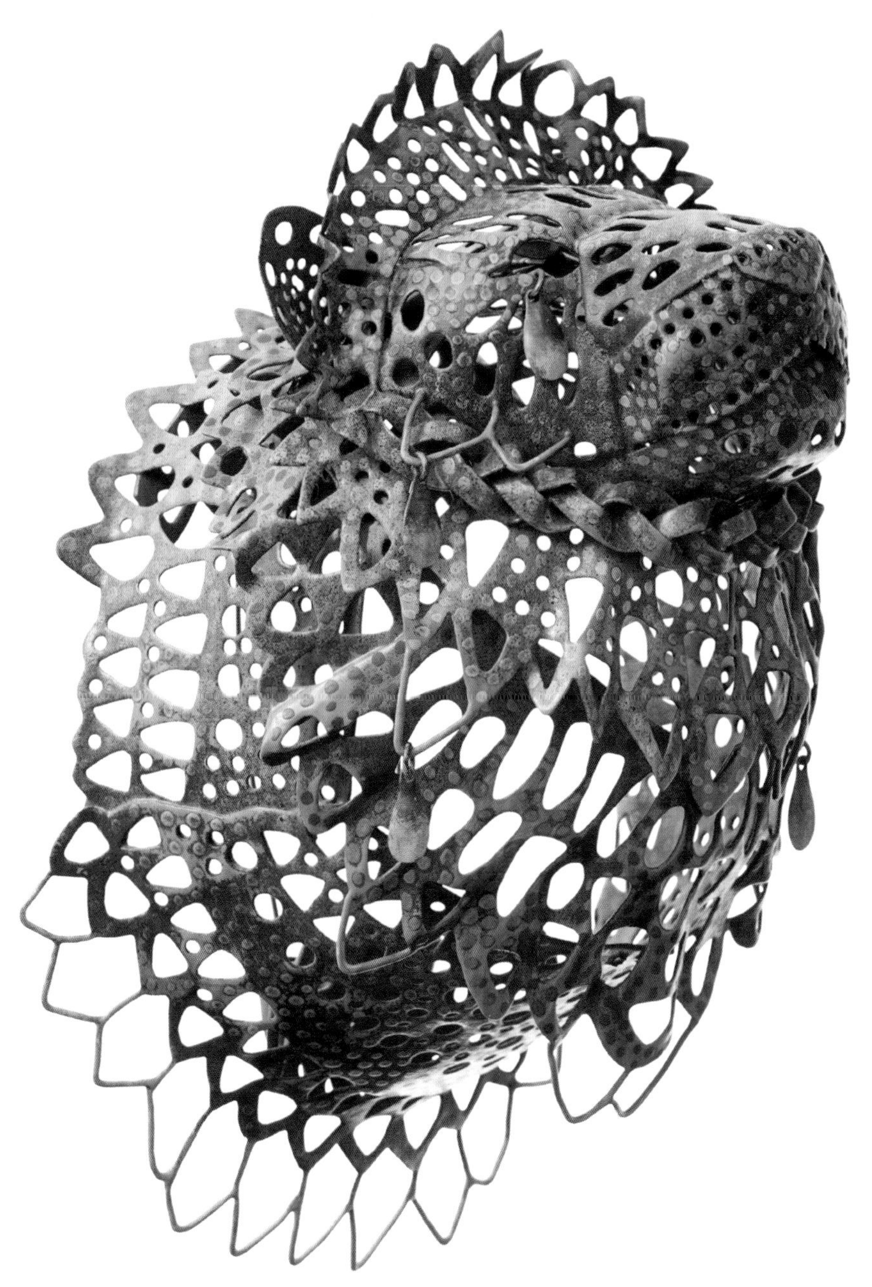

BROOCH 'PANTHERA LEO PERSICA' OXIDIZED SILVER, POWDER-COATED COPPER AND PAINT

LAURA ALVARDO / VIVIAN MELLER GERMANY

'PORTRAIT ME: RUDOLF' PHOTOGRAPHY, PAPER, FABRIC

SELECTED JUWELS

FARRAH AL-DUJAILI UK

NECKLACE COPPER, BLACKBOARD PAINT, CHALK MARKER, FAUX PEARLS

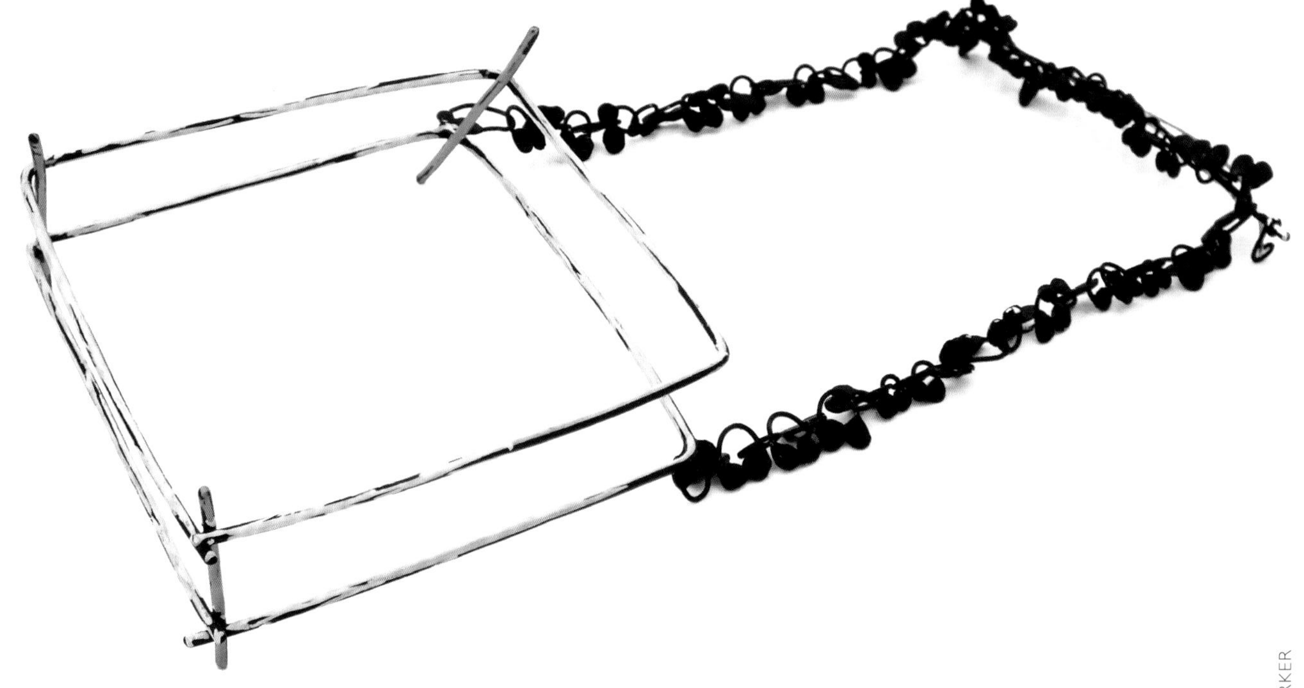

BROOCH COPPER, BLACKBOARD PAINT, CHALK MARKER

FARRAH AL-DUJAILI UK

BROOCH COPPER, BLACKBOARD PAINT, CHALK MARKER

BROOCH COPPER, BLACKBOARD PAINT, CHALK MARKER

LUIS ACOSTA THE NETHERLANDS

NECKLACE SIX STICHTED LAYERS DIFFERENT COLOURED PAPER

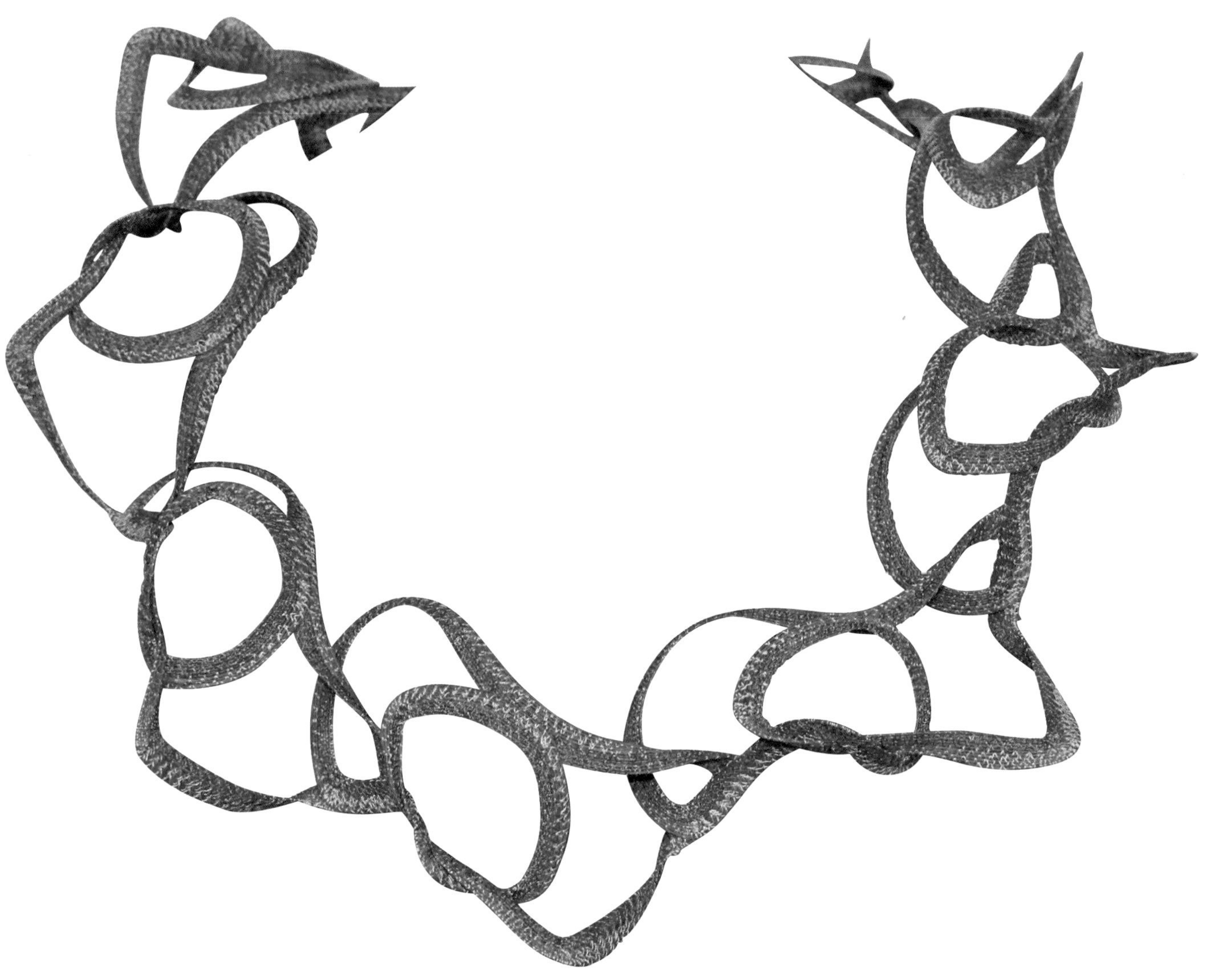

NECKLACE PAPER THREAD-STITCHED

ANA ALBUQUERQUE PORTUGAL

RING 830 GOLD 'CONCENTRIC MOVEMENTS:SOUND'

NANCY AILLERY BELGIUM

RING 'SUN-MOON' MIXED MEDIA

IRIS ALGOM CANADA

UNTITITELD MIXED MEDIA

ESTEFANIA ALMEIDA PORTUGAL

'LA PETITE MORT' SILK, GLASS, STEEL

ALIDRA ALIĆ DENMARK

'ARUM LILY 01' 925 SILVER

INÊS ALMEIDA PORTUGAL

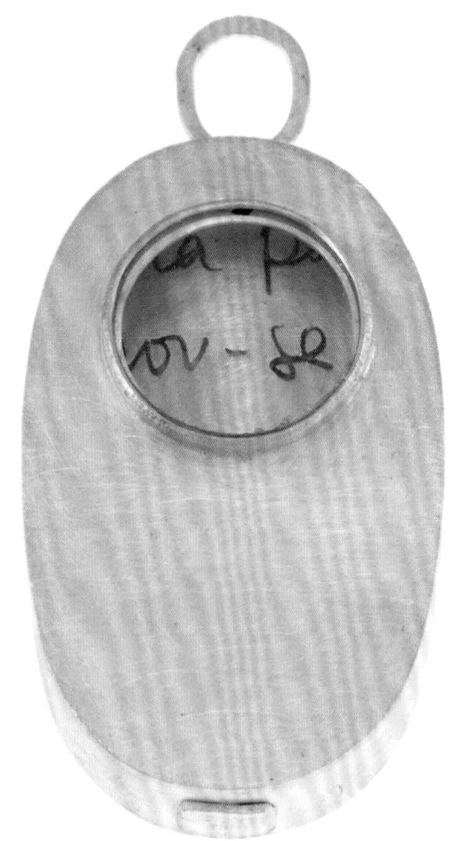

'HISTÓRIAS ÁS AVESSAS' SILVER, INK, LENS

'HISTÓRIAS DO FUNDO DO MAR' SILVER, COPPER, LENS, INK

LAURA ALVARADO / VIVIAN MELLER GERMANY

'PORTRAIT ME: MEISJE ACRYL PENDANT'
ACRYLGLAS, SILK, SILVER, BINDED-CERAMIC-LIKE-POWDER (ZPRINT)

'PORTRAIT ME: RUDOLF WOOD BROOCH'
WOOD, SILVER, RESIN, SLS NYLON

PATRICIA ALVAREZ ARGENTINA

BROOCH COPPER, SILVER 925, EBONY, OLD KEY, IAPISLAZULI

PECTORAL PAPER YARD

'SOLITUDE' BROOCH SILVER, PAPER, PLEXIGLASS, CHINA

RINALDO ALVAREZ SPAIN

PENDANT SILVER, PAPER, COTTON, THREAD

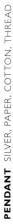

RINALDO ALVAREZ SPAIN

BROOCH SILVER, PAPER, PLEXIGLASS

'WHERE ARE YOU LOVE?' BROOCH SILVER, PAPER, PLEXIGLASS

KARIN ROY ANDERSON SWEDEN

BROOCH 'A CONSTANT GRINDING' APPLE SEEDS, TITANIUM, ALUMINIUM, SILVER, STEEL

BROOCH 'A CONSTANT GRINDING' GALIA MELON SEEDS, ROWAN WOOD, ALUMINIUM SILVER, STEEL

MIRIAM ARENTZ GERMANY

BROOCH 'RAMO', TURQOIS WOOD, RESIN, SILVER

BROOCH 'RAMO' GREY, SMALL WOOD, RESIN, SILVER

NEVIN ARIG BELGIUM

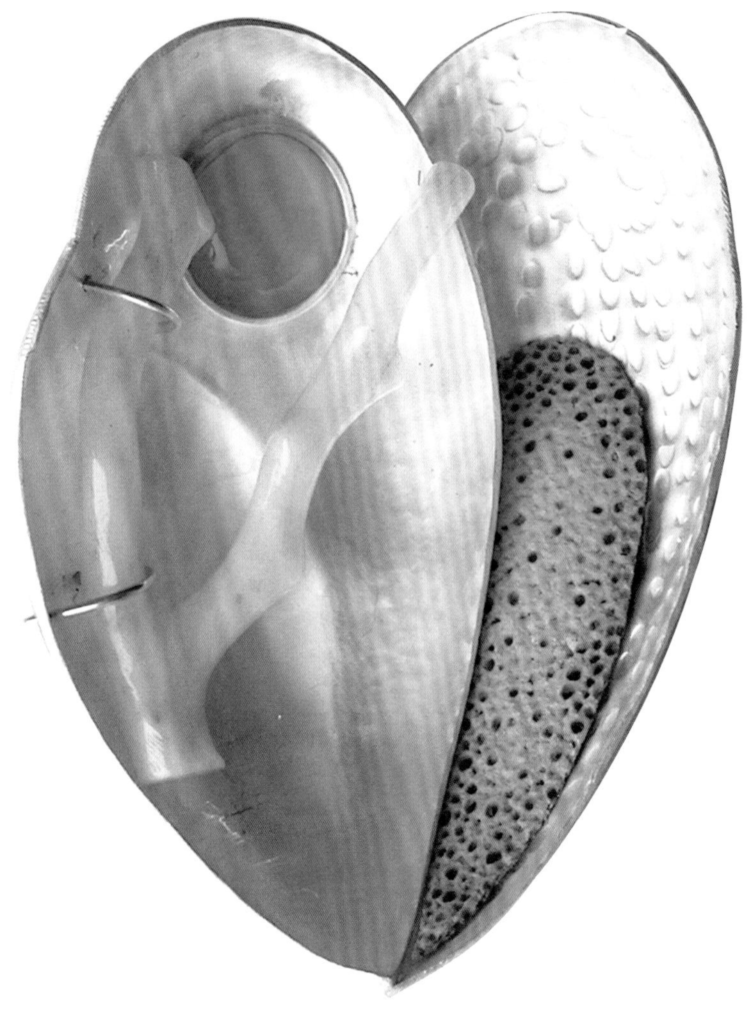

'INSIDE BROOCH' CHISELLED SILVER, CORAL, AQUAMARINE, ORANGE PEEL

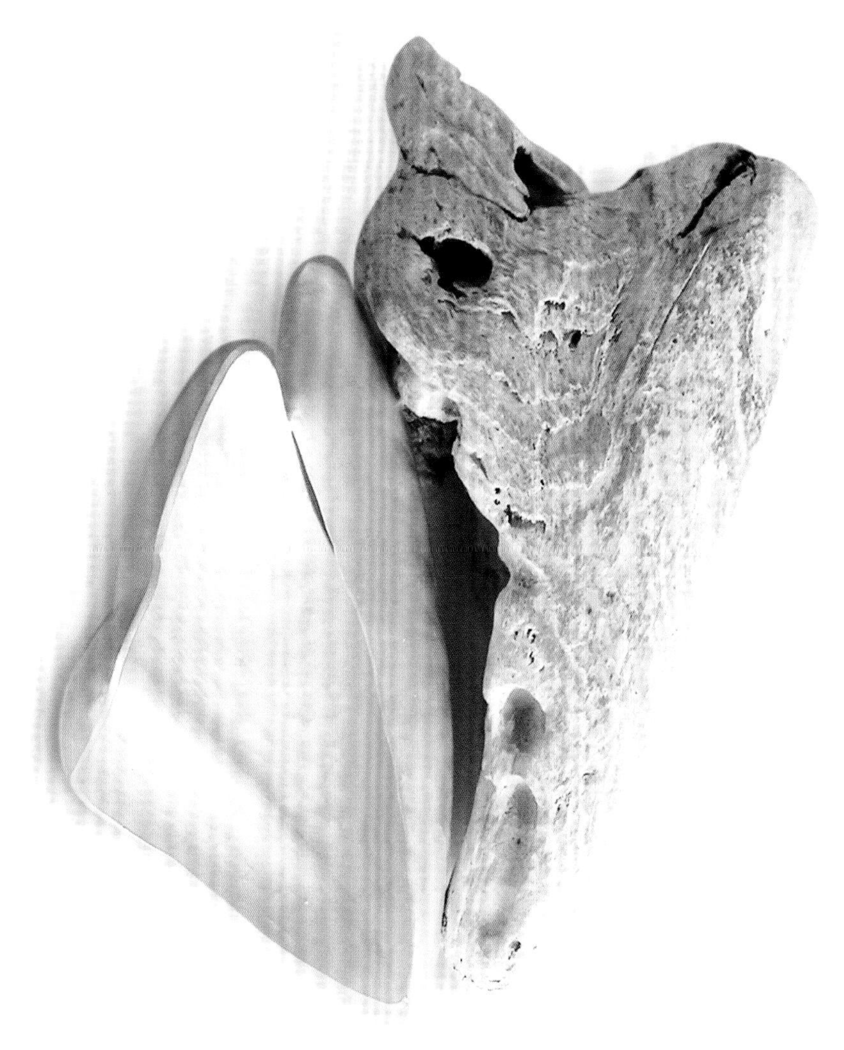

'ISLE BROOCH' CHISELLED SILVER, WOOD, PAINT

YASAR AYDIN SWEDEN

NECKLACE 'LAYERS OF PINK' LEATHER, PORCELAIN

BROOCH 'LAYERS OF PINK' LEATHER, STEEL, GLASS

IACOV AZUBEL ARGENTINA

BROOCH 'AUSTERIDAD' ROSEWOOD, BASE PAINT, POLYESTER, BRONZE NAILS, CASHEW LAQUER, 925 SILVER, NICKEL SILVER

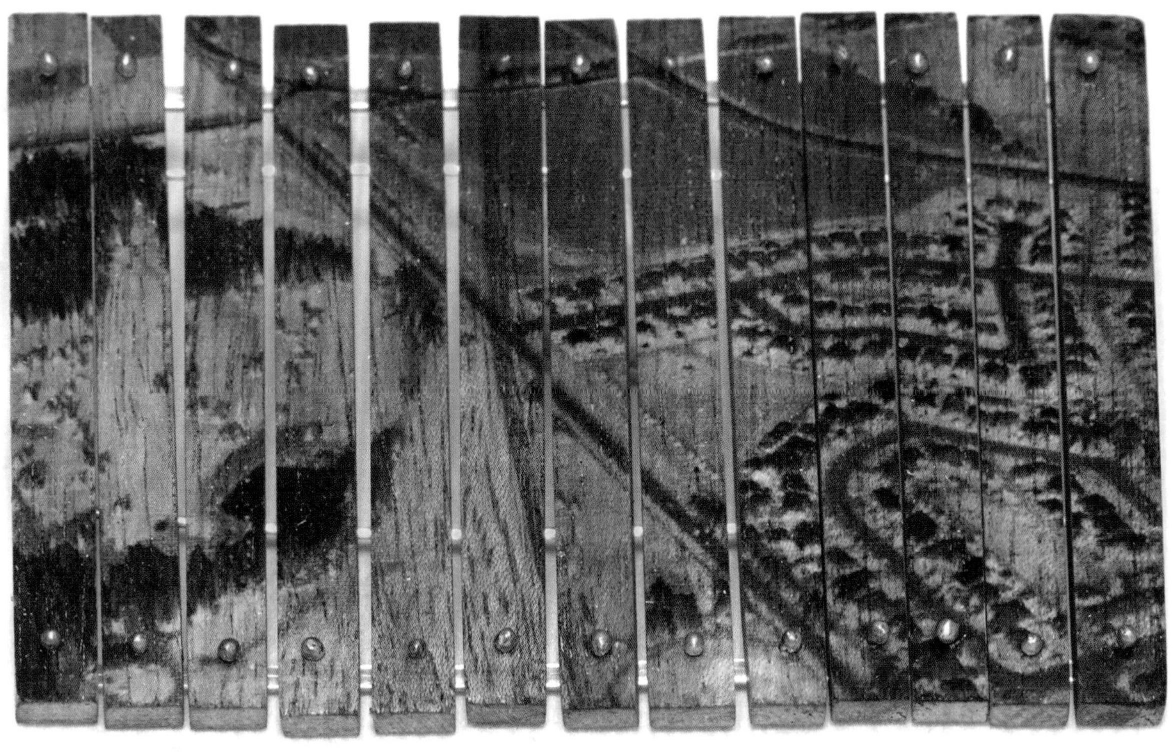

BROOCH 'URBANIZACION' PINEWOOD, POLYESTER, BRONZE, 925 SILVER, NICKEL SILVER

GIJS BAKKER THE NETHERLANDS

BROOCH 'VIRTUAL MULTIPLE' 18 K GOLD

BROOCH 'THE BLAST' TITANIUM, PERSPEX

GIJS BAKKER THE NETHERLANDS

BROOCH 'THE PRESIDENT' TITANIUM, WHITE GOLD, GREEN GOLD, ALUMINIUM, YOGO SAPPHIRES 6.22 K

BROOCH 'THE CRY' SILVER, 51 DIAMONDS 0.87 K, 3D MODEL, BASED ON PHOTOGRAPH CF FOOTBALLPLAYER HUNTELAAR

SHIRLY BAR ISRAËL

BROOCH STERLING SILVER, COPPER, TEFLON PLATING, ZIRCON GEMS, SYNTHETIC PEARLS

PENDANT STERLING SILVER, COPPER, TEFLON PLATING, ZIRCON GEMS, SYNTHETIC PEARLS

NECKLACE 'OPHIS' GOLD 18 K, TURMALINS, PEARLS, SILK, PAPER, GILDED PAPIER-MÂCHÉ WITH GOLD LEAF 22 K

GIAN LUCA BARTELLONE ITALY

BENJAMÍN BAZÁN / LOLA SOCAS SPAIN

HOLES LEATHER, STEEL, SILVER

ROSALBA BALSAMO ITALY

BRACELET SILVER IN GALVANIC PROCESS

BRACELET DIAMOND 'OMAGE TO GIO PONTI' SILVER, GOLD

ALINE BERDICHEVSKY SPAIN

BROOCH 'RECONSTRUCTION 11' ALABASTER, DYE, LACQUER, NICKEL SILVER, STERLING SILVER

BROOCH 'RECONSTRUCTION 13' ALABASTER, DYE, LACQUER, NICKEL SILVER, STERLING SILVER

ANNE-MARIE BERNHARDT SWEDEN

NECKLACE 'DYR I MÖRKA SKOVEN' JÄRN, OXIDERAT SILVER

NECKLACE 'FROSTKOG' SILVER ONYX

CECILE BERTRAND BELGIUM

UNTITLED KNITTED COTTON, OLD TIES LABELS

UNTITLED SILK TOURISTIC SCARF

'LAYERS (ROSE GARDEN) II' STERLING SILVER, COPPER, ENAMEL, IMAGE TRANSFER ON TO FABIC, TEXTILLE

RAQUEL BESSUDO MEXICO

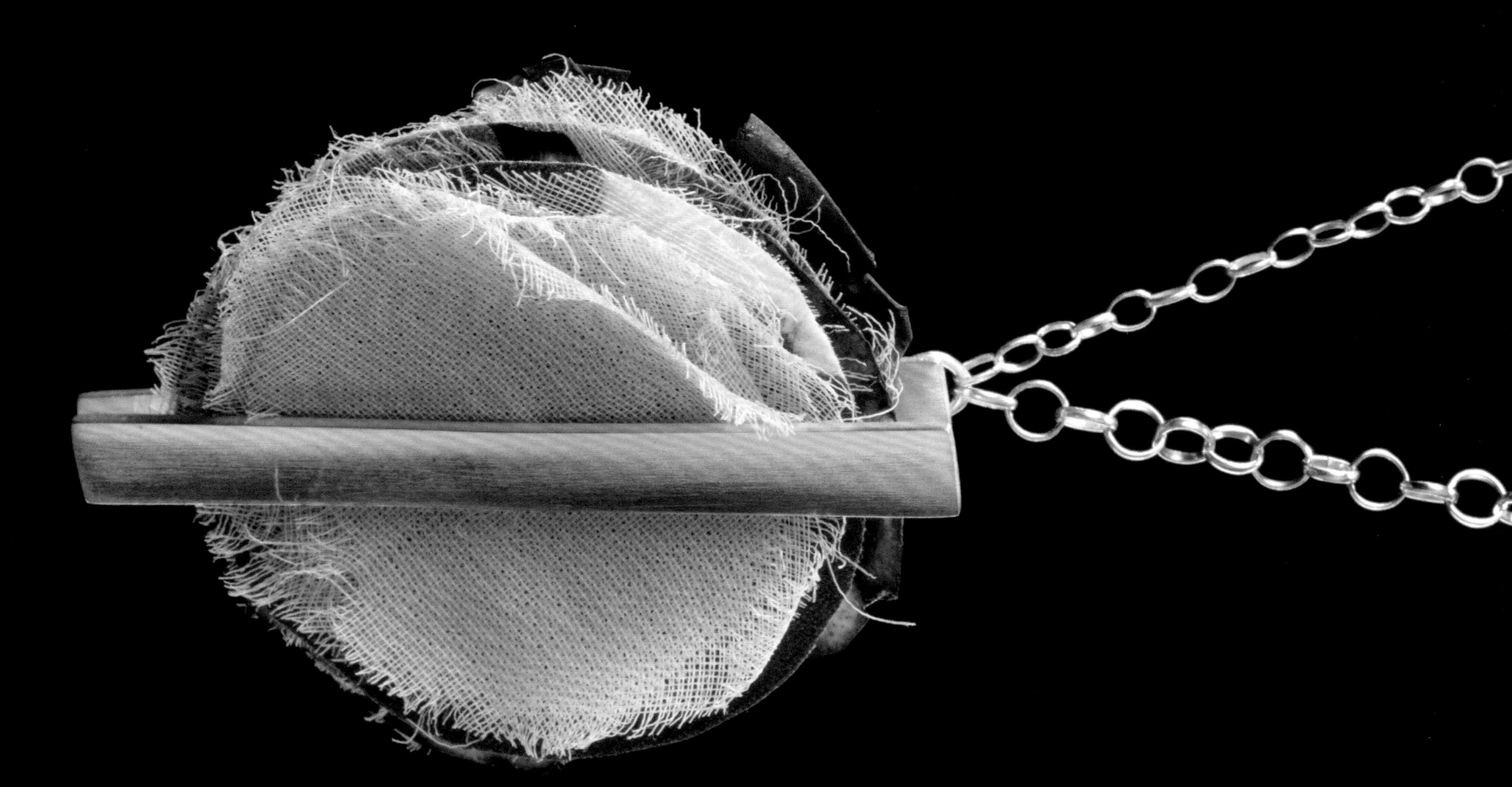

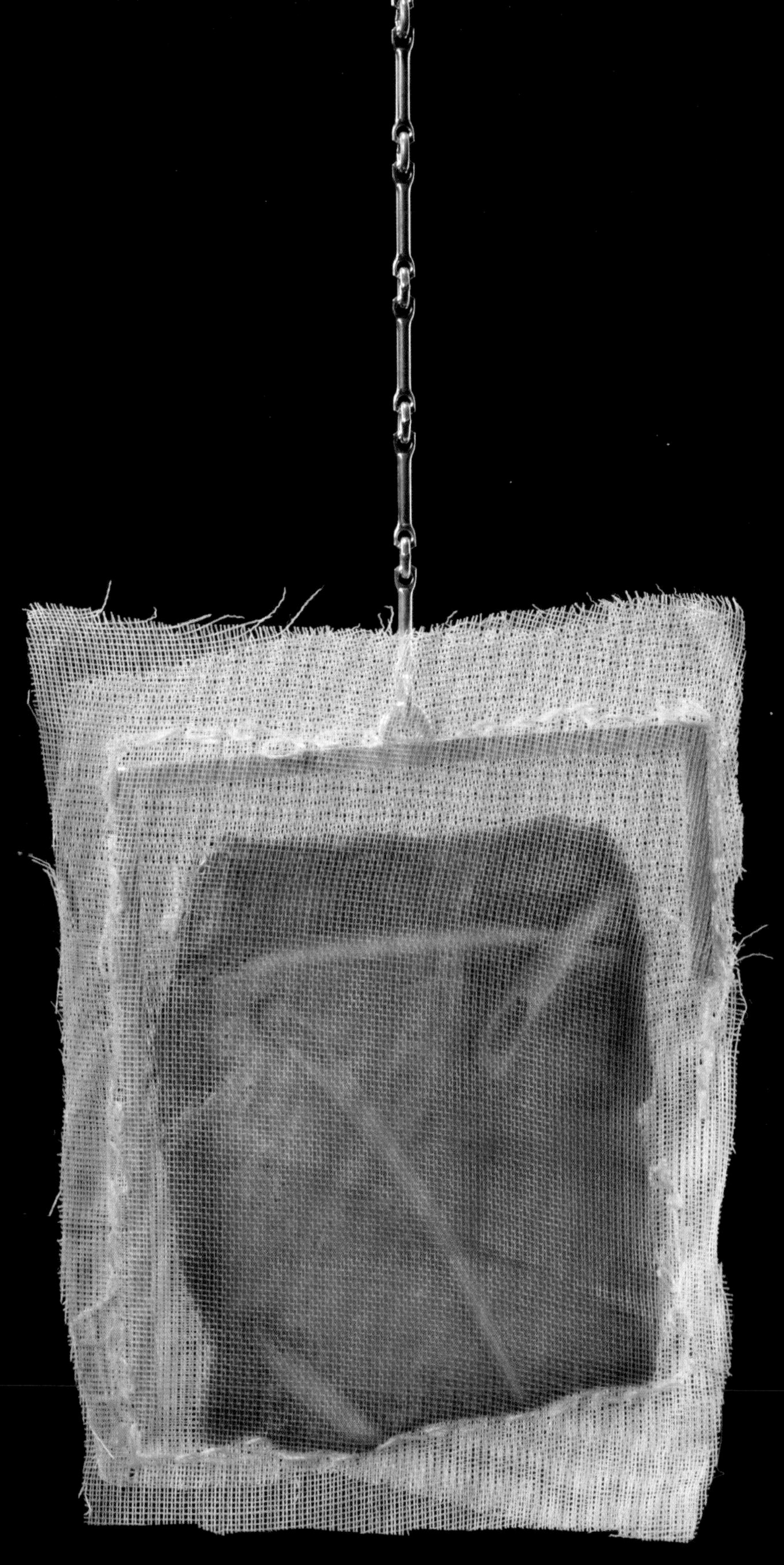

'NEEDLES (INSIDE) I' STERLING SILVER, SILVER PMC, TEXTILE

CHRISTINA BIZZARRO DENMARK

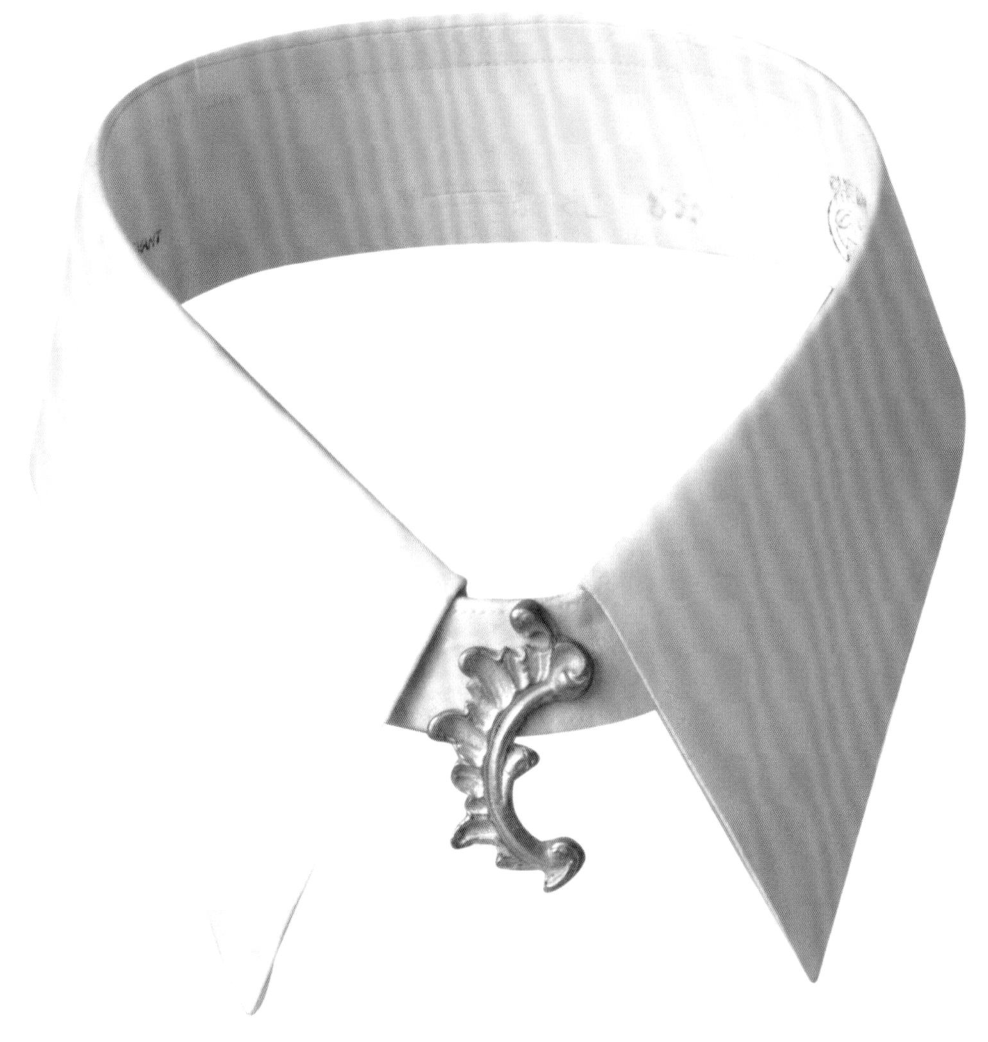

UNTITLED VINTAGE GENTS COLLAR, COTTON, SILVER ORNAMENT

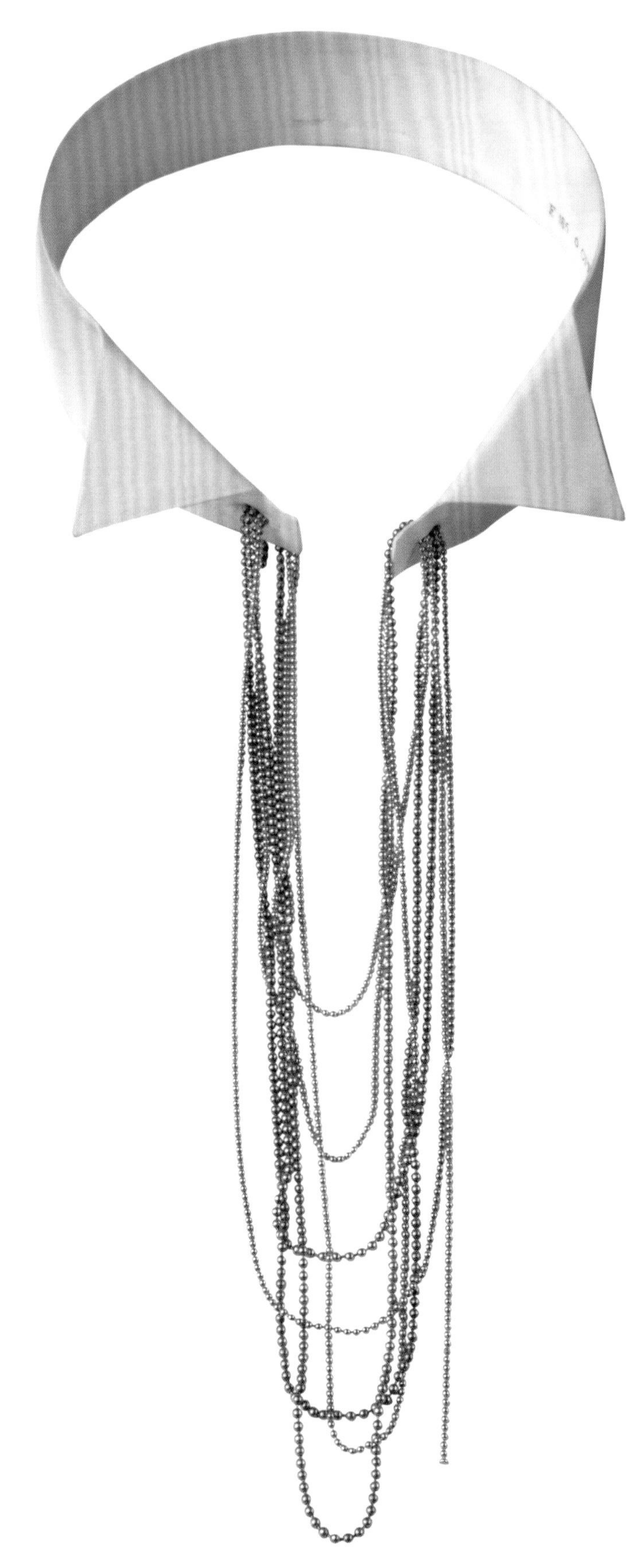

UNTITLED VINTAGE GENTS COLLAR, COTTON VARIONS, SILVER CHAINS

RING 'STREET DIAMONDS', SILVER, GLASS SPLINTERS (FOUND ON THE STREET)

TITTI BJERNÉR SWEDEN

RING 'STREET DIAMONDS', SILVER, GLASS SPLINTERS (FOUND ON THE STREET)

LISA BJÖRKE SWEDEN

BROOCH 'SOPHIA' COPPER, BRASS, LAQUER, BEAO CORO, DENTAL WIRE

BROOCH 'VIKTORIA' COPPER, BRASS, LAQUER, DENTAL WIRE

ALEXANDER BLANK GERMANY

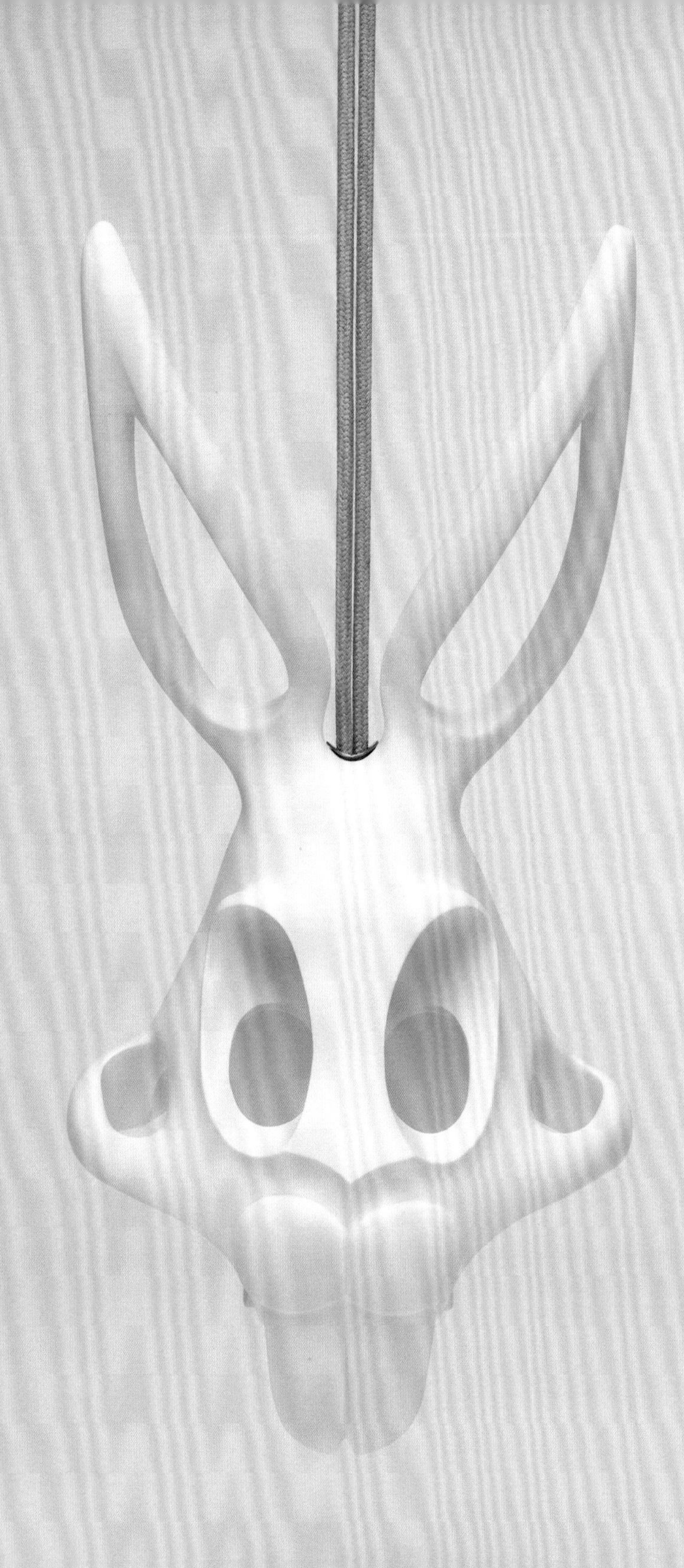

'MEMENTO JUNIORI (BUGS)' PENDANT HANDCARVED RIGID FOAM, SILVER, STRING

'MEMENTO JUNIORI (WILE E)' PENDANT HANDCARVED RIGID FOAM, SILVER, STRING

RING PORCELAIN, SILVER

JUDITH BLOEDJES THE NETHERLANDS

COLLIER PORCELAIN, PEARLS, TRANSFERS

MARTA BOAN SPAIN

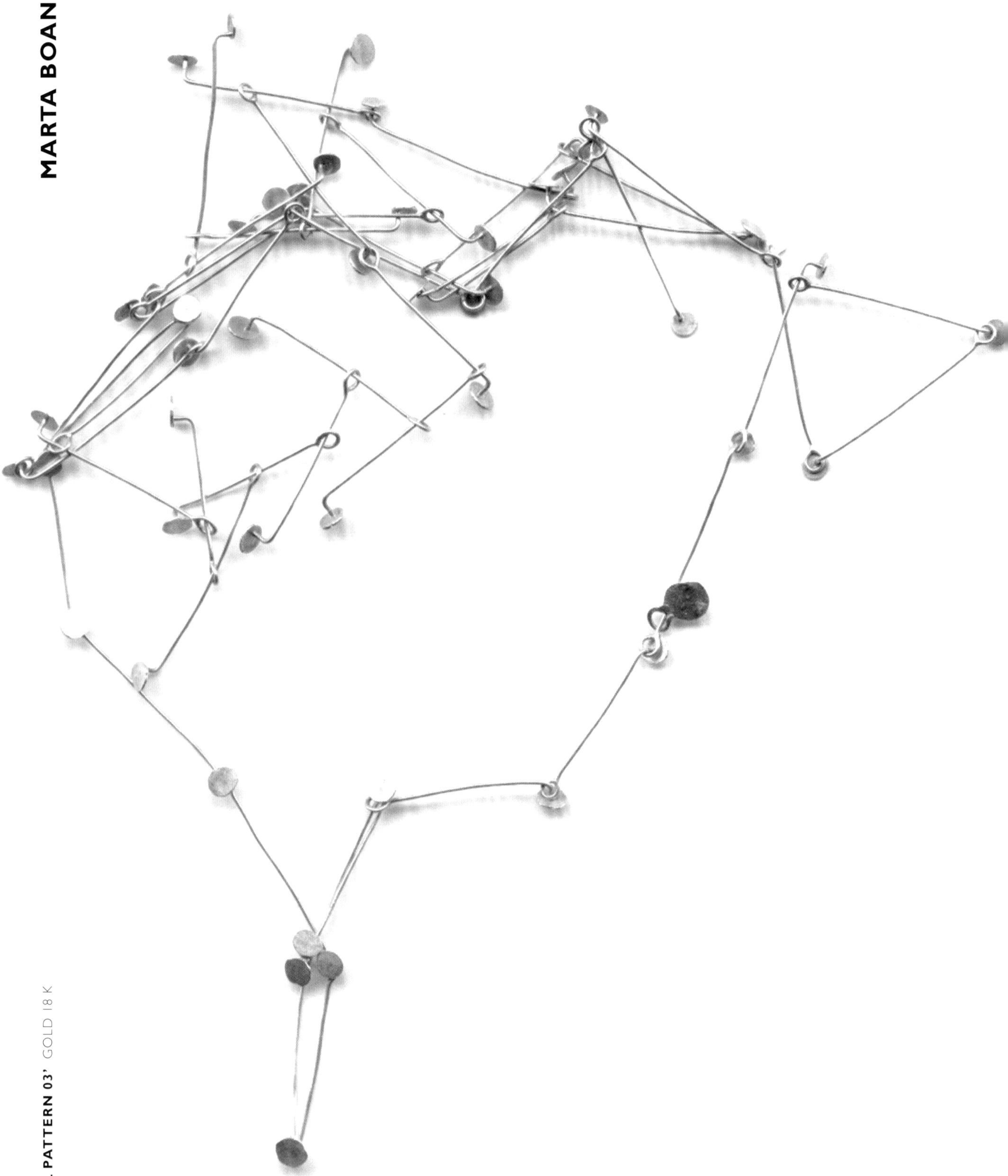

'CYCLICAL PATTERN 03' GOLD 18 K

SOFIE BOONS UK

'PERFUME' NECKLACE MADE OF A SCENTED WAX THAT DISSOLVES IN A FEW MONTHS TIME DUE TO CONTACT WITH AIR

SOFIE BOONS UK

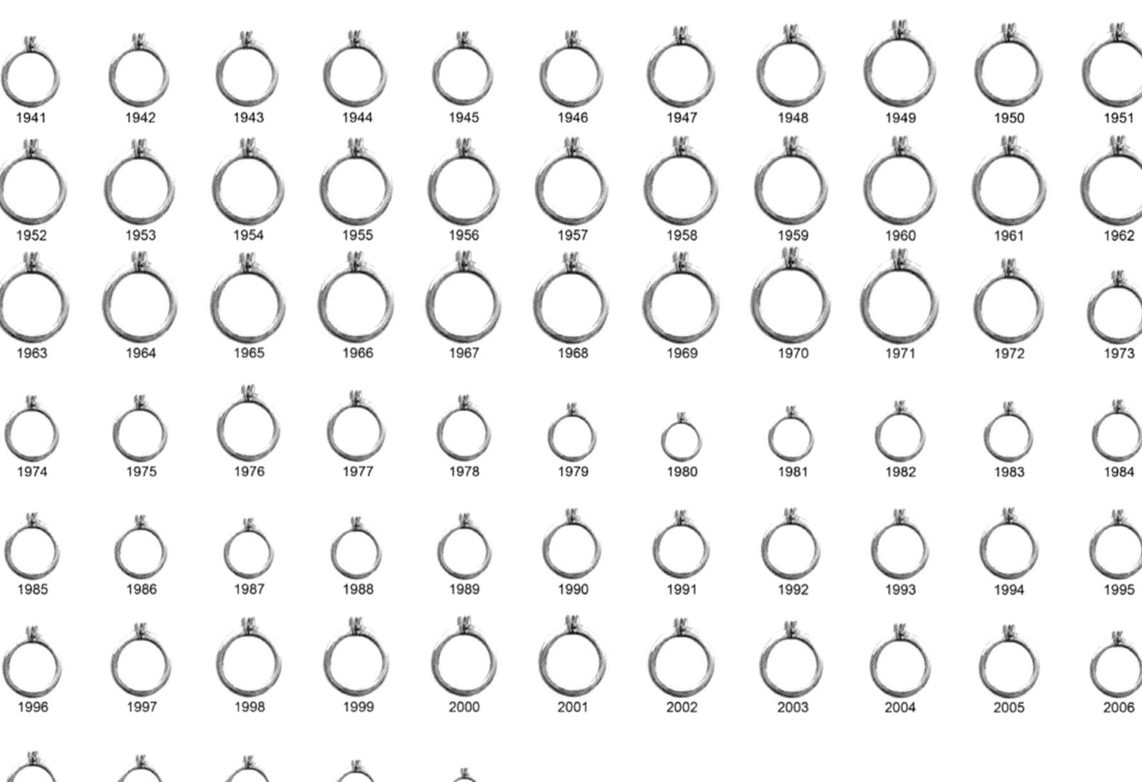

'GOLD PRICE'

'GOLD PRICE' A RING SCALED DOWN IN COMPARISON WITH THE GOLD-PRICE, GOLDEN SCALED RING, DIAMOND

ELEANOR BOLTON UK

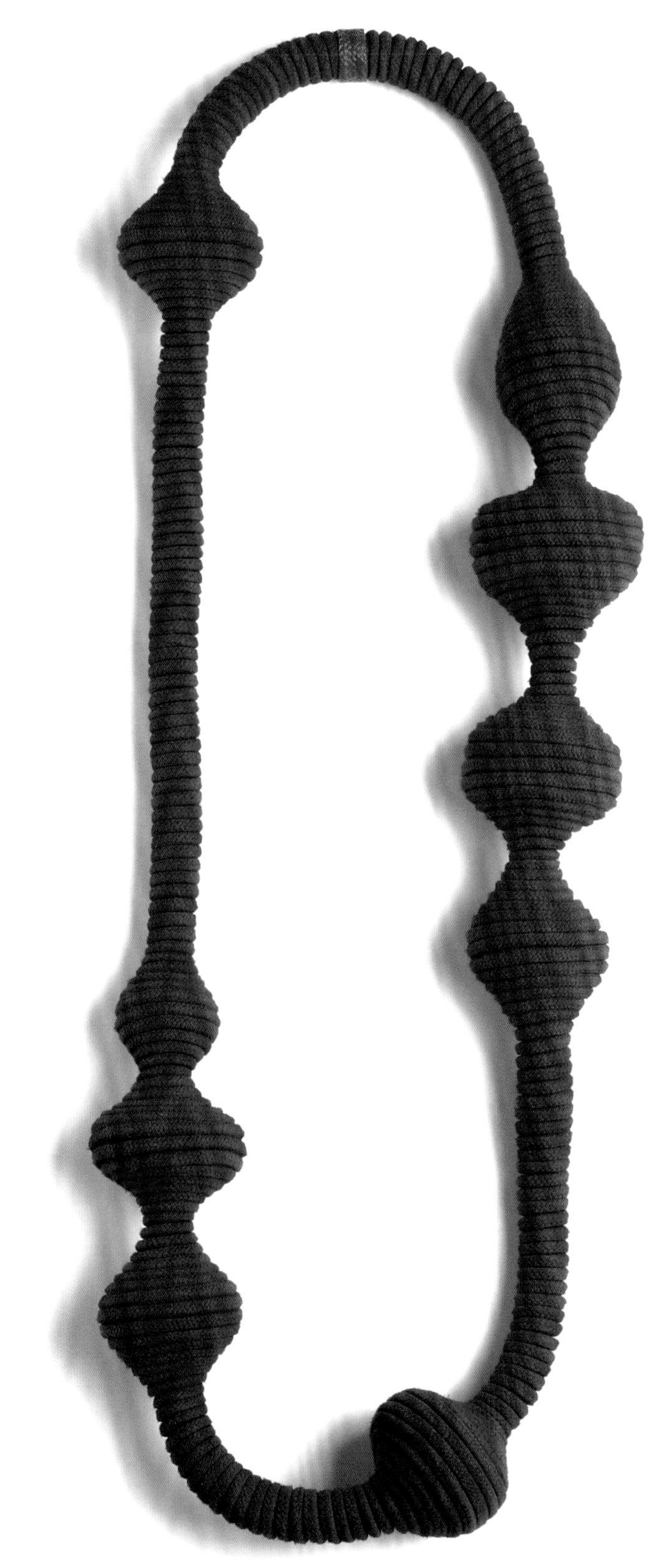

RED NECKPIECE COILED COTTON ROPE AND YARN

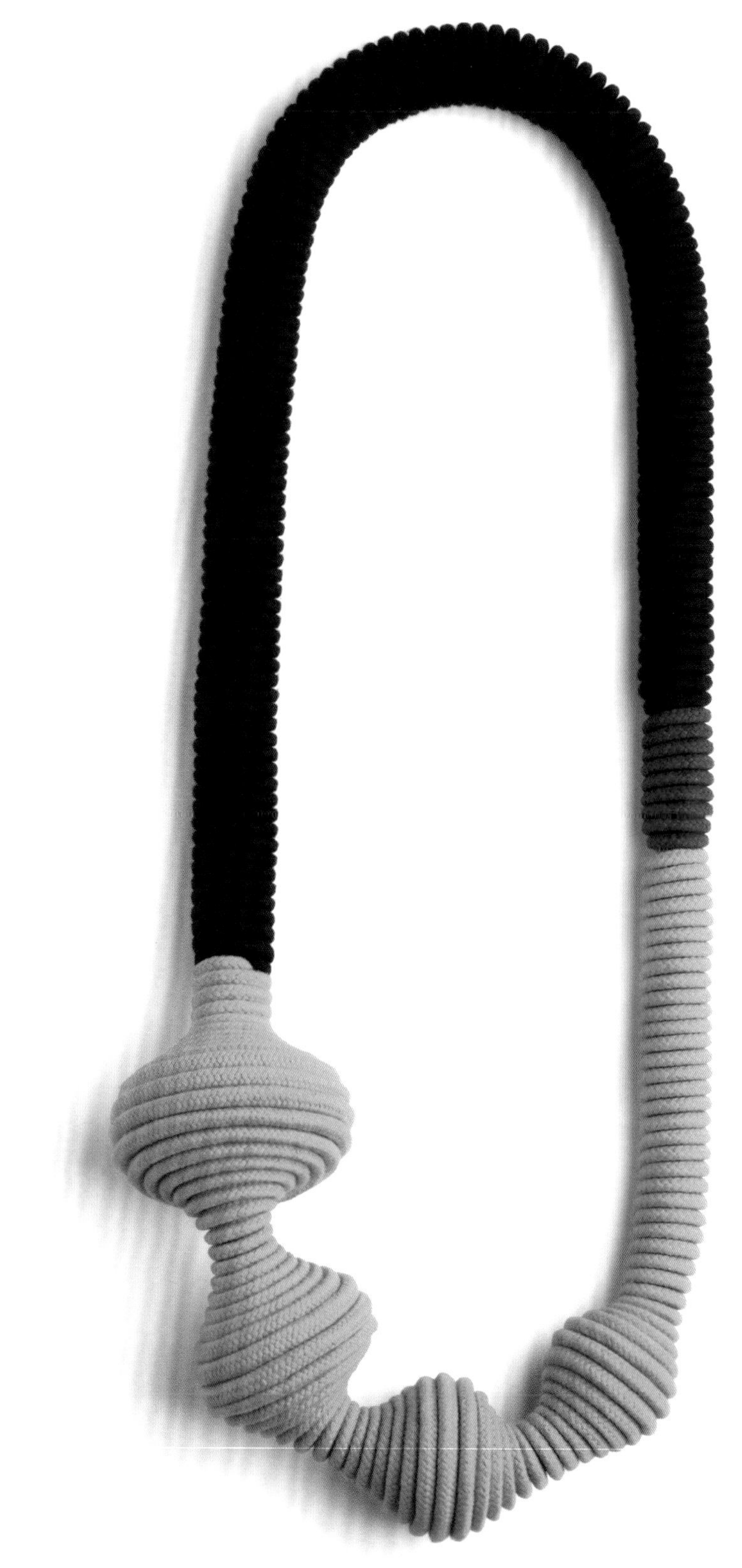

'BLUES COLLECTION I' NECKPIECE COILED COTTON ROPE AND YARN

FEMKE BOSCHKER THE NETHERLANDS

NECKLACE 'HOME IS WHERE THE HART IS'
SILVER, 14 K YELLOW GOLD, SOLAR QUATZ

STEPHEN BOTTOMLEY UK

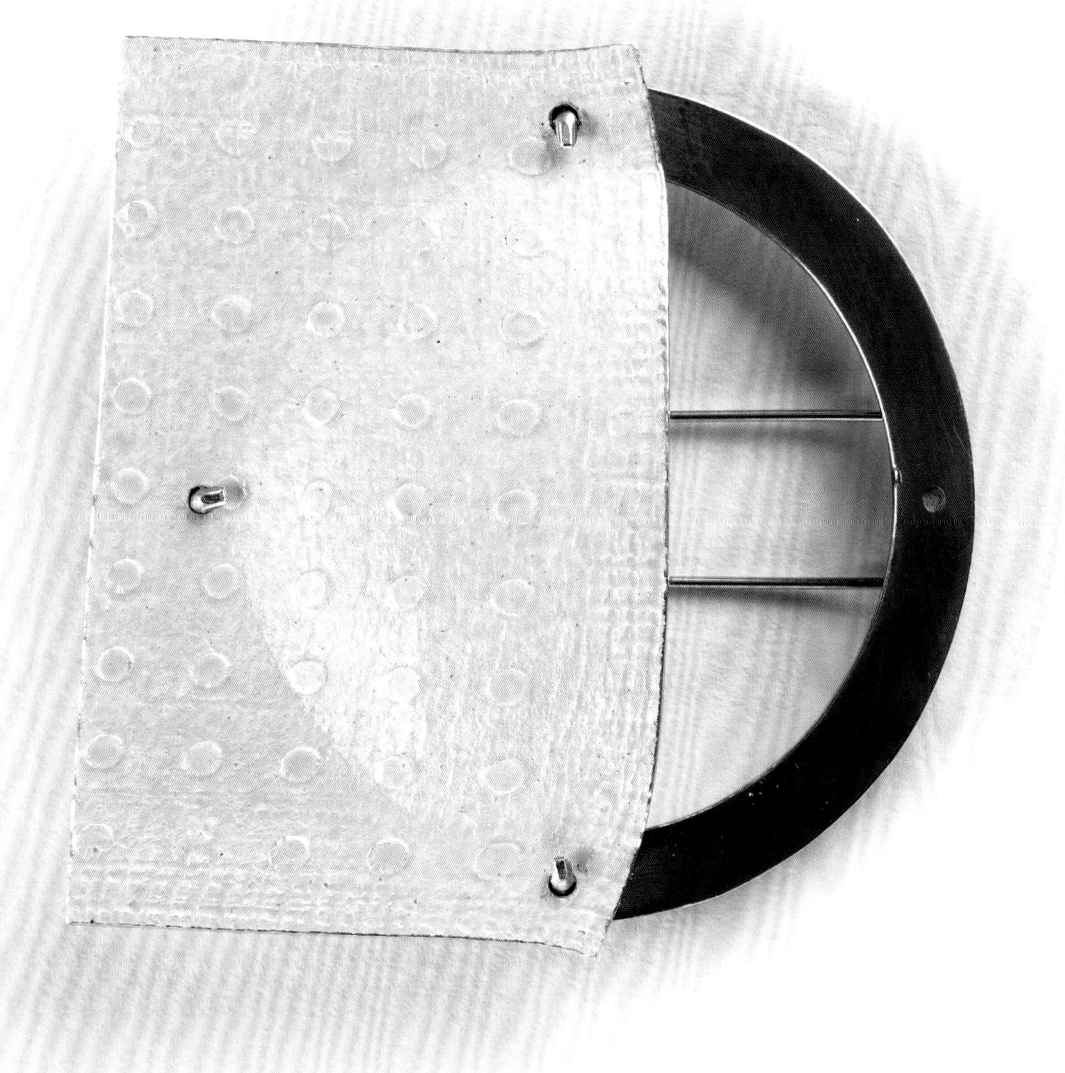

BROOCH ENAMEL, SILVER, GOLD, STEEL

JONATHAN MATHEW BOYD UK

'RING III' OXIDISED SILVER

BROOCH/PENDANT 'CIRCULATING GOSSIP' OXIDISED SILVER

FRÉDÉRIC BRAHAM FRANCE

BROOCH 'SKIN DEEP'
POLYURETHANE CHAMELEON PAINT AND GLOSSY POLYURETHANE VARNISH ON NICKEL-SILVER,SILVER, STAINLESS STEEL

BROOCH 'SKIN DEEP'
POLYURETHANE, CHAMELEON PAINT AND GLOSSY POLYURETHANE, VARNISH ON NICKEL-SILVER, SILVER, STAINLESS STEEL

'A' RING SILVER, QUARTZ, RED GLASS

CATALINA BRENES ITALY

'AGOSTO' BRACELET BRASS AND SHIBUICHI (JAPANESE ALLOW OF COPPER AND SILVER)

'BINARY NECKLACE' FINE SILVER WIRE, STERLING SILVER, MANUAL LOOM-FABRICATED-SEW

LILIA BREYTER ARGENTINA

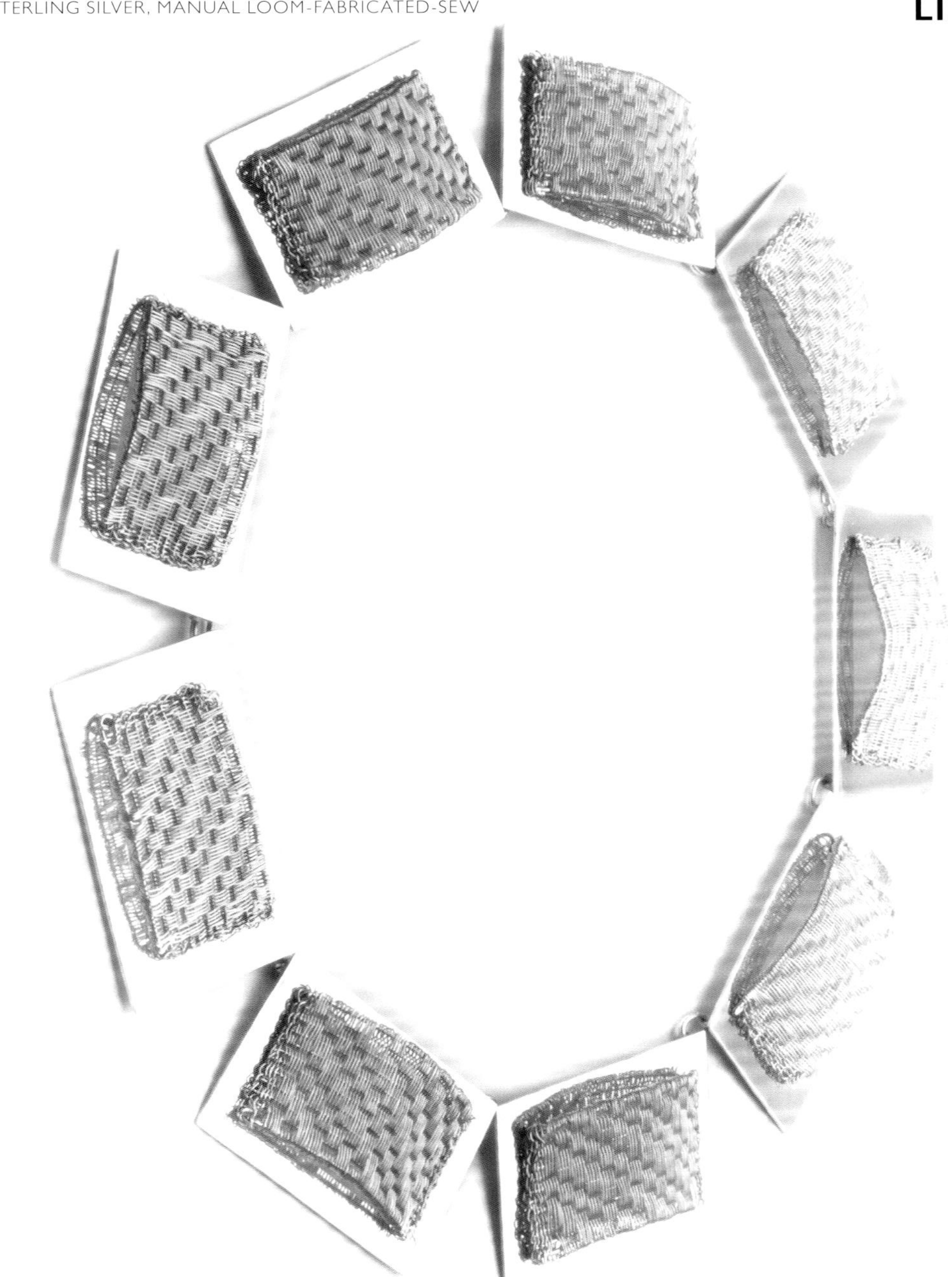

'BITONE NECKLACE' FINE SILVER WIRE, STERLING SILVER, MANUAL LOOM-SPOOL KNITTING FABRICATED

HELEN BRITTON GERMANY

'GREYLILAC' SILVER, GLASS, PAINT

'BIG GOLD' SILVER, GOLDPLATED, PLASTICS

HELEN BRITTON GERMANY

'ORANGEGREY' SILVER, PAINT, GLASS

'GREYPLANES' SILVER, PAINT, PLASTICS, WOOD, BRASS WIRE

SIGURD BRONGER NORWAY

'CARRYING DEVICE FOR A OSTRICH EGG' GOLD PLATED BRASS, STEEL, LEATHER CORD OSTRICH EGG SHELL

'BALLON RING' SILVER, STEEL, BALLOON VALVE

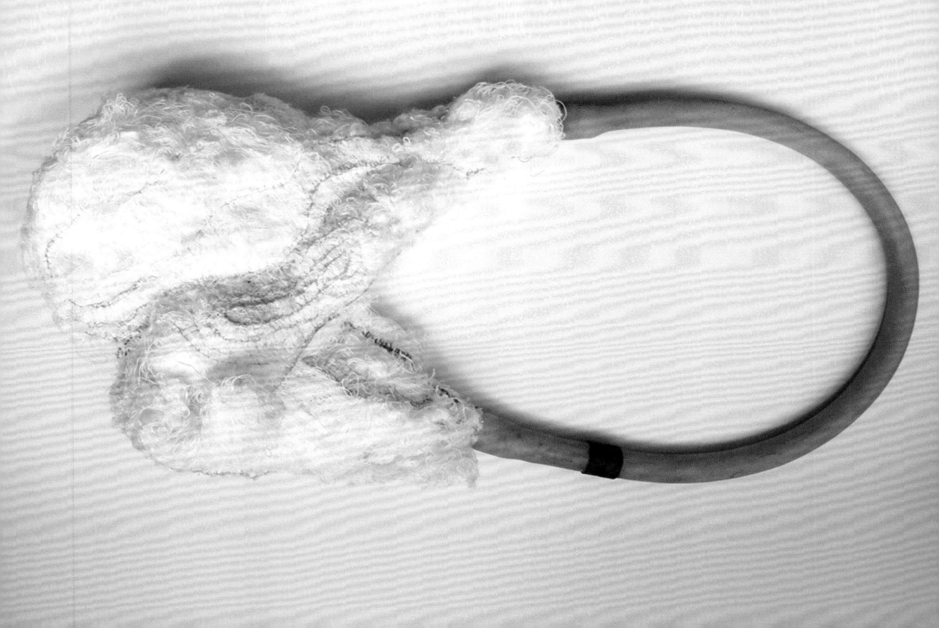

BEATRICE BROVIA SWEDEN

'BINDING WORKS'
SILK FIBERS, SILK THREADS, LATEX, OXIDIZED SILVER, MAGNETS

'THE UNAVOIDABLENESS OF EDUCATION'
NATURAL RESIN, LATEX, SILK/FLAX THREADS

KIM BUCK DENMARK

'PUMPOUS II' 24 K GOLD, HOT AIR

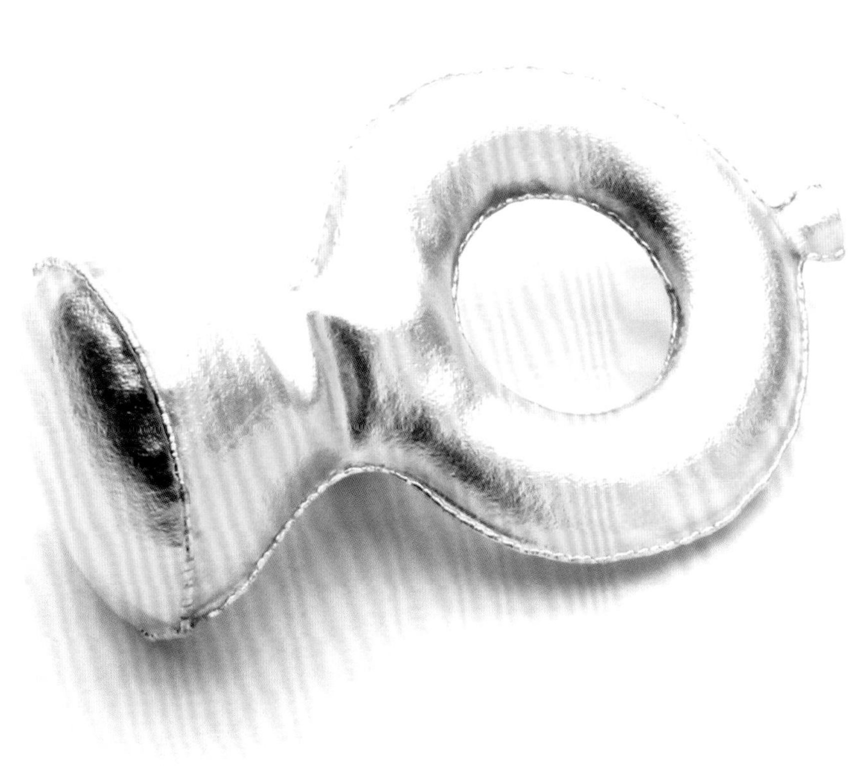

'PUMPOUS III' 24 K GOLD, HOT AIR

EVA BURTON SPAIN

BROOCHE 'INVISIBLE MAPS' METHACRYLATE, NIQUEL SILVER, PAINT

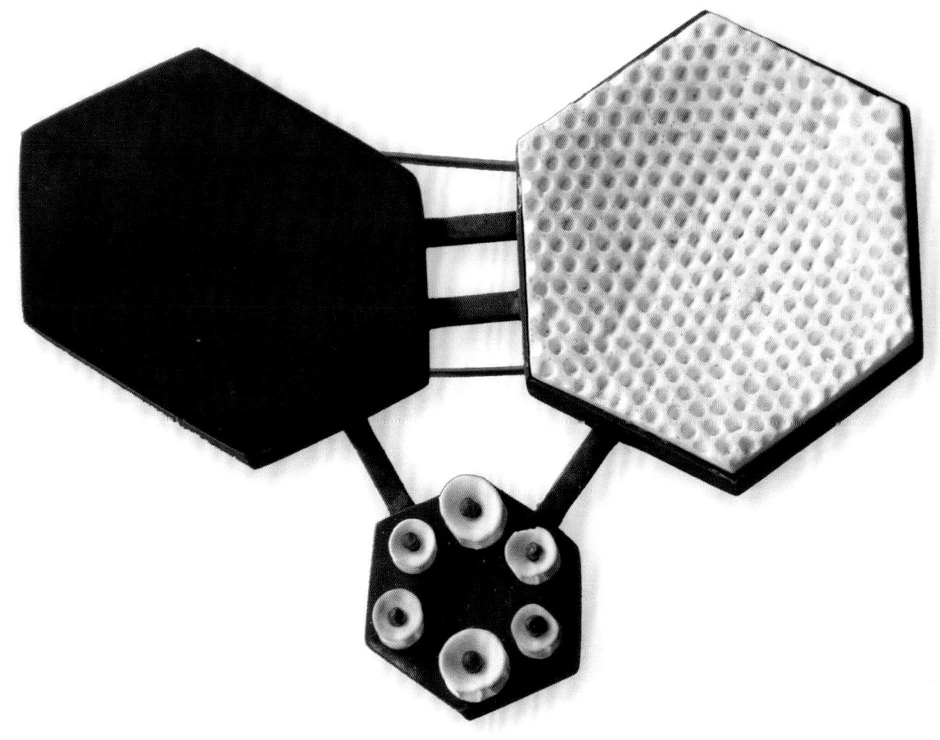

BROOCH 'MITOSIS' ACRYLIC RESIN, FISH VERTEBRAE, NIQUEL SILVER, PATINA

YURY BYLKOV RUSSIA

RING 'RUFS' BRASS, SILVER, CASTING

RING 'SEGMENTS' TITANIUM, SILVER

NECKLACE 'BLUE AND WHITE POTTERY' FOUND FIELD POTTERY, FABRIC AND HEMP STITCHWORK

AMANDA CAINES UK

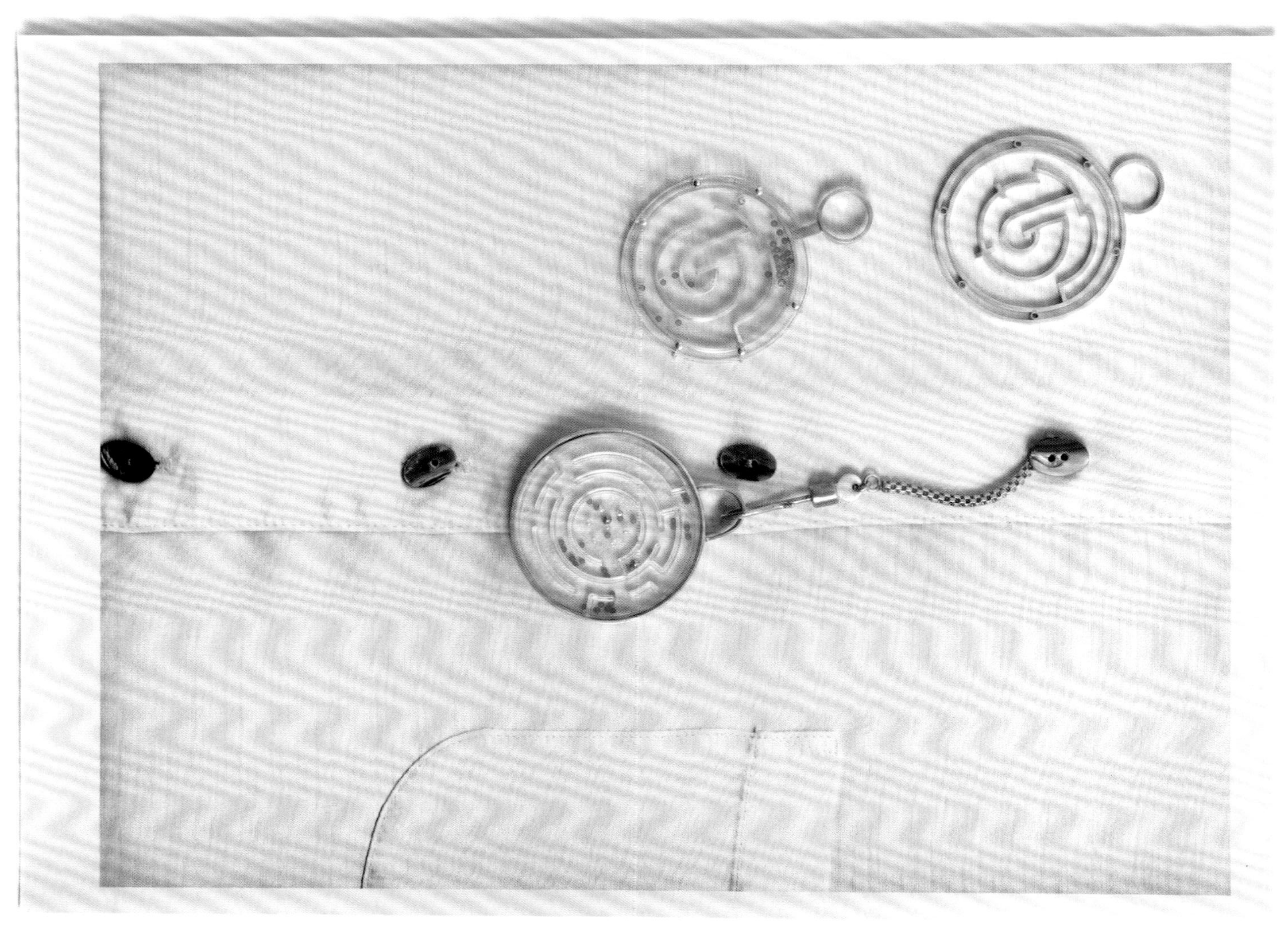

BROOCH/PENDANT STERLING SILVER AND ACRYLIC

ROXANNE CASALE ARGENTINA

MELISSA CAMERON USA

'POINT, LINE, PLANE PENTANT I' STAINLESS STEEL, VITREOUS ENAMEL, 925 SILVER

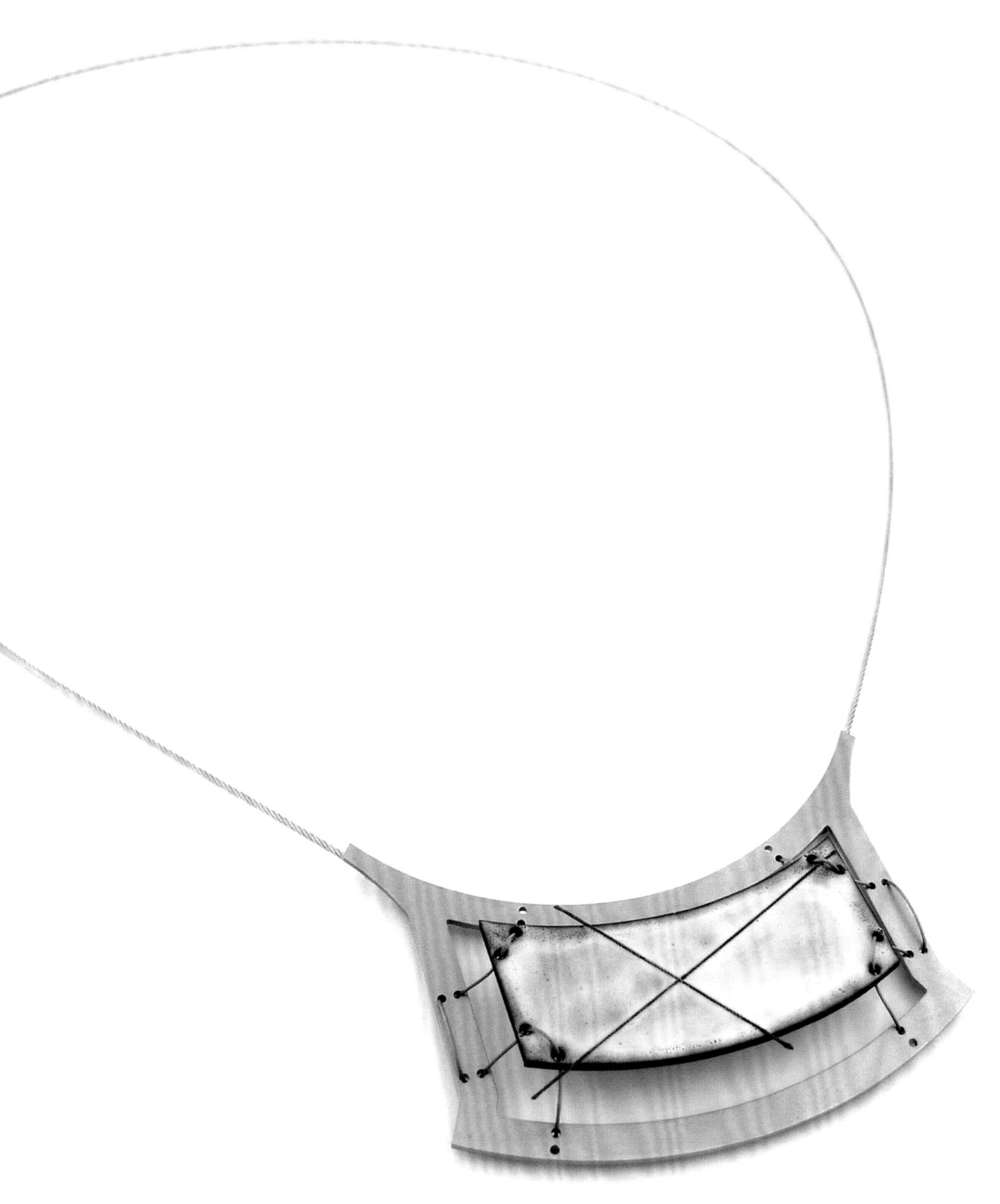

'AXIS NECKPIECE' STAINLESS STEEL, VITREOUS ENAMEL, 925 SILVER

H 'COLLECTION CONTRAPUNT' GOLD, SILVER, ACRYLIC ON CANVAS

JOAQUIM CAPDEVILLA SPAIN

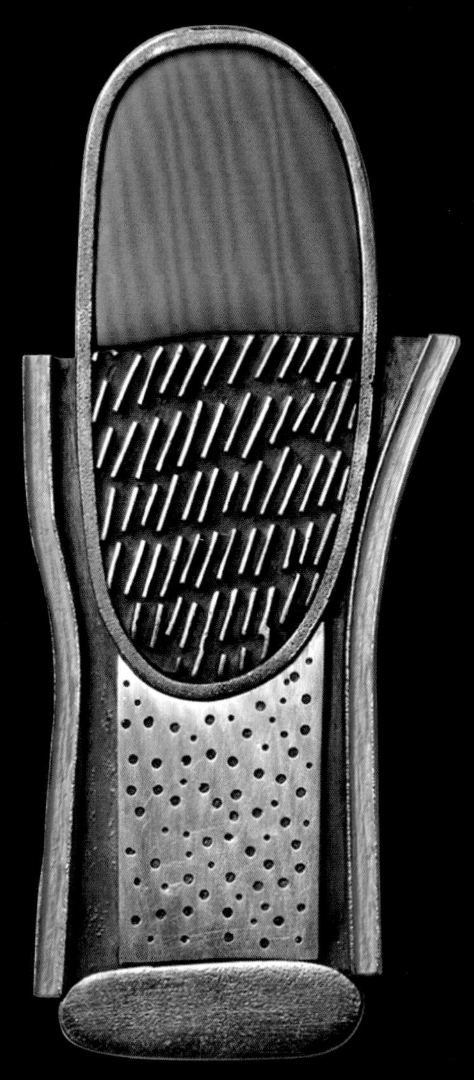

BROOCH 'AGNES' SILVER, GOLD, JAPANESE LACQUER AND ACRYLIC

JOAQUIM CAPDEVILLA SPAIN

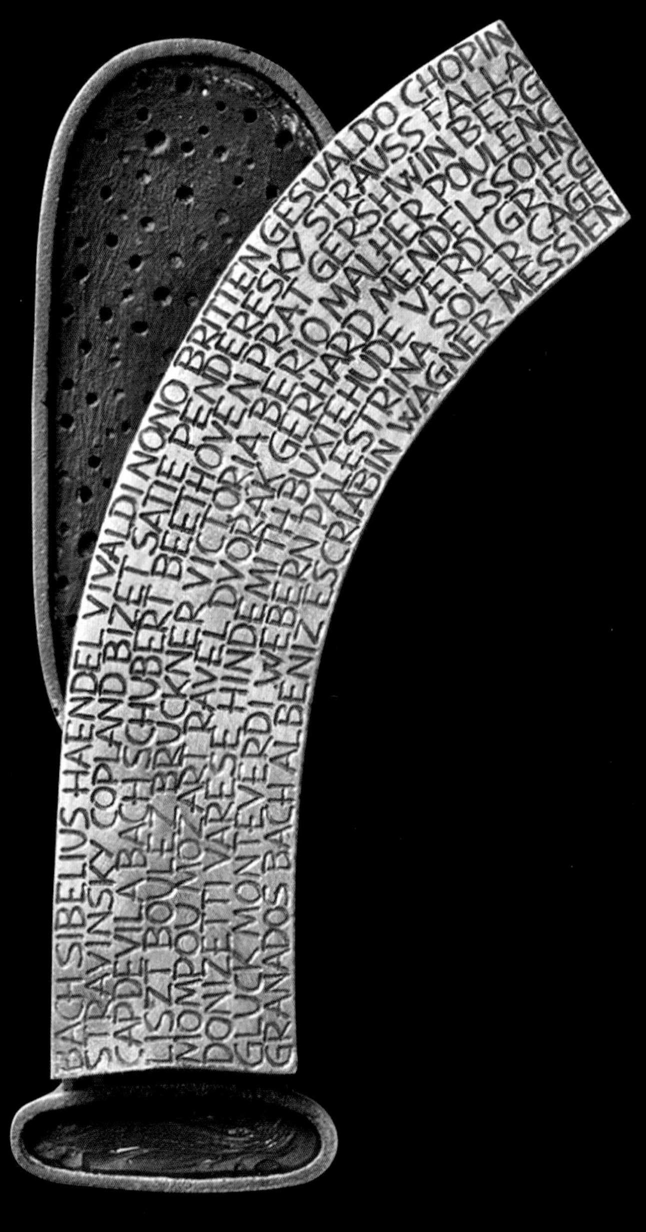

BROOCH 'COLLECTION CAMINS INTERIORS' GOLD AND SILVER

BROOCH 'ANGELS' SILVER, WOOD AND ACRYLIC

JICHANG CHAI UK

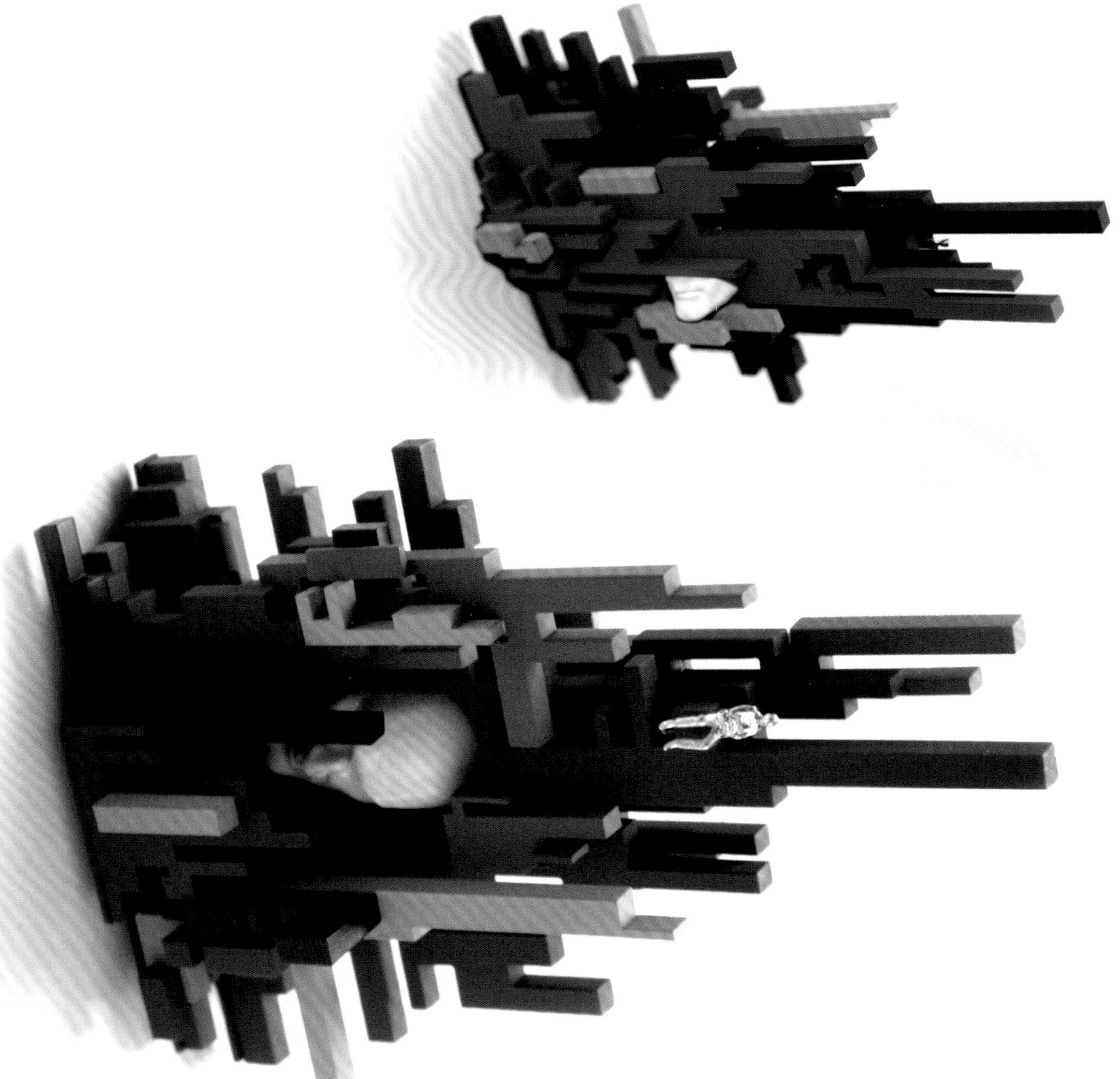

'THE BABEL' SILVER, ACRYLIC, RESIN, METAL PAINT, MAGNET

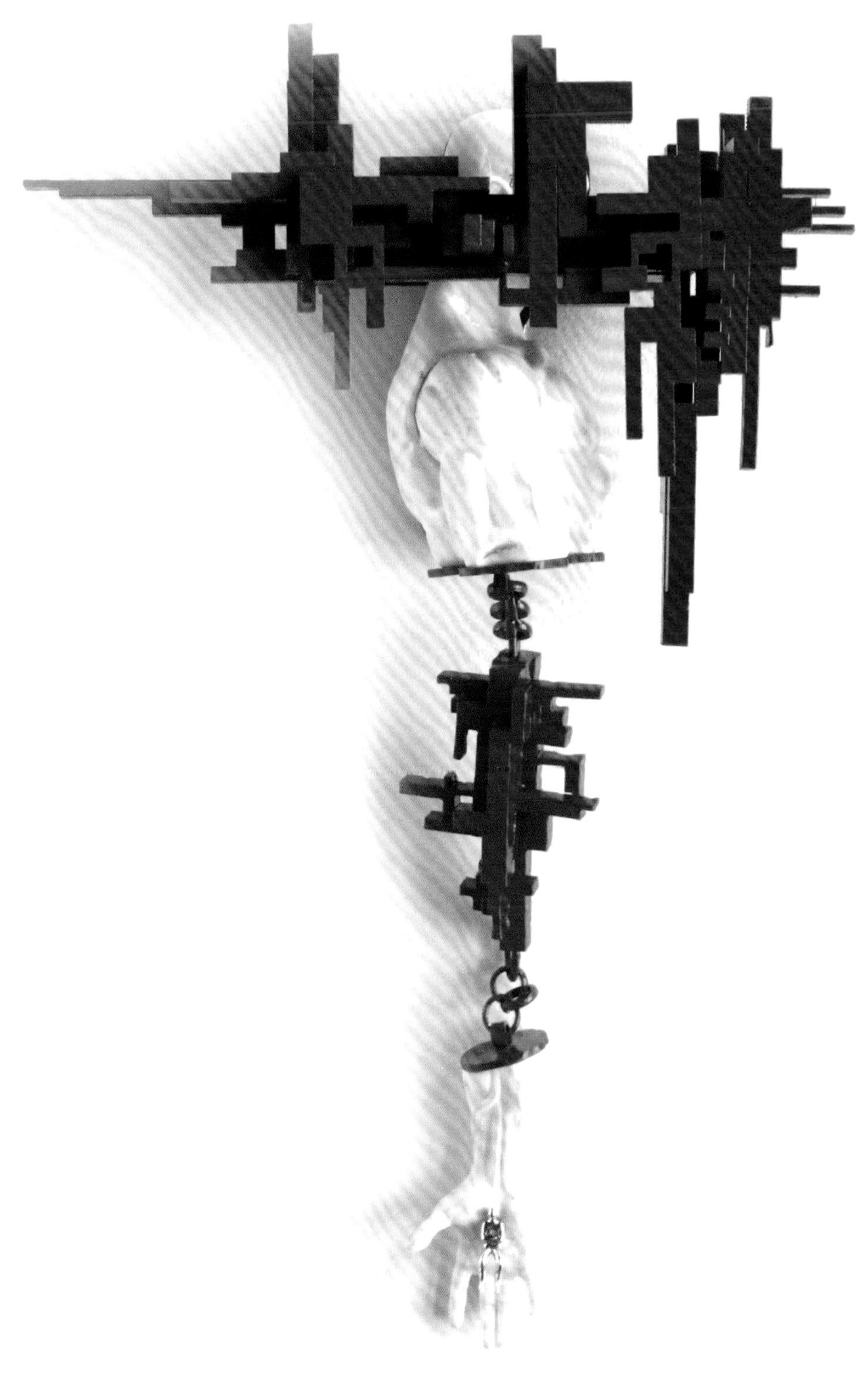

'RULE' SILVER, ACRYLIC, RESIN, METAL PAINT

JACQUI CHAN AUSTRALIA

BROOCH FROM PUBLIC PROJECT 'HOST A BROOCH' BURNT FLOORBOARDS, BRASS, GAS HEATER (STEEL), STAINLESS STEEL PIN

BROOCH FROM PUBLIC PROJECT 'HOST A BROOCH' ROAD CONE, BRASS TUBE RIVETS, GAS HEATER (STEEL), STAINLESS STEEL PIN

DANIA CHELMINSKY ISRAËL

BROOCH EPOXY, SILVER, PHOTOS, THREADS

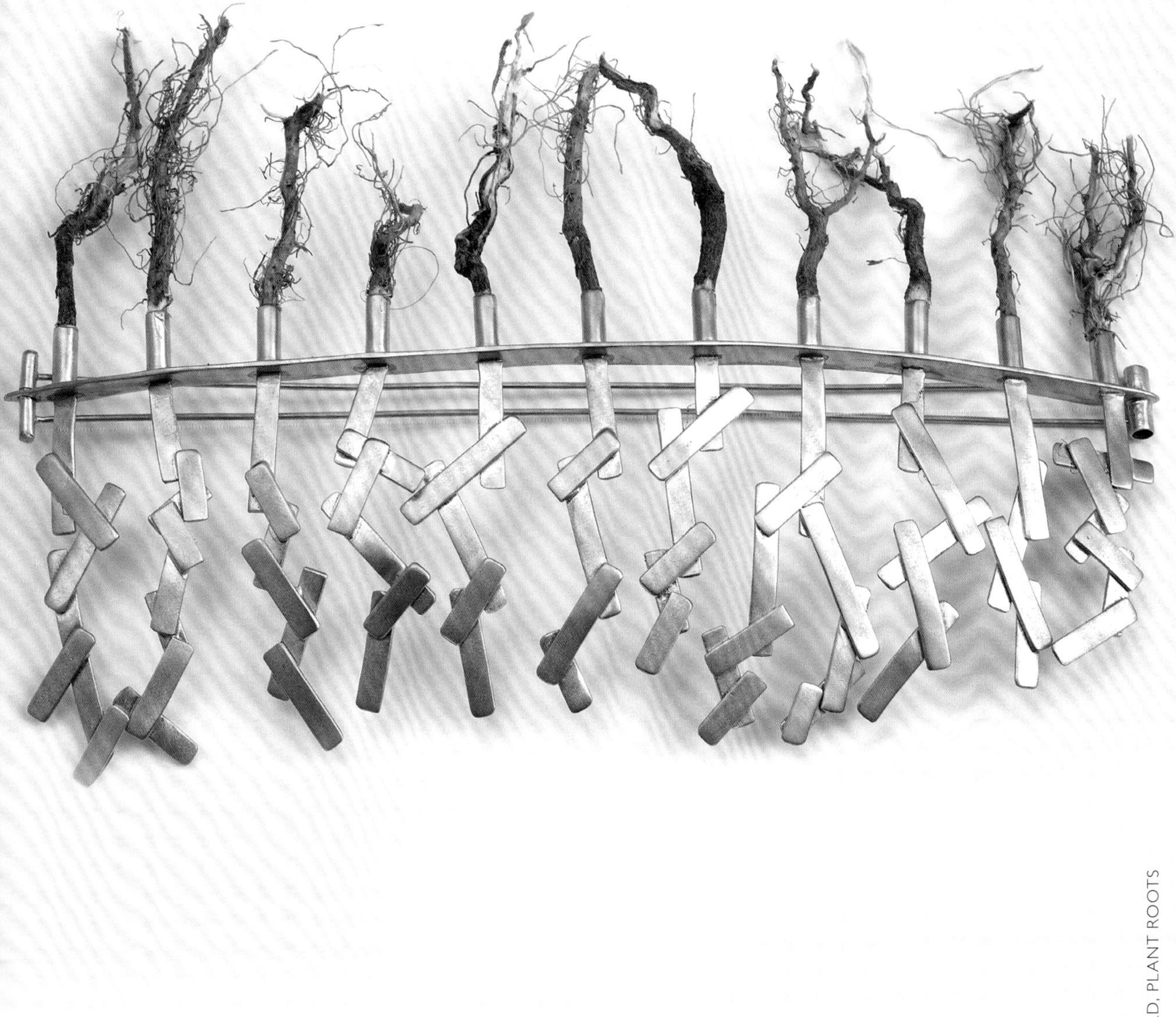

BROOCH BRASS, GOLD, PLANT ROOTS

ATTAI CHEN GERMANY

UNTITELD BROOCH PAPER, PAINT, GRAPHITE, GLUE, SILVER, BRASS, STAINLESS STEEL

NICOLAS CHENG SWEDEN

'BEAUTY OF NOTHINGLESS' COPPER, NATURAL SPONGE, SISAL FIBRE, COTTON, SILK

UNTITLED BRACELET SILVER, AQUAMARINE - CAD (RHINO)HAND FOLDED, FABRICATED

DAVID CHOI USA

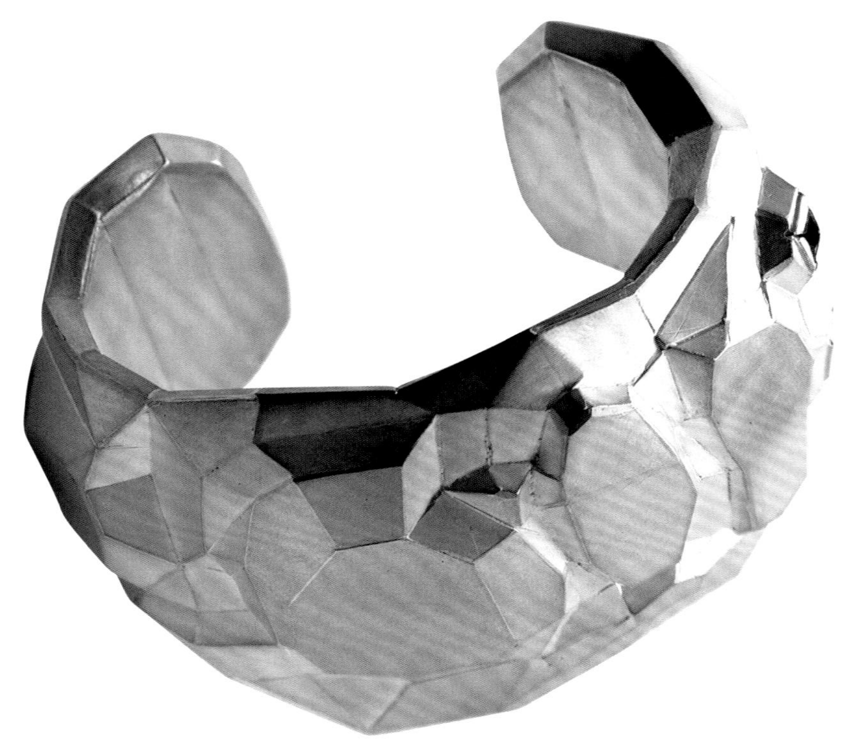

CARINA CHITSAZ-SHOSHTARY GERMANY

PENDANT 'WHAT'S LEFT OF KRYPTON-STAINED' GRAFFITI, SILVER

JEEHYUN CHUNG UK

'ROOF AND I 1' NECKLACE ELASTIC AND COTTON THREADS, OXIDISED SILVER

'ROOF AND I 2' NECKLACE ELASTIC AND COTTON THREADS, OXIDISED SILVER

THEA CLARK USA

'ROOT' PENDANT CYANOTYPE ON SILK, FOUND PLASTIC, WOOD, NICKEL, TINTED PLASTIC, OXIDIZED SILVER, COTTON TREAD

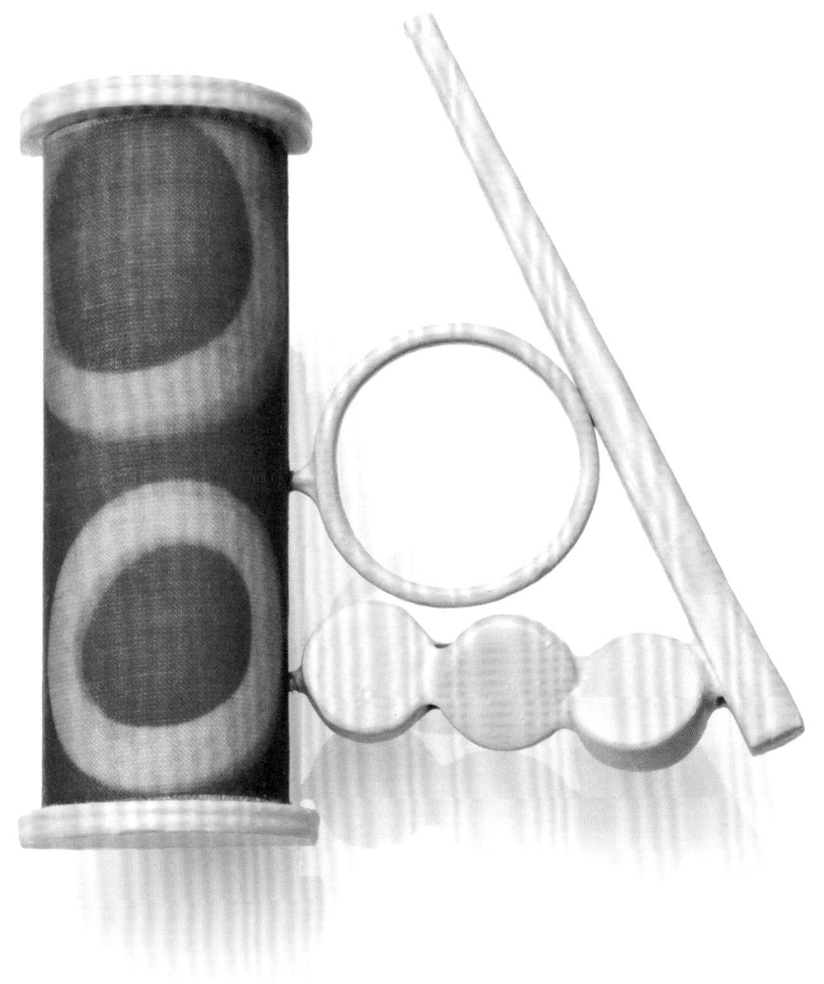

BROOCH 'SIX DEGREES' CYANOTYPE ON SILK, WOOD, COPPER, PVC, TINTED PLASTIC, ACRYLIC

EIMEAR CONYARD IRELAND

'JEWELLERY IS NOT MERELY ADORNMENT' COPPER AND GARNET GEMSTONE BOWL WITH 18 K GOLD AND PEARL RING INSET

'JEWELLERY IS NOT MERELY ADORNMENT' COPPER AND GARNET GEMSTONE BOWL WITH 18 K GOLD AND PEARL RING INSET

ANA COUTO PORTUGAL

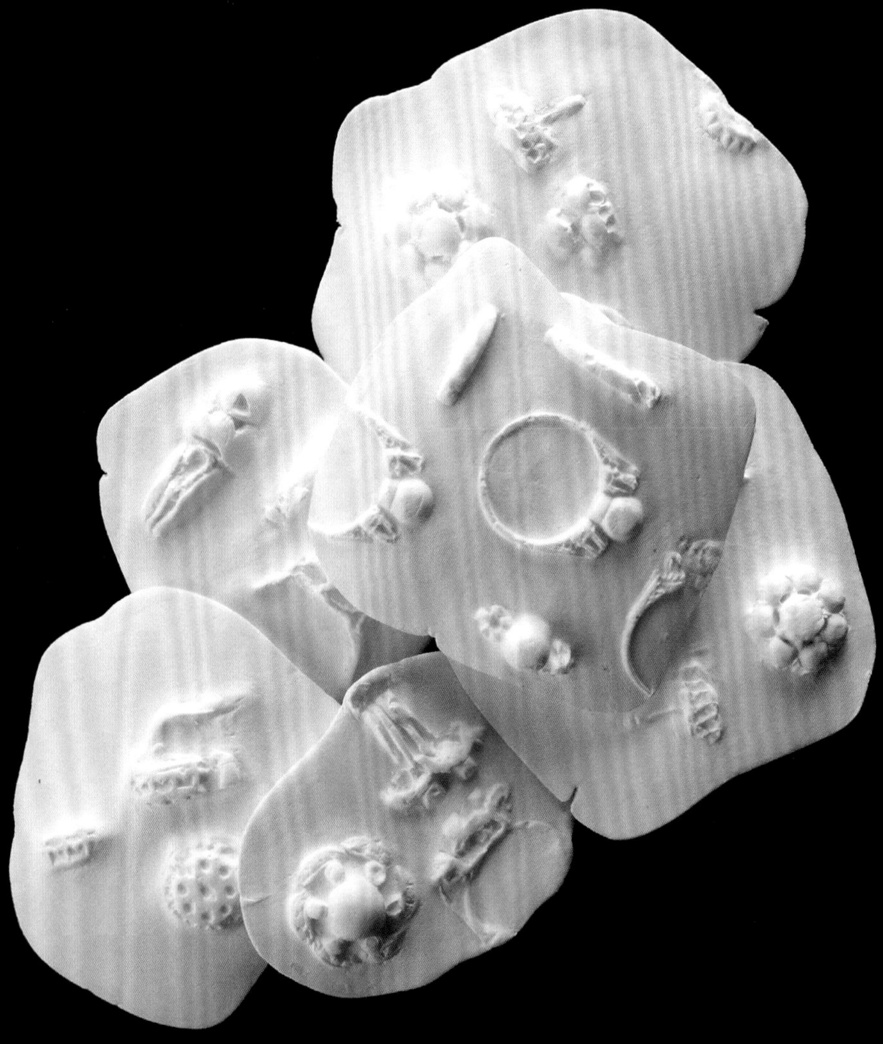

PAPER BROOCH PAPER PULP, MAGNETS, MANUFACTURE

FRÉDÉRIQUE COOMANS BELGIUM

RESURRECTION 'REPEAT AFTER ME' NECKLACE SILVER, DOLL'S MOUTH/NOSE, SOUND BOX, LEATHER

ELS CUVELIER THE NETHERLANDS

RING 'ELECTRIC PLUG'
LEFT: HANDMADE SILVER WITH GOLDEN PINS
RIGHT: 3D PRINTED IN POLYAMIDE, COLOURED BLACK

RAMÓN PUIG CUYÀS SPAIN

BROOCH NICKEL, OXIDIZED SILVER

RAMÓN PUIG CUYÀS SPAIN

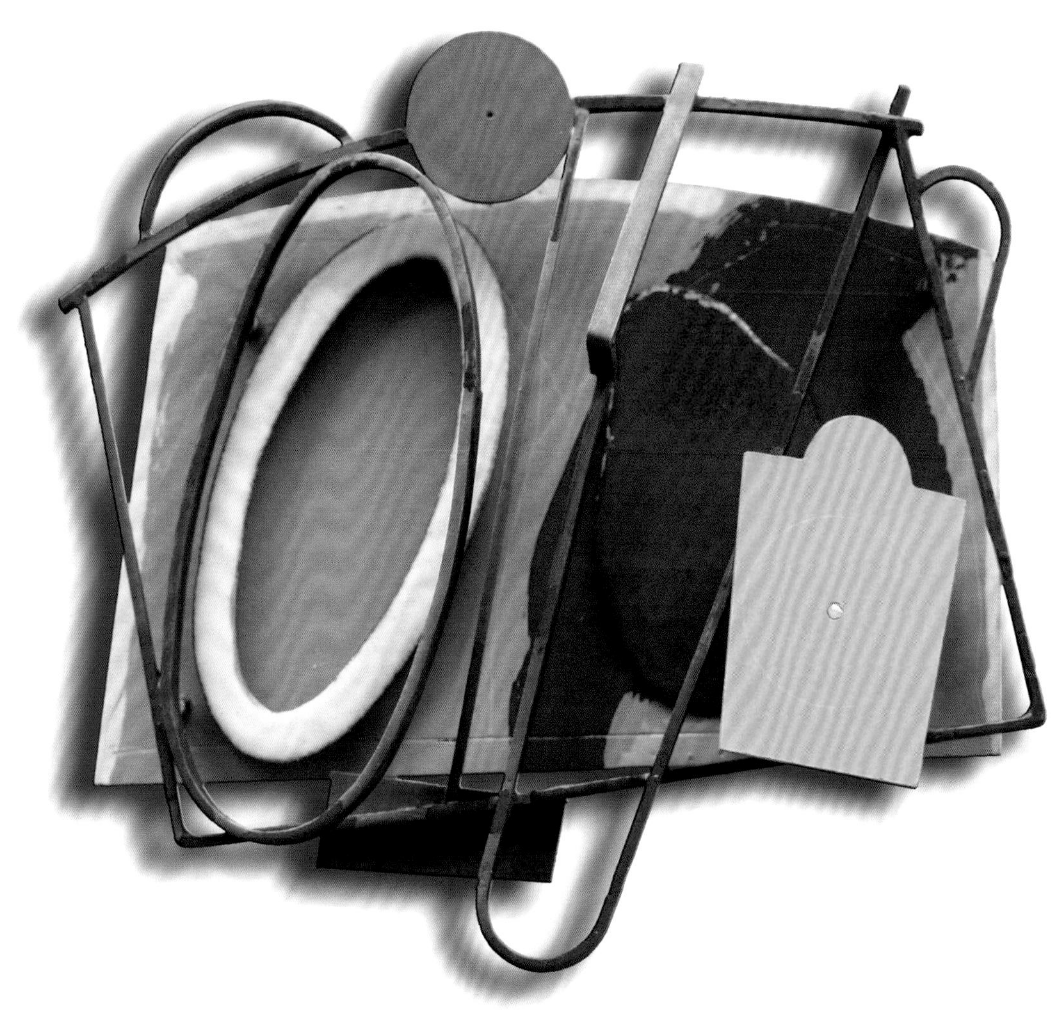

BROOCH SILVER, PLASTIC, ENAMEL, NICKEL SILVER, ACRYLIC PAINTED

BROOCH NICKEL SILVER, OXIDIZER, RECONTSTRUCTED STONE

JOHANNA DAHM SWITZERLAND

RING 'ENHANCEMENT'
PURE GOLD 24 K, FRESH WATER PEARLS, PURE SILVER 999,9 - 'FAST ASHANTI' RING, MODELLED IN CLAY IN THE NEGATIVE.
CAST IN THE 'CLOSED CYCLE' CASTING TECHNIQUE OF THE ASHANTI, GHANA AND THE DOKRA, INDIA

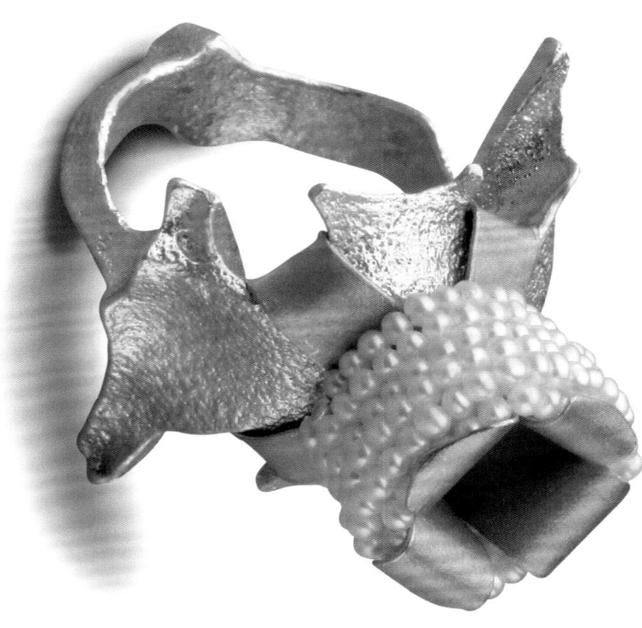

RING 'ENHANCEMENT'
PURE GOLD 24 K, PURE SILVER 999,9 - 'FAST ASHANTI/HERITAGE' RING WITH TRACES FROM A 1950 DIAMOND RING, MODELLED IN CLAY IN THE NEFATIVE. CAST IN THE 'CLOSED CYCLE' CASTING TECHNIQUE OF THE ASHANTI AND THE DOKRA

UNTITLED SILVER, PLASTIC BOXES, PEARLS, CORALS, SILK TREAD AND A LOT OF GEMSTONES

ANNETTE DAM DENMARK

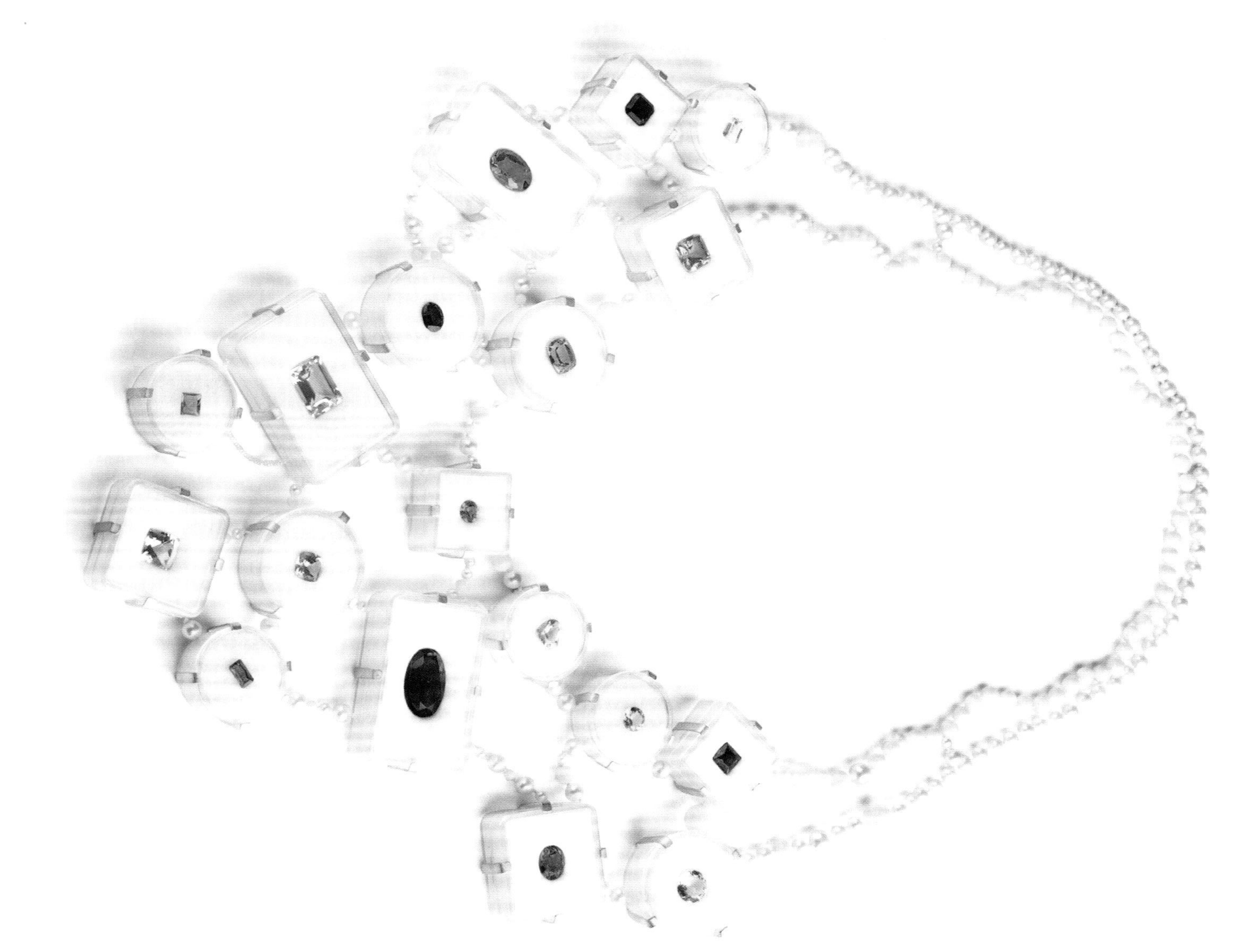

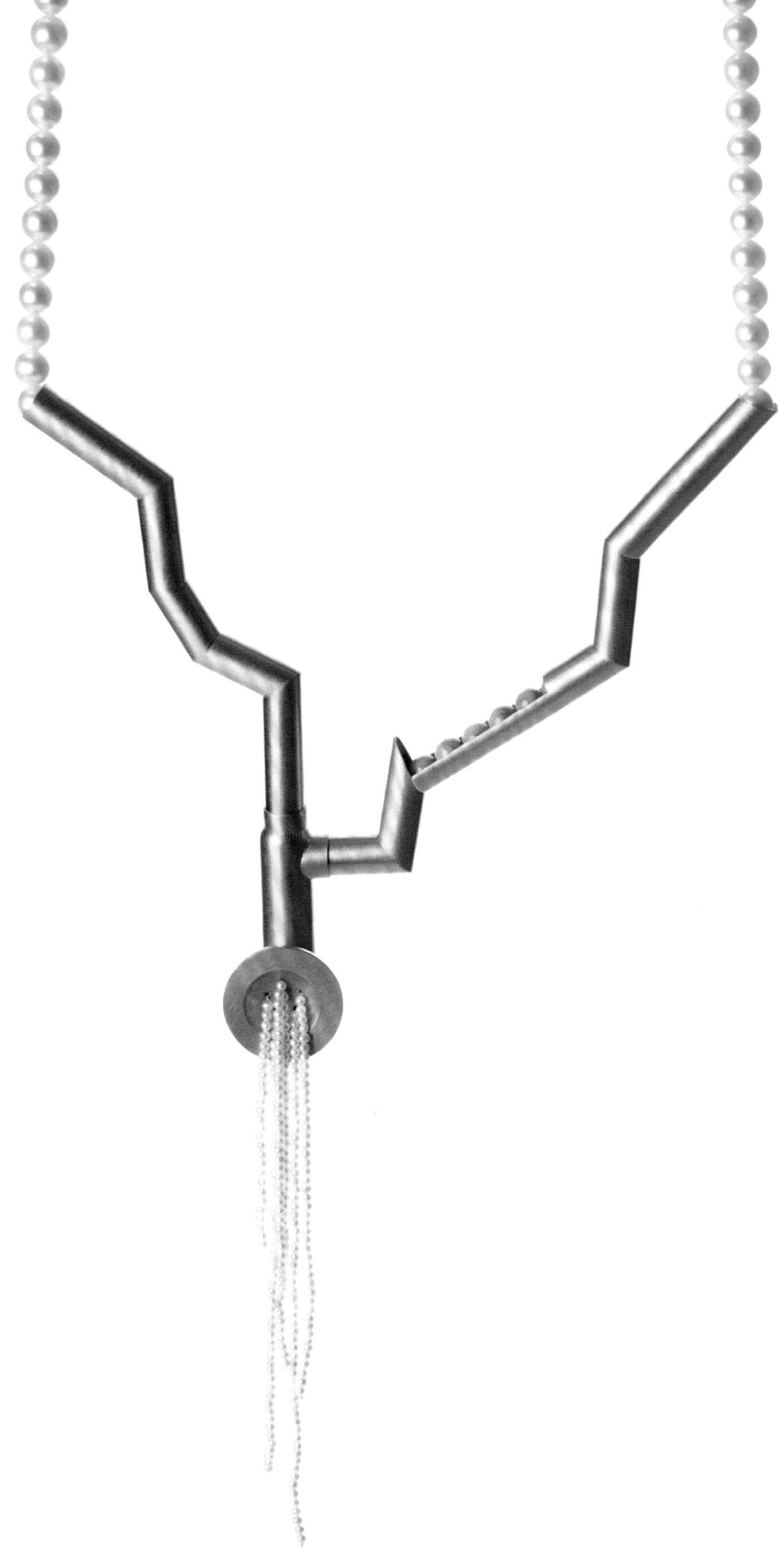

UNTITLED GOLDPLATE SILVER, GOLD 18 K, PEARLS, CORALS

PIN 'THE SOWING' BREAD, LOBSTER , PAW, SILVER

TERESA DANTAS PORTUGAL

'FOUNTAIN OF LIFE' SILVER OXIDIZED AND BLEACHED - OPAL (RAW)

ALEXANDER DAUVIT UK

'A FOREST'

FOUND, CORRODED IRON SHEET 'RECYCLED NICKEL FROM INDUSTRIAL ELECTRODES' RECLAIMED COPPER, SILVER, GOLD, PURE IRON, PORCELAIN, VICTORIAN GLASS TILE, ENAMEL, CARVED ONYX SKULL, EMERALDS, RUBIES, BACK SPINELS, JADE, GARNET, CITRINE, RECLAIMED AFRICAN BLACKWOOD, AMBER

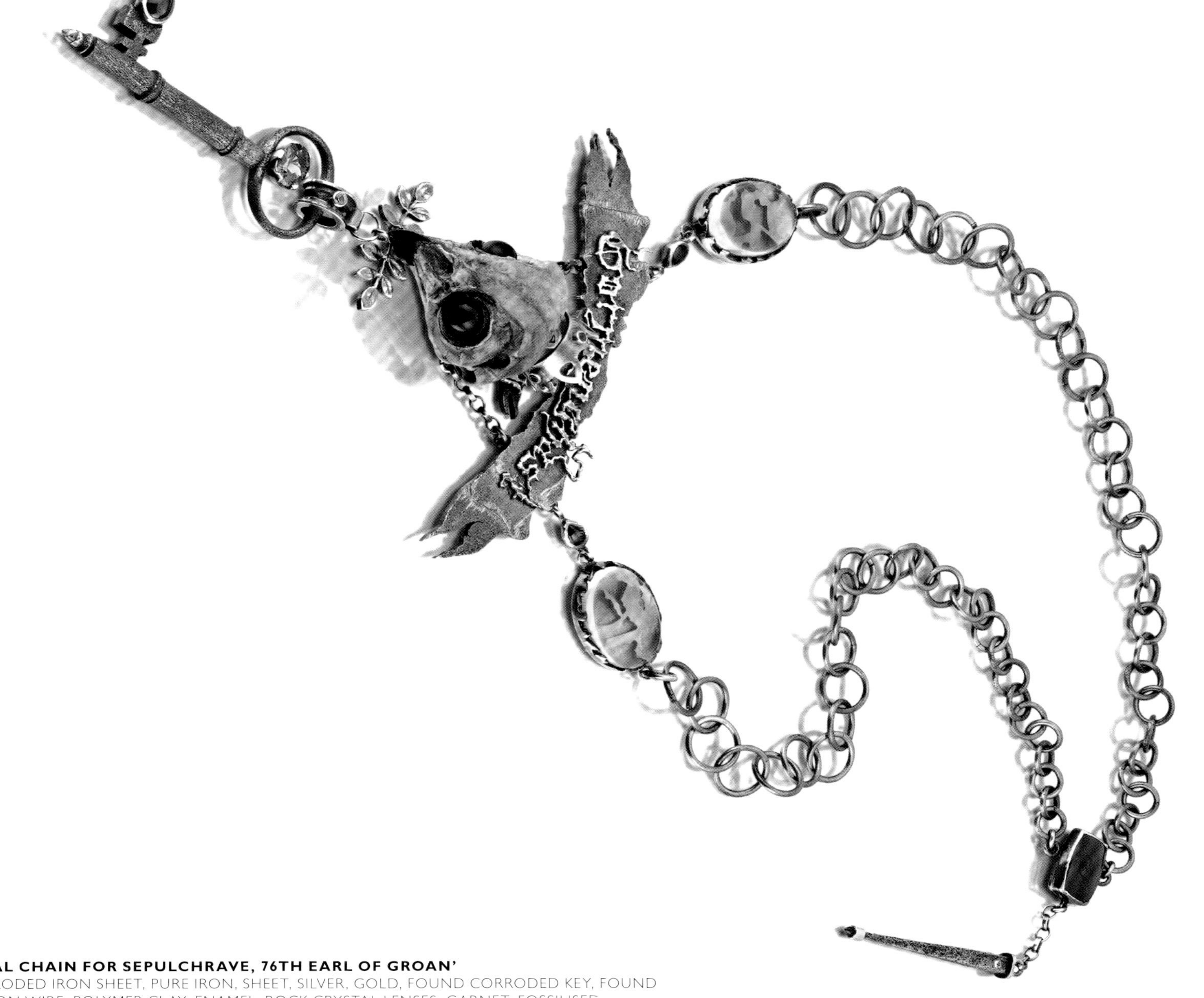

'CEREMONIAL CHAIN FOR SEPULCHRAVE, 76TH EARL OF GROAN'
FOUND, CORRODED IRON SHEET, PURE IRON, SHEET, SILVER, GOLD, FOUND CORRODED KEY, FOUND IRON NAIL, IRON WIRE, POLYMER CLAY, ENAMEL, ROCK CRYSTAL LENSES, GARNET, FOSSILISED DINOSAUR BONE, GREEN GARNET, CHRYSOPRASE

SYLVIA DE LAVEGA SPAIN

UNTITLED YELLOW AND WHITE GOLD, GREEN TOURMALINE

DAAN DE DECKER BELGIUM

BROOCH 'CONSTRUCTION I WITH MOTHER OF PEARL' SILVER (PLATINATED) AND MOTHER OF PEARL

TINE DE RUYSSER UK

'NZ BRACELET' 16 POLYMER BANKNOTES OF 5 NEW ZEALAND DOLLAR

'CHINA-DOUBLE' 68 PAPER BANKNOTES OF 1/10 CHINA YUAN (YI JIAO)

JULIA DE VILLE AUSTRALIA

'CLAW RING BLACK' STERLING SILVER, BLACK SAPPHIRES

'LILY CLAW BROOCH' STERLING SILVER, BLACK RHODIUM, GOLD PLATE

PENDANT SILVER, GERMAN SILVER, COTTON

MARIELLE DEBETHUNE FRANCE

BROOCH SILVER, COPPER, GERMAN SILVER, STEEL

SIEGFRIED DEBUCK BELGIUM

RING 'SPINA' GOLD

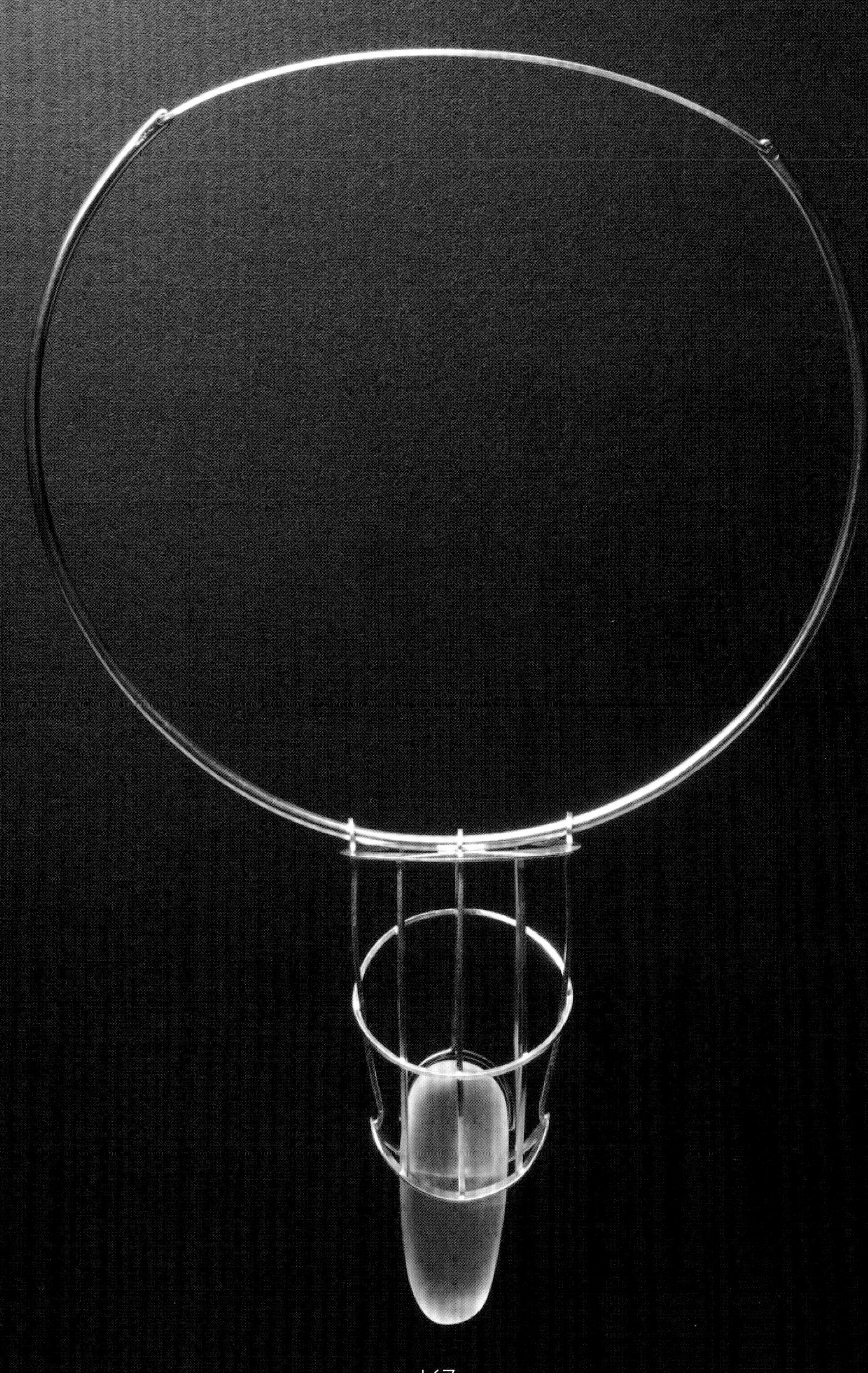

PENDENTIEF 'TOISON D'OR' GOLD, PLEXI, STEEL

MARIE CLAIRE DESMEDT BELGIUM

NECKLACE 'KISSES' RED SILK FROM A JAPANESE KIMONO, SILVER CHAIN (RECYCLED)

MARION DELARUE FRANCE

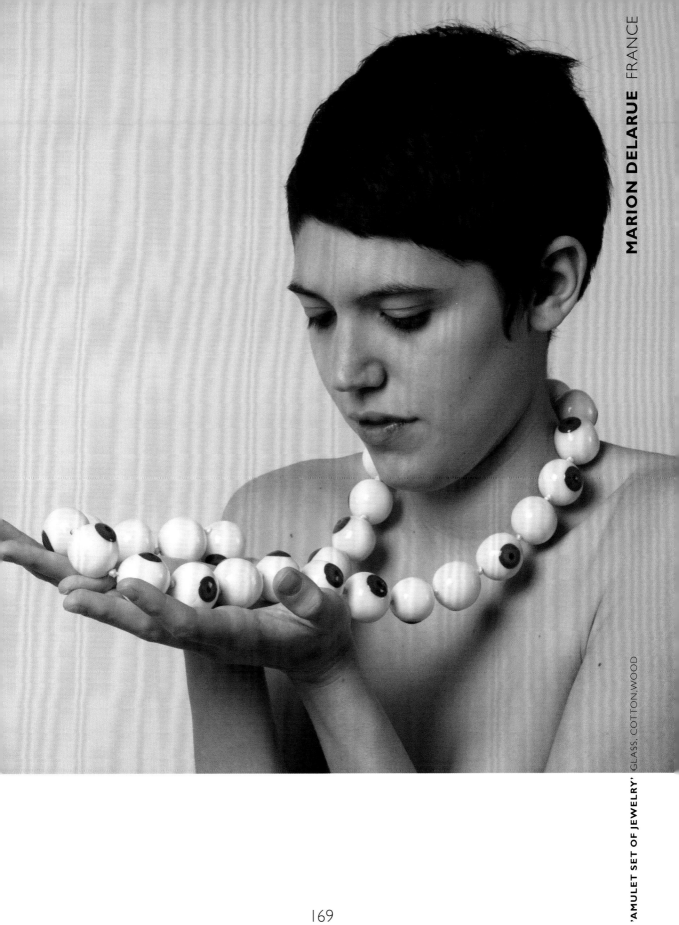

'AMULET SET OF JEWELRY' GLASS, COTTON, WOOD

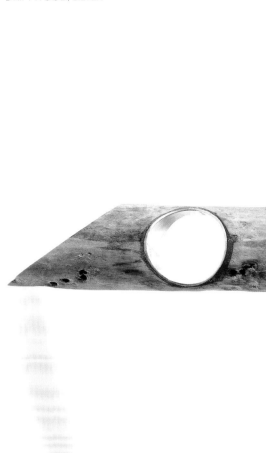

MARTINA DEMPF GERMANY

RING 'FINGER OF GOD' DRIFTWOOD, SILVER

PENDANT 'BODY AND SOUL' EBONY WOOD, SWEET WATER PEARLS, SILVER

PENDANT 'ARGONAUTS' TIN, SWEET WATER PEARLS, BRONZE, GOLD

MARTINA DEMPF GERMANY

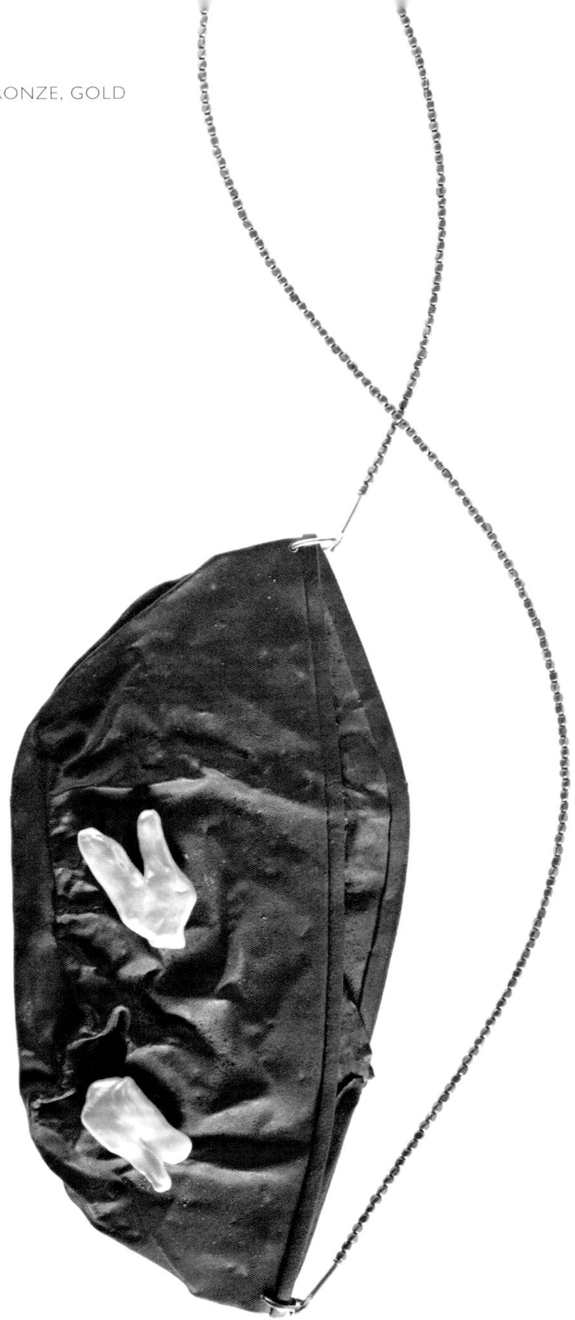

BROOCH 'COCOONING' DRIFTWOOD, SILVER, SMOKED QUARTZ

IRIS MONDELAERS BELGIUM

RING 'EIRTH COLLECTION'
GOLD 750/1000 AU, 8 MARQUISE SHAPED DIAMONDS (0.56 K) 1 BRILLIANT CUT DIAMOND (0.02 K)

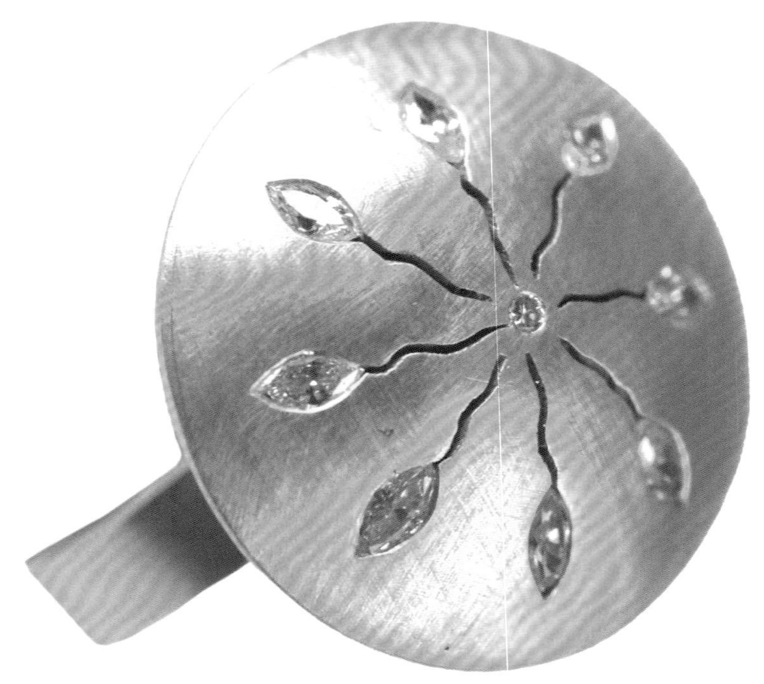

CATARINA DIAS PORTUGAL

'SOLDADOS 2' DOUBLE PIN SILVER AND GOLD PLATED

LAURENT DIOT BELGIUM

NDANT 'BISSO NA BISSO' ALUMINIUM, TITANIUM, GOLD (YELLOW 18 K), STAINLESS STEEL

PENDANT 'PROPAGANDA' IVORY, TITANIUM, GOLD (YELLOW 18 K), STAINLESS STEEL, CABLES

JOUNGMEE DO AUSTRALIA

'LONGEVITY BROOCH' STEEL, STAINLESS STEEL, FINE SILVER

'LONGEVITY BROOCH' STEEL, FINE SILVER, FINE GOLD

'INFANT OF PRAGUE' STERLING SILVER, GOLD 14 K, BRASS, COTTON, PLASTIC

JAN DONALDSON AUSTRALIA

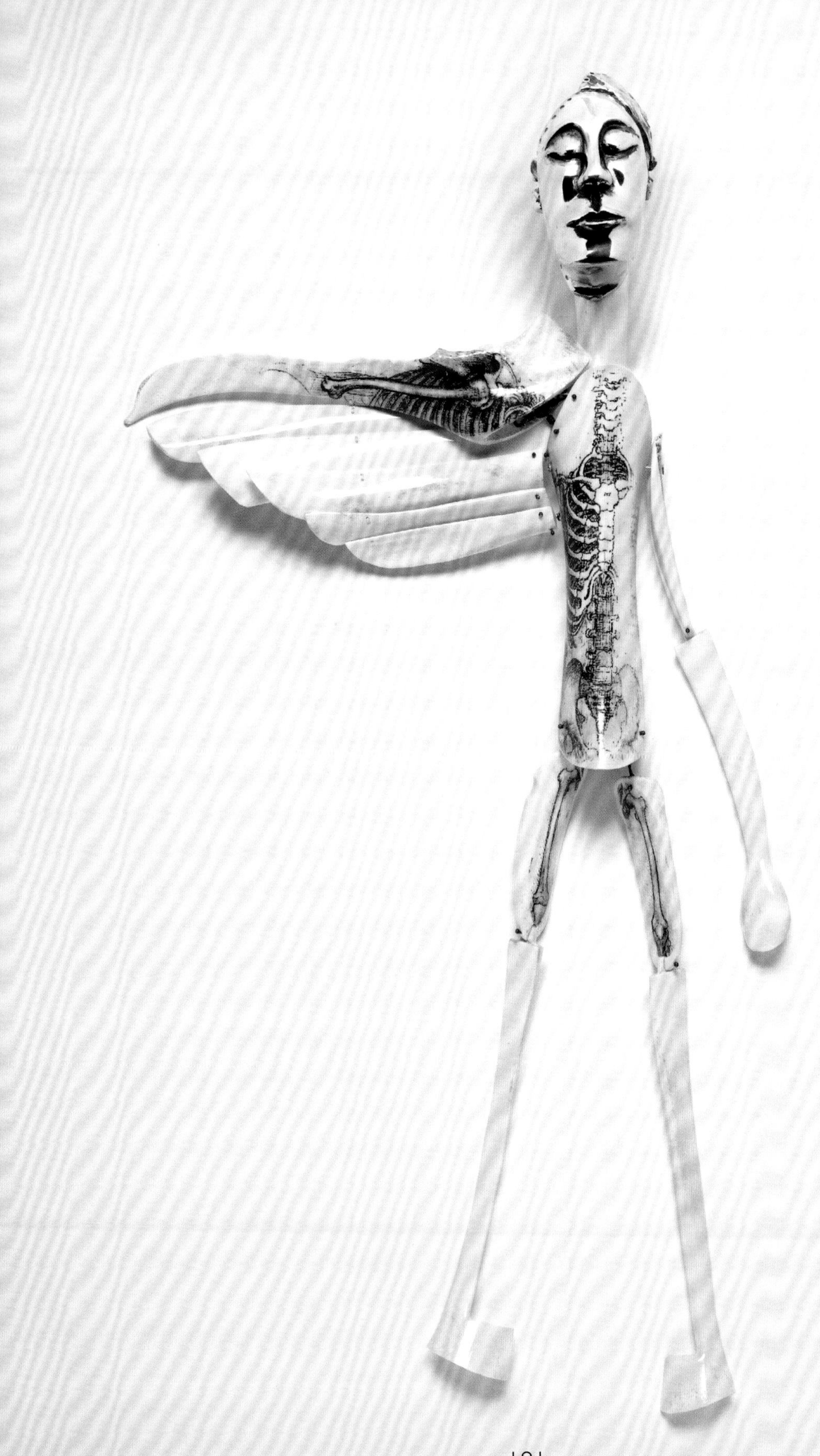

'ME AND YOU' BONE, STERLING SILVER, PAPER, LAQUER

JANEA DRESLER GERMANY

'KONFRONTIERT' PORCELAIN, COTTON BAND

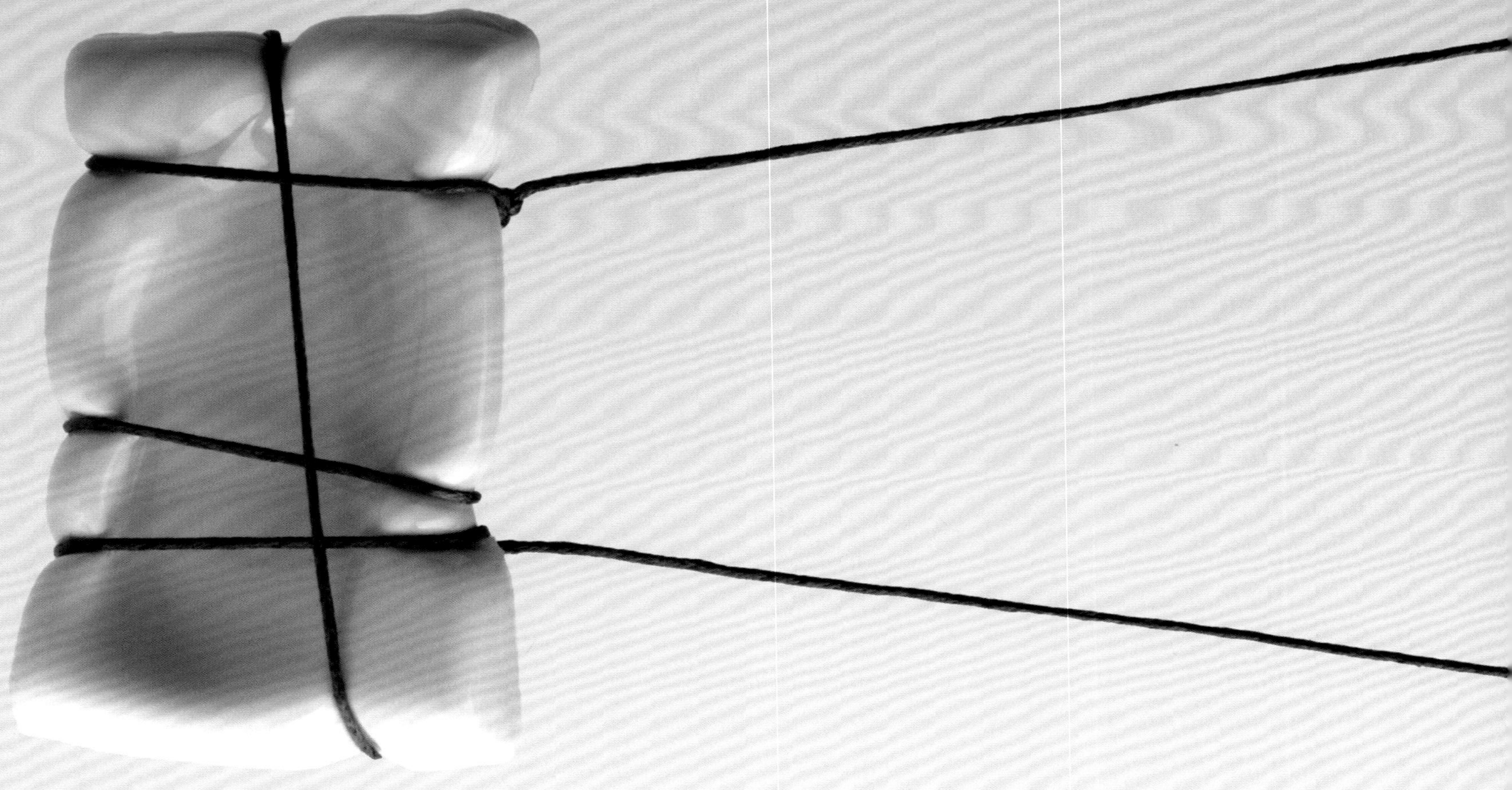

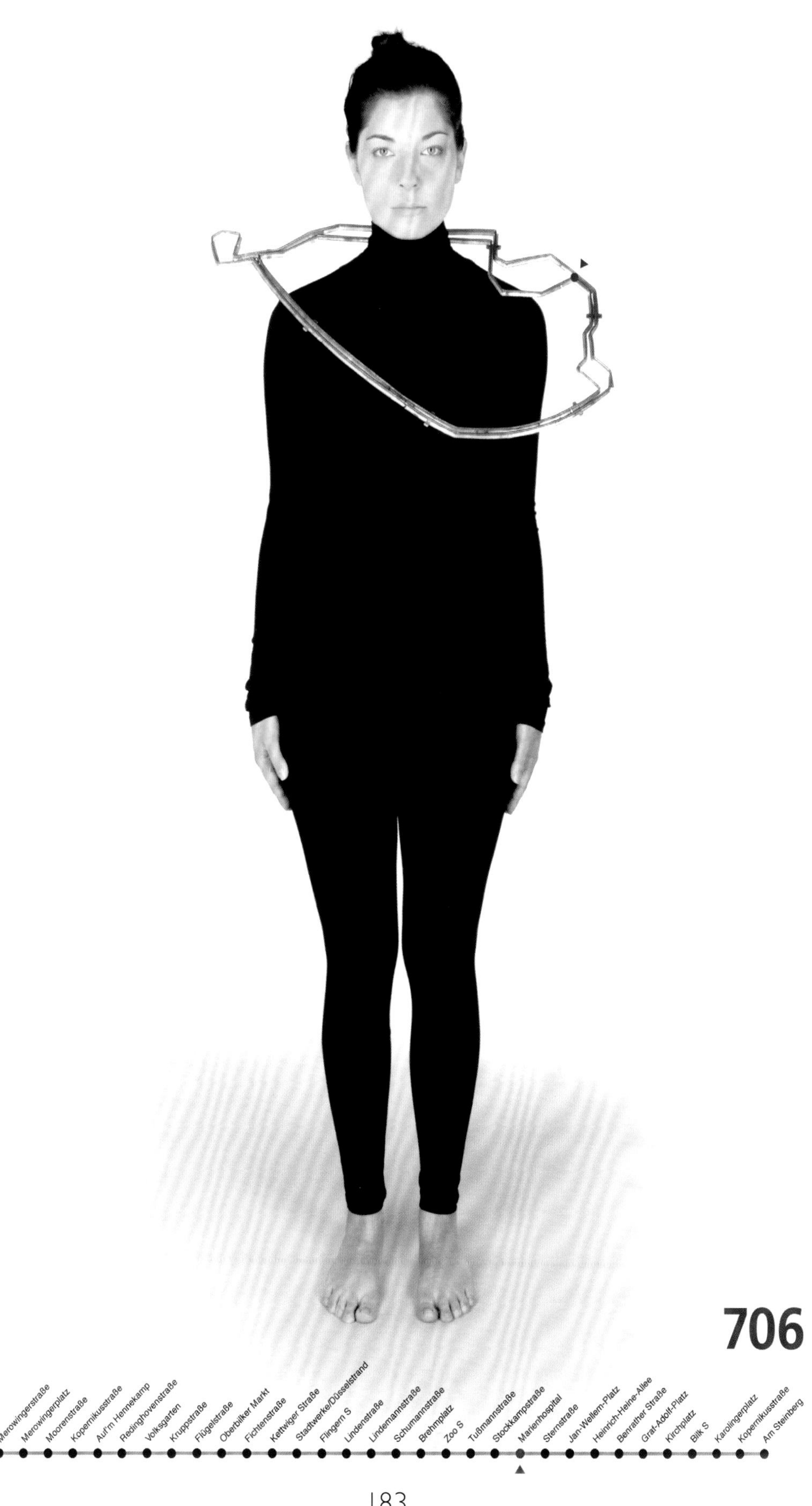
706
Merowingerstraße
Merowingerplatz
Moorenstraße
Kopernikusstraße
Auf'm Hennekamp
Redinghovenstraße
Volksgarten
Kruppstraße
Flügelstraße
Oberbilker Markt
Fichtenstraße
Kettwiger Straße
Stadtwerke/Düsselstrand
Flingern S
Lindenstraße
Lindemannstraße
Schumannstraße
Brehmplatz
Zoo S
Tußmannstraße
Stockkampstraße
Marienhospital
Sternstraße
Jan-Wellem-Platz
Heinrich-Heine-Allee
Benrather Straße
Graf-Adolf-Platz
Kirchplatz
Bilk S
Karolingerplatz
Kopernikusstraße
Am Steinberg

MARIE-ANGE DUMONT BELGIUM

'COUCOU_CLOCK' MIXED MATERIALS

'PRECIOUS_PIGS' PEARLS, FLOWERS, TISSUE, EDGINGS, TOYS, MEDAL

SAM THO DUONG GERMANY

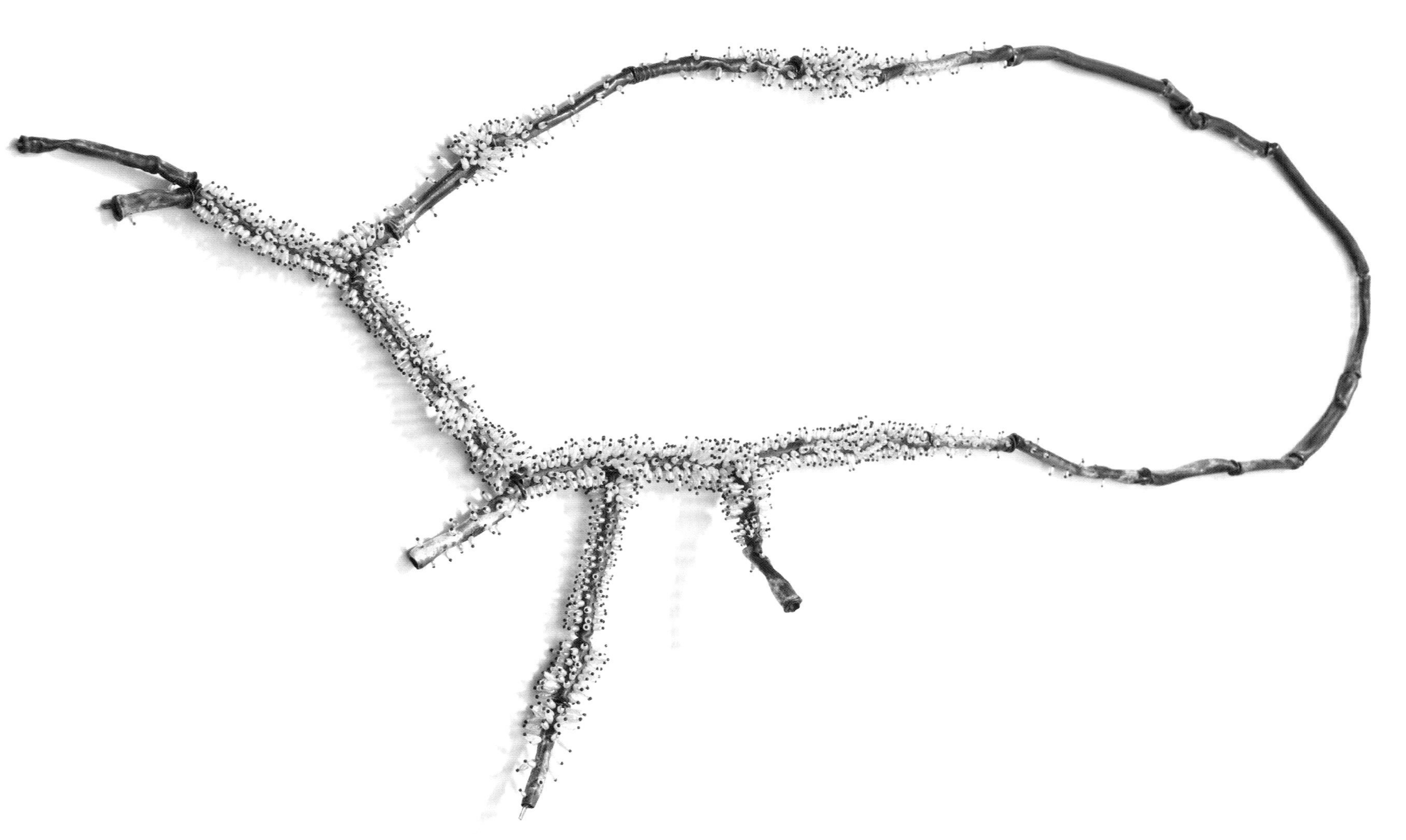

'NECKLACE-FROOZEN' SILVER, FRESHWATER PEARLS, NYLON

'NECKLACE-FROOZEN' SILVER, FRESHWATER PEARLS, NYLON

SUSANNE ELSTNER GERMANY

BROOCHE 'FONDLE ME' GOLD 24 K, SILVER OXIDIZED, COLOUR

BROOCH 'FONDLE ME' GOLD 18 K, SILVER OXIDIZED

SINA EMRICH GERMANY

BROOCH WOOD, GOLD 14 K

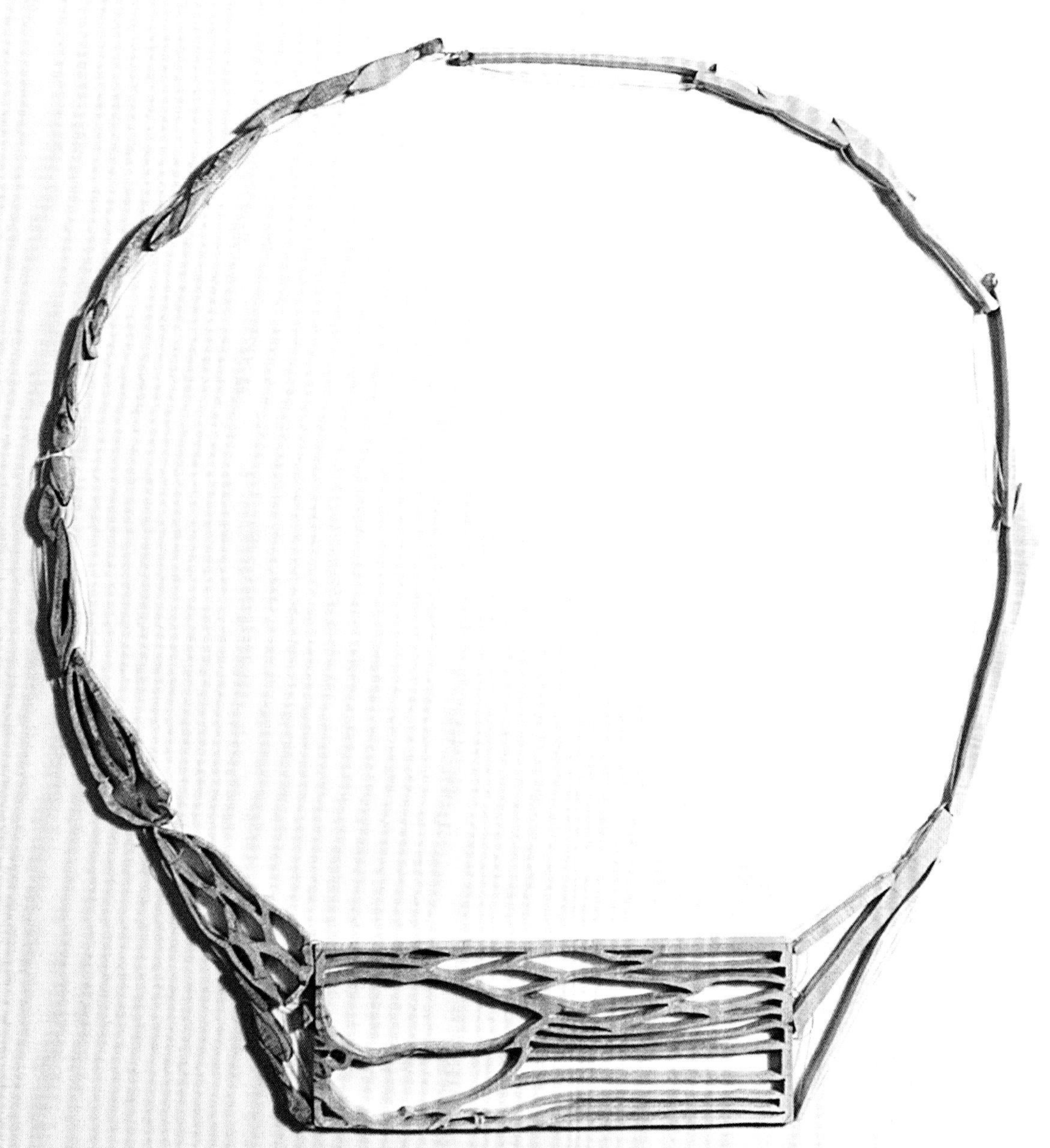

NECKLACE WOOD, QUILT THREAD

LINDA EZERMAN THE NETHERLANDS

'STUMBLE ACROSS A TENTACLE'
FELT, SILICONE, INK, RUBBER, GLASS BEADS, MIYUKI BEADS

LINNÉA ERIKSSON SWEDEN

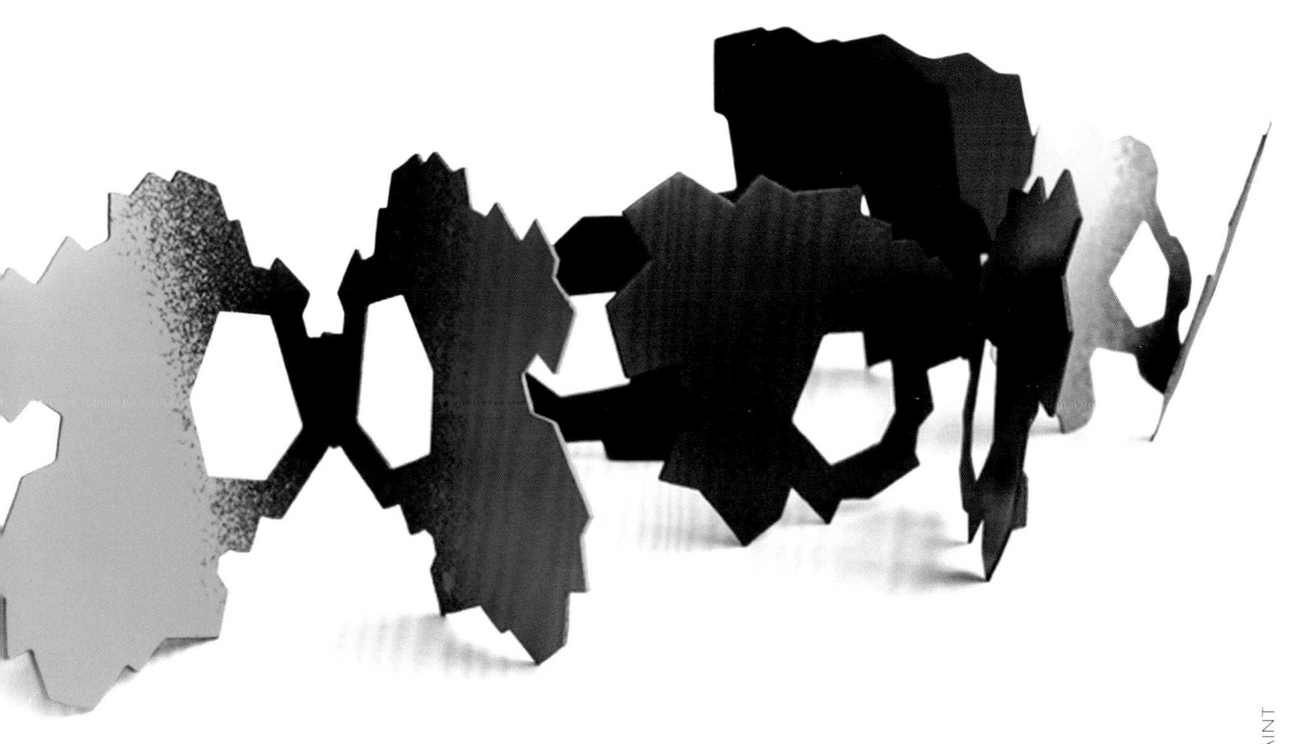

'LET YOUR COLORS BURST' STEEL, SILVER, SPRAY PAINT

TERESA FARIS USA

NECKPIECE 'COLLABORATION WITH A BIRD II'
STERLING SILVER, WOOD ALTERED BY A BIRD

BROOCH 'COLLABORATION WITH A BIRD II'
STERLING SILVER, WOOD ALTERED BY A BIRD

RÉKA FEKETE THE NETHERLANDS

NECKLACE 'WINDOW' (FOUND) WOOD, SASH CORD, HOOK, STEEL PINS

BROOCH 'BEHIND THE DOOR' (FOUND) WOOD, ENAMELLED STEEL, ZINC, SILVER, PAINT

MIRLA FERNANDES BRAZIL

'DOMESTIC:CAMEO' FROM DEVOUT SERIES
LASERCUT TEXTILES, VANED THREADS, READY-MADE PORCELAIN, PAINT, VIDEO PROJECTION OF ANIMATION

'MOUTH SAID NO WORD' FROM DEVOUT SERIES
LASERCUT TEXTILES, VANED THREADS, READY-MADE PORCELAIN, PAINT

JANTJE FLEISCHUT THE NETHERLANDS

'INTERFACE CONTROL' GOLD 14 K, FOUND PLASTIC, AGALITE, RESIN

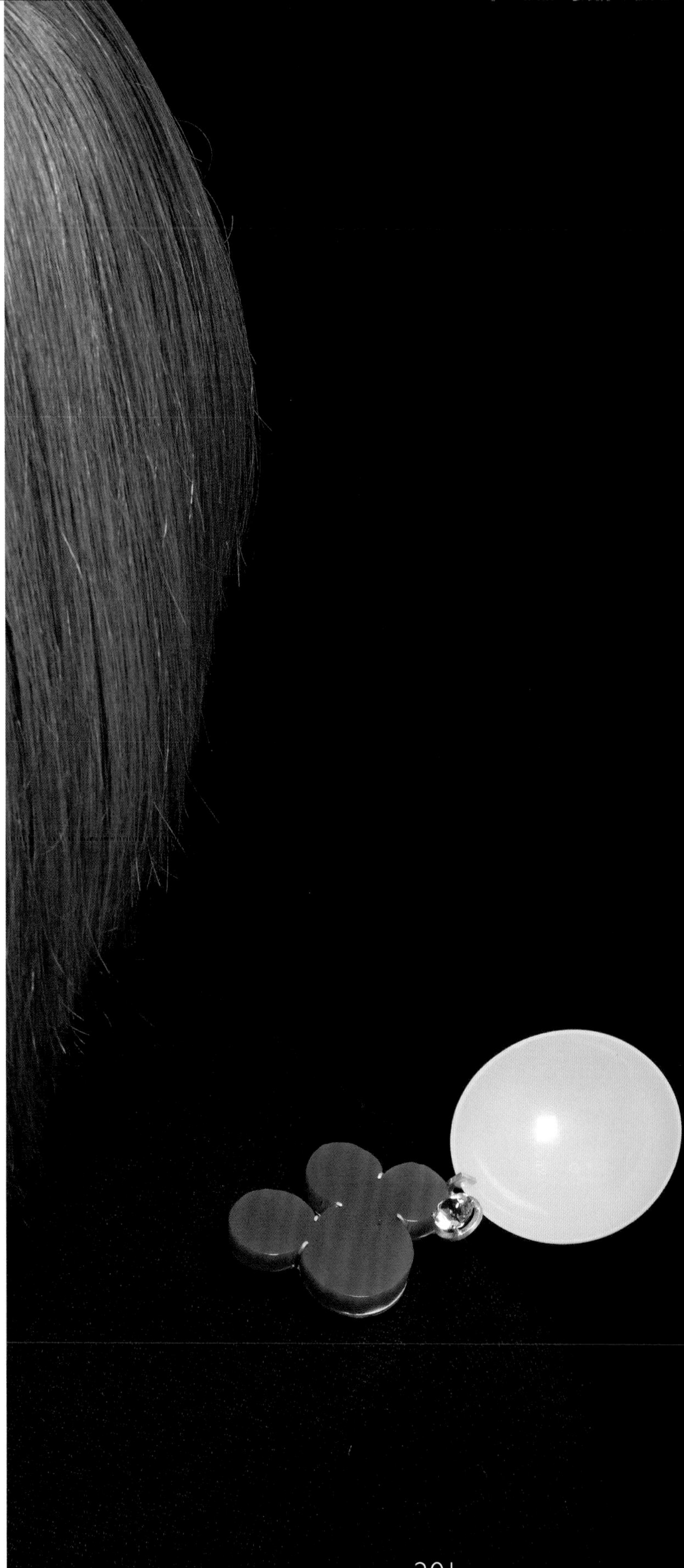

ELINE FRANSEN BELGIUM

'PLAYINGGAMES'
GLASS, GOLD 18 K, GOLDEN GRANULES

'ISEEMMYSELFINYOU'
GLASS, SILVER, GRANULES, SILVER

ARATA FUCHI ITALY

RING SILVER 925, SILVER POWDER, FINE GOLD

RING SILVER 925, SILVER POWDER, FINE GOLD, NIELLO

MOTOKO FURUHASHI USA

RING ROAD SEGMENT FROM GERTY STREET, BRASS

RING ROAD SEGMENT FROM N. BROADWAY AVENUE, BRASS

GISELE GANNE UK

'BIRD OF PREY' 18 K GOLDPLATED STERLING SILVER WITH BLACK FOX TAIL

BETTINA GEISTLICH SWITZERLAND

'CIRCULUS RING' YELLOW GOLD 750, DIAMOND

KAREN GILBERT USA

UNTITLED NECKPIECE STERLING SILVER, RAW SILVER, BOROSILIGATE GLASS

NECKPIECE 'COLLECTION' STERLING SILVER, ENAMEL, CORAL, BOROSILIGATE GLASS

SUZANNE GOLDEN USA

'POLKA DOTTY' ACRYLIC BEADS, JAPANESE SEED BEADS RIGHT ANGLE WEAVE, EMBELLISHMENT

'CLOWN TIE' JAPANESE SEED BREADS, VINTAGE BEADS, SWAROVSKI CRYSTALS PEYOTE STITCH AND CROSS WEAVING

CAROLINE GORE USA

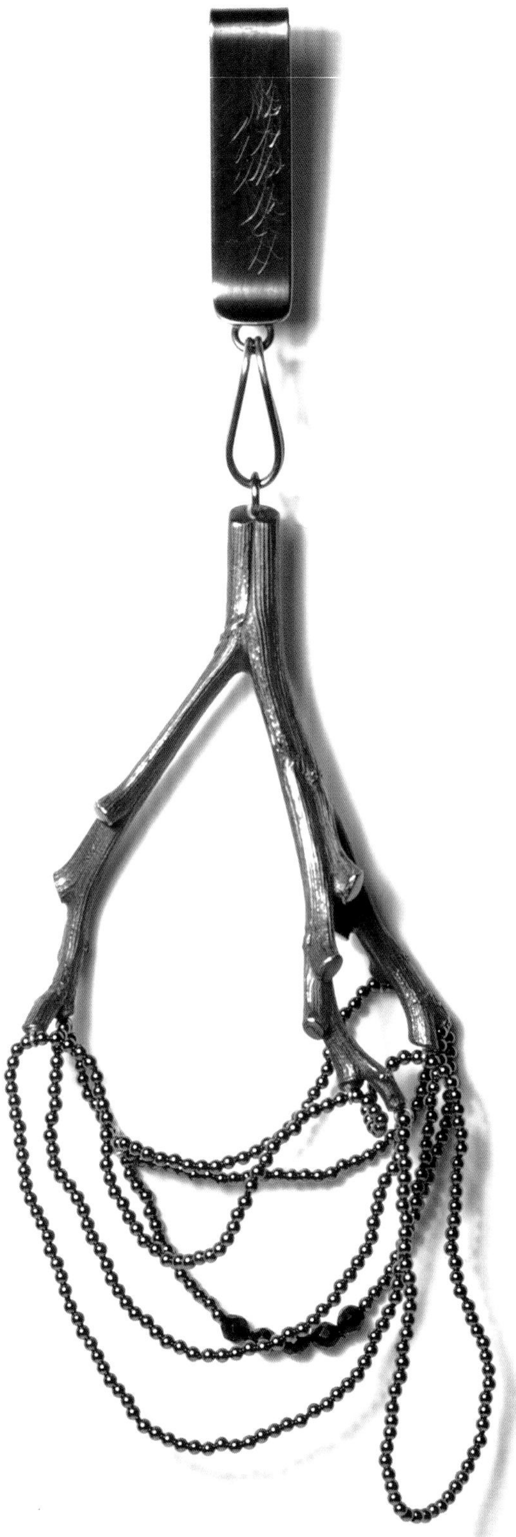

CHATELAINE '...DEW...' 18 K GOLD, OXIDIZED STERLING SILVER, JET, HEMATITE, SILK

NECKLACE '...AFTER...' 18 K GOLD, OXIDIZED STERLING SILVER, JET, RECLAIMED LEATHER, BOROSILICATE GLASS, HEMATITE, SILK

JED GREEN UK

'BANGLE' GLASS, SILVER, PAINT, CERAMIC TRANSFER

'BANGLE' GLASS, SILVER, PAINT, PEARLS, CERAMIC TRANSFER

KATIE GRUBER AUSTRIA

'INNOCENCE' SHIBUICHI, CHIFFON

'20 CENTIMETERS OF SNOW' COPPER, SILVER, ACRYLIC, TILE PAINT

TAMARA GRÜNER GERMANY

BROOCH 'CRYSTAL GOLD'
HISTORICAL METAL PIECES, SILVER,
GLASS, MOTHER OF PEARL, STEEL

NECKLACE 'BERMUDA BLUE'
HISTORICAL PIECES, SILVER BLACKENED, GLASS

MICHAEL GUERISSE / PHILIPPE HUMBEECK BELGIUM

'PULSE GENERATOR' STERLING SILVER 925, BIOCOMPATIDLE TITANIUM, ACRYLIC POLYMER + ALUMINA TRIHYDRATE, MICROCHIP

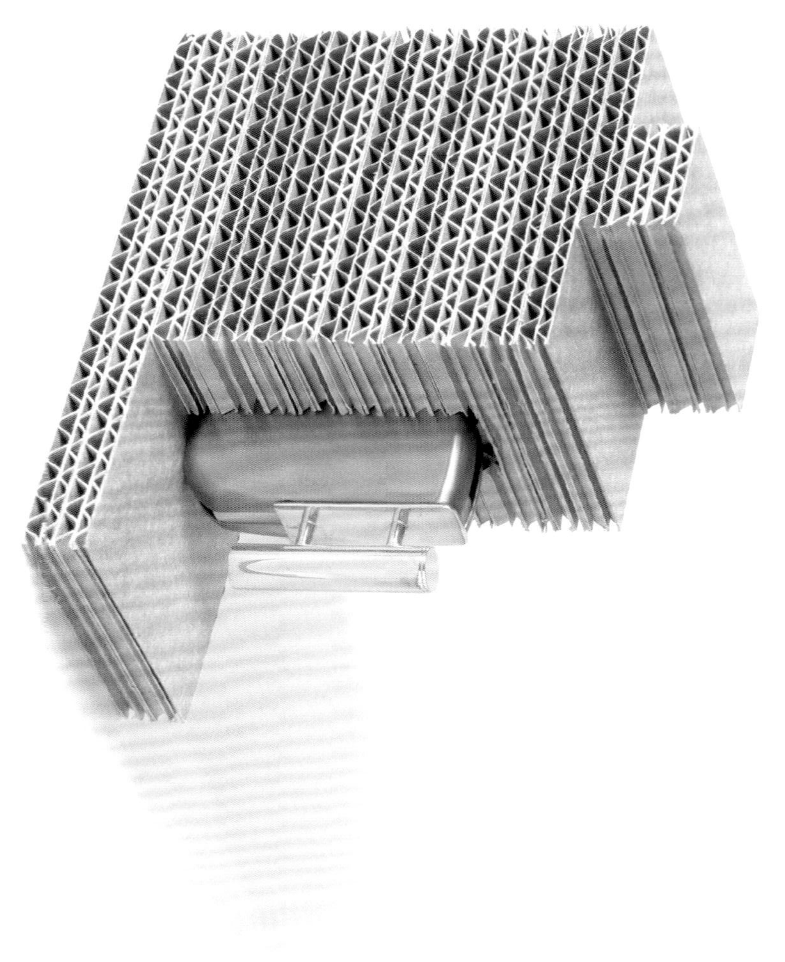

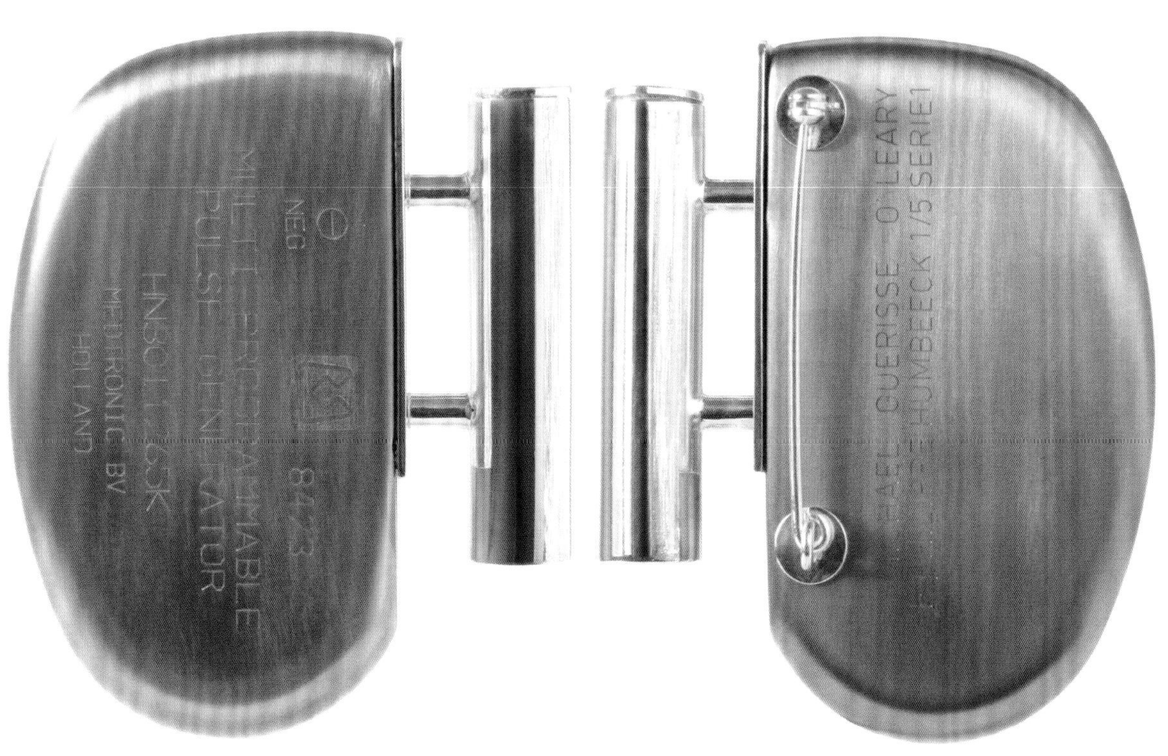

PREETI GUPTA / VIVEK PRASAD INDIA

'LEAF PENDANT' ORIGINAL TEAK LEAF, BRASS WIRE, NATURAL COLOUR

'TWIN LEAVES' PAPER PULP, WHITE CLAY, NATURAL RESIN, LEATHER STRING WITH NON-TOXIC COLOUR

GÉSINE HACKENBERG THE NETHERLANDS

'DELFT BLUE LILY' NECKLACE
(ANTIQUE) DELFT BLUE EARTHENWARE PLATE, THREAD

'FRISIAN SHIP KITCHEN' NECKLACE
(OLD) DUTCH EARTHENWARE PLATE, THREAD

'LONG' NECKPIECE LAMINATE, CABLE

REBECCA HANNON CANADA

'BALANCE' NECKPIECE LAMINATE, CABLE

MARGIT HART AUSTRIA

BROOCH 'SHADOW WITH YELLOW' PHOTO ON DIBOND, SILVER, PAINT

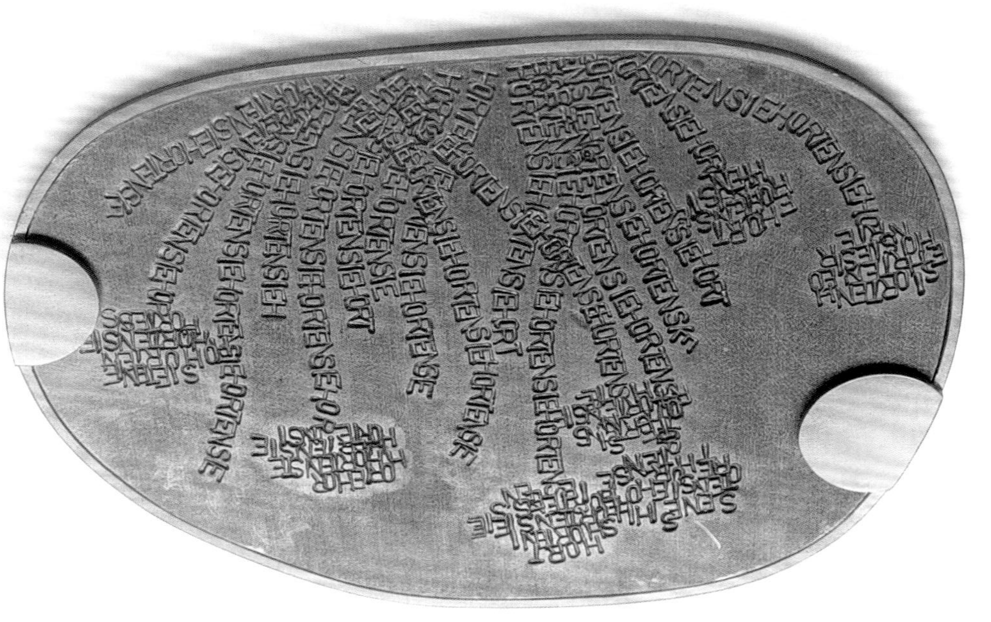

'WITHIN WORD-HYDRANGEA' 935 AG

ARIANE HARTMANN GERMANY

LIISA HASHIMOTO JAPAN

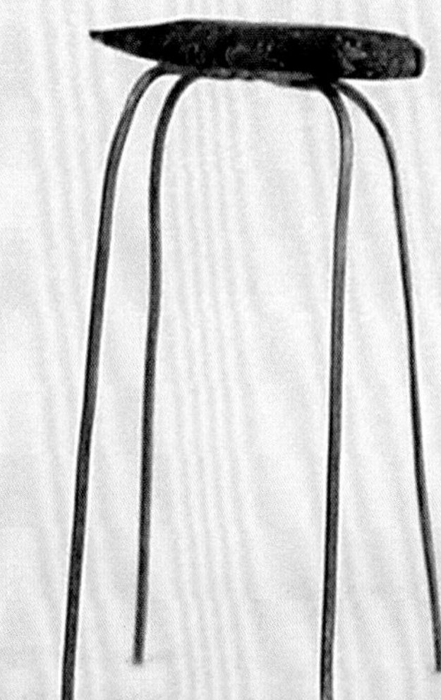

'JUNK YARD PENDANT TOPS' SILVER

INEKE HEERKENS THE NETHERLANDS

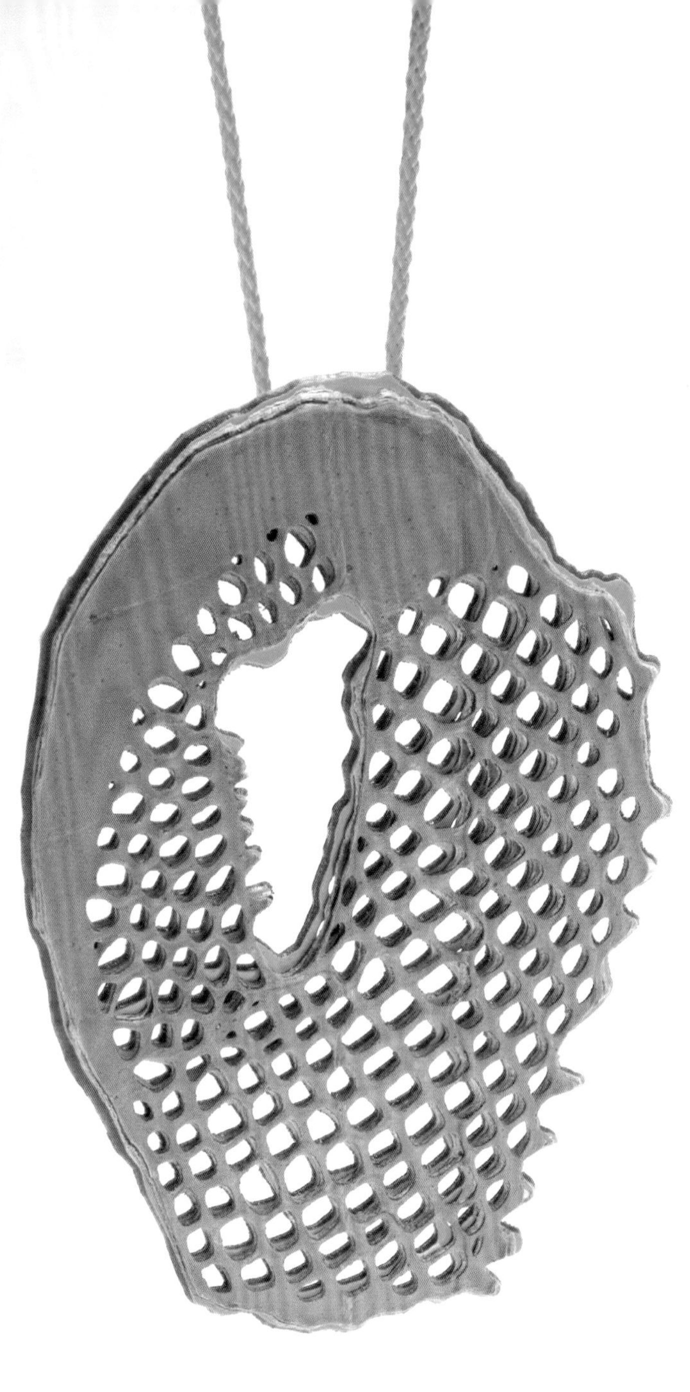

PENDANT 'LOW TIDE' POLYETHYLENE, STAINLESS STEEL, TEXTILE CORD

COLLIER 'WHIRLING LEAVE' POLYETHYLENE, STAINLESS STEEL, OXIDIZED SILVER

MIA HEBIB USA

'IN CYCLES' STERLING SILVER, FABRICATED

MARIA HEES THE NETHERLANDS

NECKLACE 'BLACK FOAM' PORCELAIN, RUBBER

ANNA HEINDL AUSTRIA

COLLIER 'TREASURE' GOLD 14 K, STAINLESS STEEL, CITRIN, CORALS PEARLS, AMANDINES, LAPISLAZULI

'FLOWER OF THE NIGHT' ETERNAL RING STAINLESS STEEL, REDGOLD 14 K, PEARLS

MARLEEN HENOT BELGIUM

RING 'VALUES II' ALLOY OF BRONZE, SILVER, COPPER, PLASTIC, ACRYLPAINT

UNTITLED GILDED SILVER 925, ACRYLPAINT, PLASTIC

HEIDEMARIE HERB ITALY

COLLECTION HERB'S GARDEN, BROOCH ORGANIC, RESIN

COLLECTION HERB'S GARDEN RINGS, ORGANIC FRAGMENT, RESIN, 925 AG

LOLA MOLINA HERNANDEZ SPAIN

'HORREO' PYRITE, SILVER 925

'RAMAS' PYRITE, SILVER 925

PAVEL HERYNEK CZECH REPUBLIC

BROOCH FROM THE OSTREV SERIES WOOD, GOLD LEAF, PAINT, STAINLESS STEEL

SOPHIE HEYMANS BELGIUM

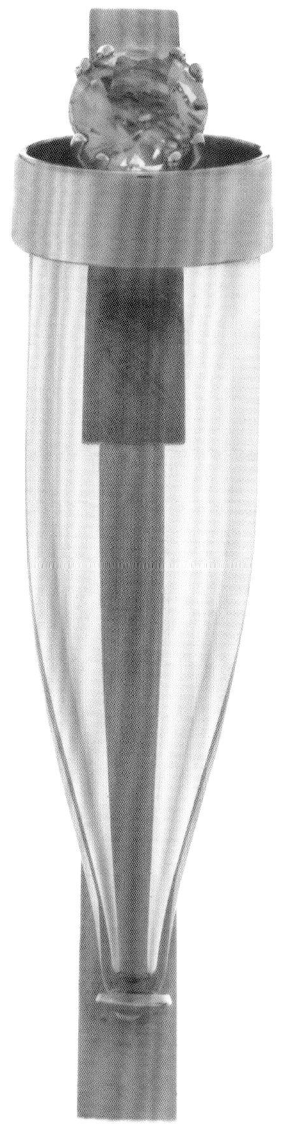

'FIRE' CITRINE, PYREX, YELLOW GOLD 18 K

LEONOR HIPOLITO PORTUGAL

UNTITLED GILDED BRASS, LEATHER

UNTITLED SIVER, LEATHER

LYDIA HIRTE GERMANY

UNTITLED FINE DRAWING CARD, DRAWING AND CALLIGRAPHIC INK WITH VERY HIGH LIGHT RESISTANCE GLAZED, PEARL SILK

UNTITLED FINE DRAWING CARD, DRAWING AND CALLIGRAPHIC INK WITH VERY HIGH LIGHT RESISTANCE, GLAZED, PEARL SILK

SUSANNE HOLZINGER GERMANY

BROOCHES 'PODS' PAPER, GOLD PLATED MAGNET, LAYERED GLUED PAPER BLOCK, HAND CARVED AND SANDED

BRACELET 'GREEN MOEBIUS' PAPER, LAYERED GLUED PAPER BLOCK, HAND CARVED AND SANDED

PETER HOOGEBOOM THE NETHERLANDS

NECKLACE 'WESTLAND' TERRACOTTA, SILVER, NYLON, CERAMIC TECHNIQUES AND SILVERSMITHING

NECKLACE 'CLAY FEET' CERAMICS, TERRACOTTA, SILVER, CORK, CERAMIC TECHNIQUES AND SILVERSMITHING

PETER HOOGEBOOM THE NETHERLANDS

BROOCH 'NORTH SEA 8'
FUSED CERAMICS, SILVER, STEEL, CERAMIC TECHNIQUES, KILN CASTING, SILVERSMITHING

BRACELET 'ONE FOR THE ROAD'
CERAMICS, CORK, CERAMIC TECHNIQUES

KARINA HUNNERUP DENMARK

'COLIBRI EARRINGS' UPCYCLED BLACK LEATHER, OXIDISED STERLING SILVER

HEEJIN HWANG USA

'TACTILE SENSATION I' STEEL WIRE, ENAMEL, GROUND ROCK, HAND-DYED YARN

FRANCESC OLIVERAS I BALLUS SPAIN

'ENTRE SOMNIS' YELLOW GOLD, BRASS MICRO-PARTICLES FRAGMENTED, RESIN

'COMPOSITE' GOLD CHIPPINGS (WHITE, YELLOW, PINK), RESIN

IRIS SAAR ISAACS AUSTRALIA

'COCOON' BROOCH STAINLESS STEEL, 22 K MATT GOLD PLATING

REIKO ISHIYAMA USA

'TEN PAPERS' BROOCH 18 K YELLOW GOLD, STERLING SILVER

'EMPTY' NECKLACE STERLING SILVER

'CAVEA (5)' NECKLACE STAINLESS STEEL, PULVERIZED HEMATITE, CRUSHED PEARLS, LACQUER, ACRYLIC, COTTON STRING

MELANIE ISVERDING GERMANY

'CAVEA (9)' STAINLESS STEEL, ENAMEL, PULVERIZED PYRIT AND SMOKY QUARTZ, LACQUER

MARGIT JAESCHKE GERMANY

BROOCH CARDBOARD, PLASTIC, SILVER, SYNTH. SPINELLE

BROOCH SILVER, PLASTIC, IVORY, CARDBOARD

HELENA JOHANSSON SWEDEN

UNTITLED COPPER, TEXTILES

UNTITLED COPPER, TEXTILES

BROOCH 'NOKOMIS' MADE OUT OF SURFACE, THREATED POLYCARBONAT, COLOURED AND CRAFTED BY HAND

SVENJA JOHN GERMANY

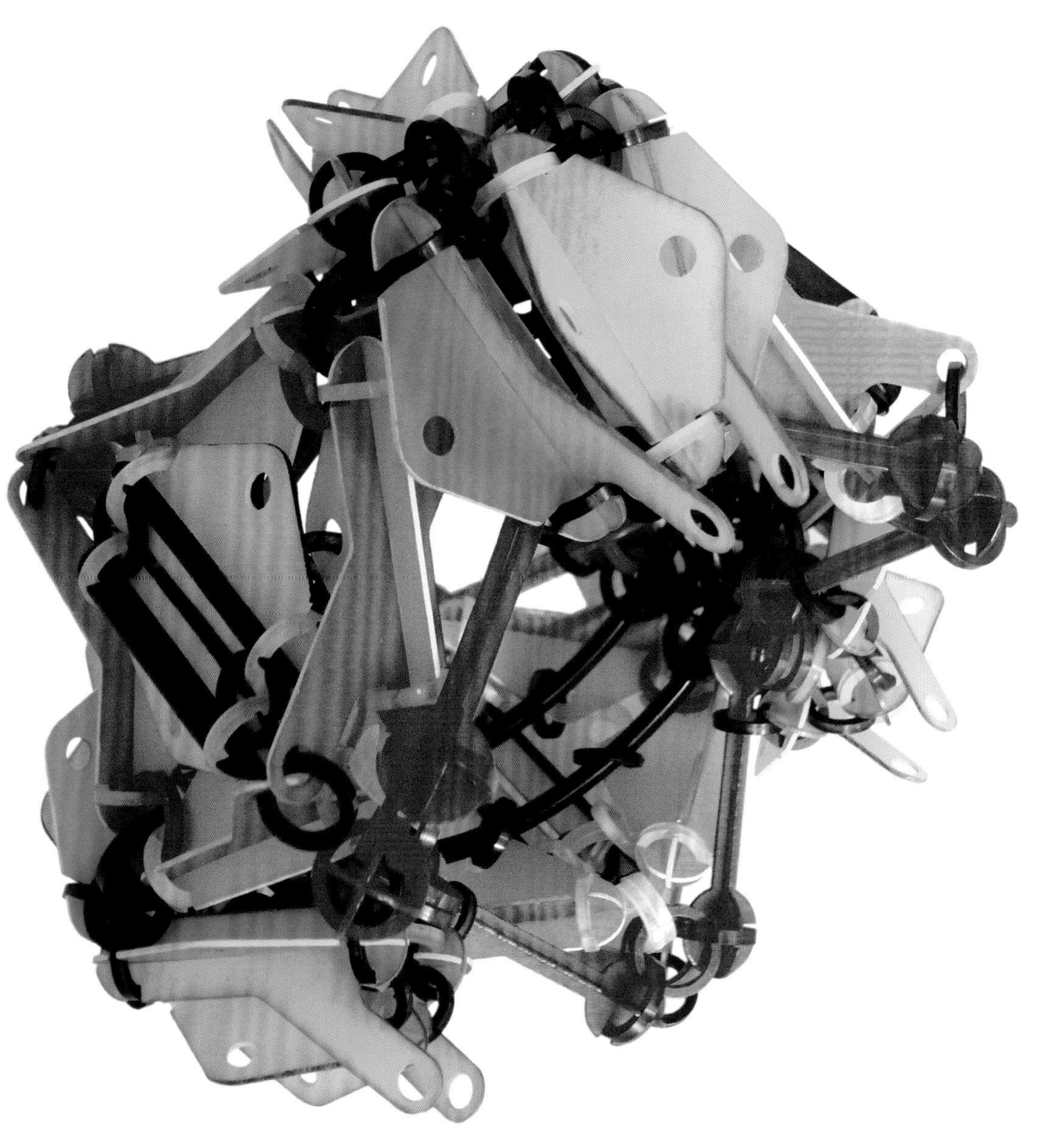

BRACELET 'ZAMIST' MADE OUT OF SURFACE, THREATED POLYCARBONAT, COLOURED AND CRAFTED BY HAND

HILDUR YR JONSDOTTIR ICELAND

RING CASTED SILVER

NECKLACE HIGH FIRED PORCELAIN, IRON, CHAIN

HANNAH JORIS BELGIUM

'CURA POSTERIOR V (NI DIEU, NI MAÎTRE)' PENDANT/BROOCH/OBJECT WHITE YAM, PARCHMENT, IRON, STEEL, NYLON

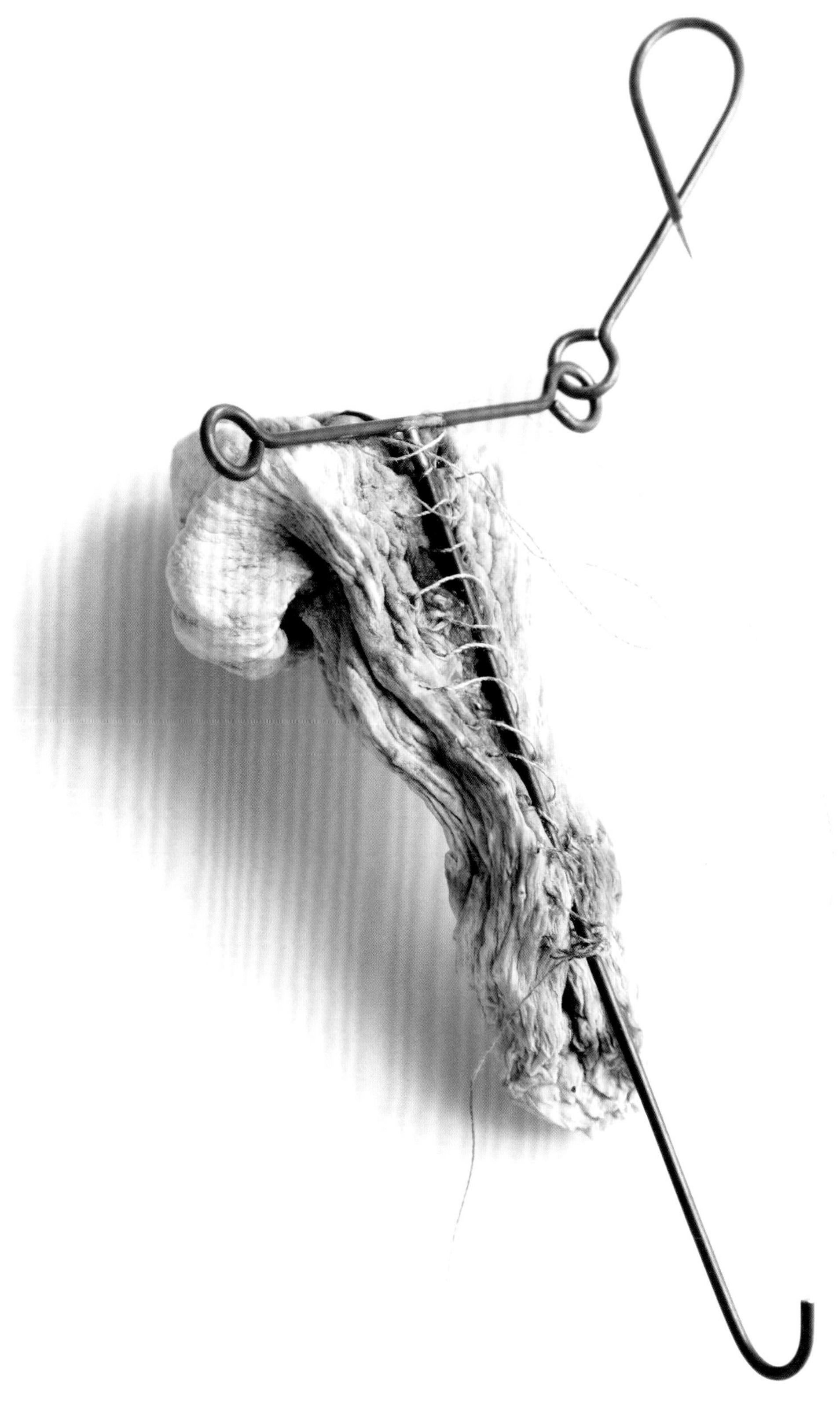

BROOCH (PART OF INSTALLATION 'OUR VULNERABLE POSITION') 'CRUCIFIX' (1/99) SWEET POTATO, IRON, THREAD, CHINESE INK

KAORI JUZU DENMARK

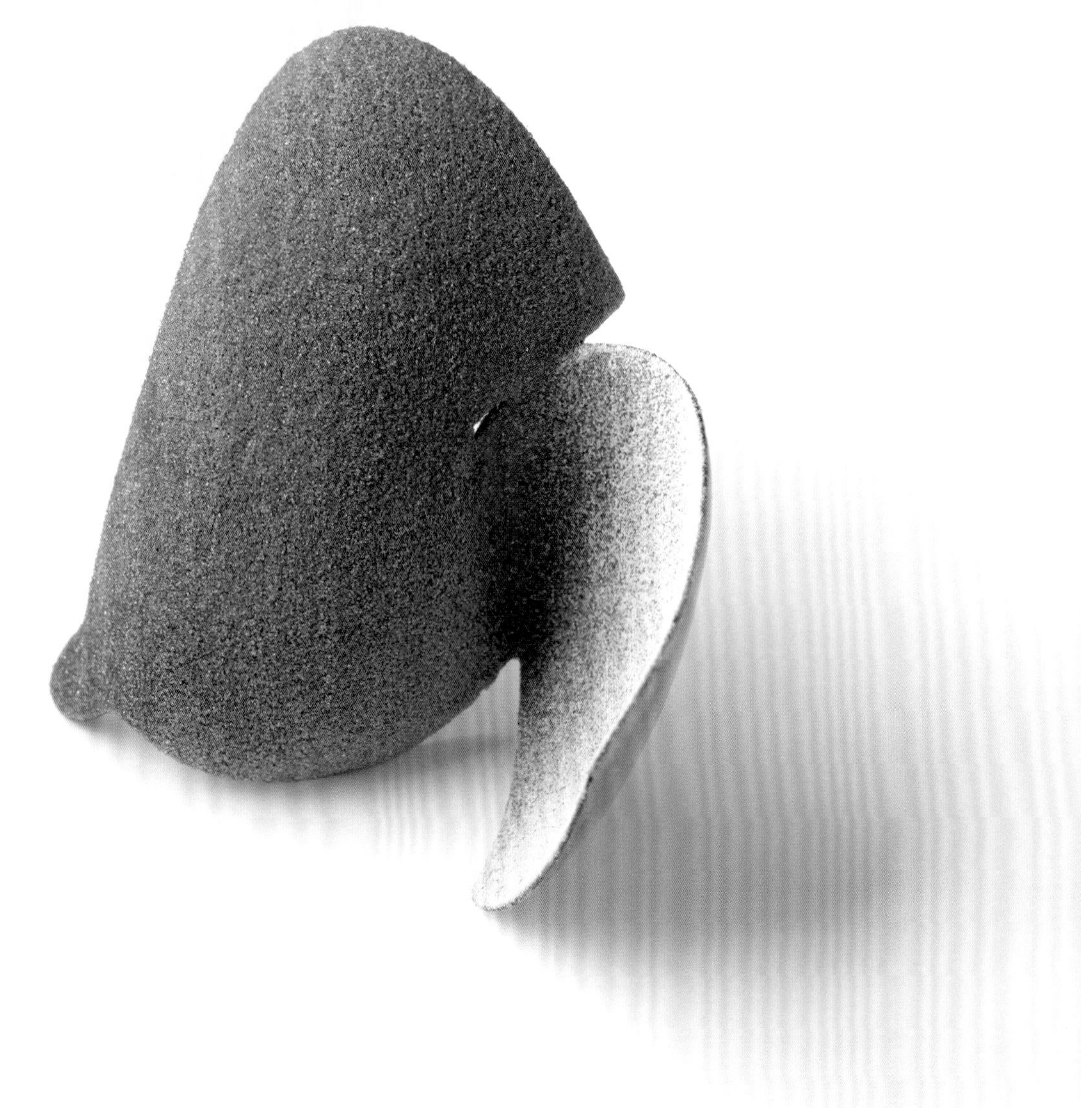

BROOCH 'NOT ME, BUT STORYTELLER' ENAMEL, COPPER, GOLD 14 K

BROOCH 'NOT ME, BUT STORYTELLER' ENAMEL, COPPER, GOLD 14 K

JIRO KAMATA GERMANY

UNTITLED CAMERA LENSES, PAINTED, SILVER

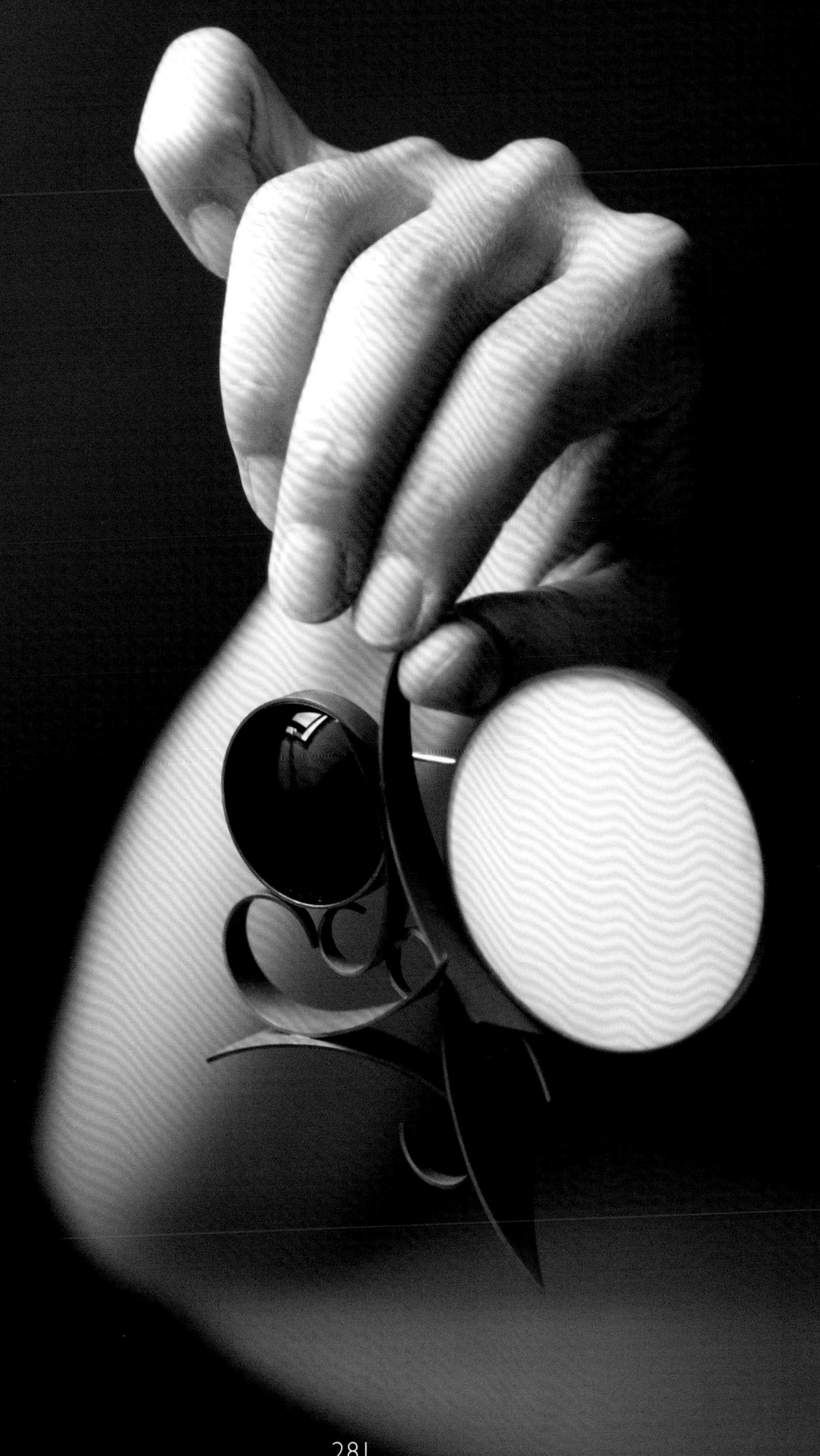

UNTITLED CAMERA LENS, PAINTED, SILVER

DAEHOON KANG AUSTRALIA

PENDANT/BROOCH 'THE CONDIMENT BAY' FINE SILVER, FINE GOLD, STERLING SILVER

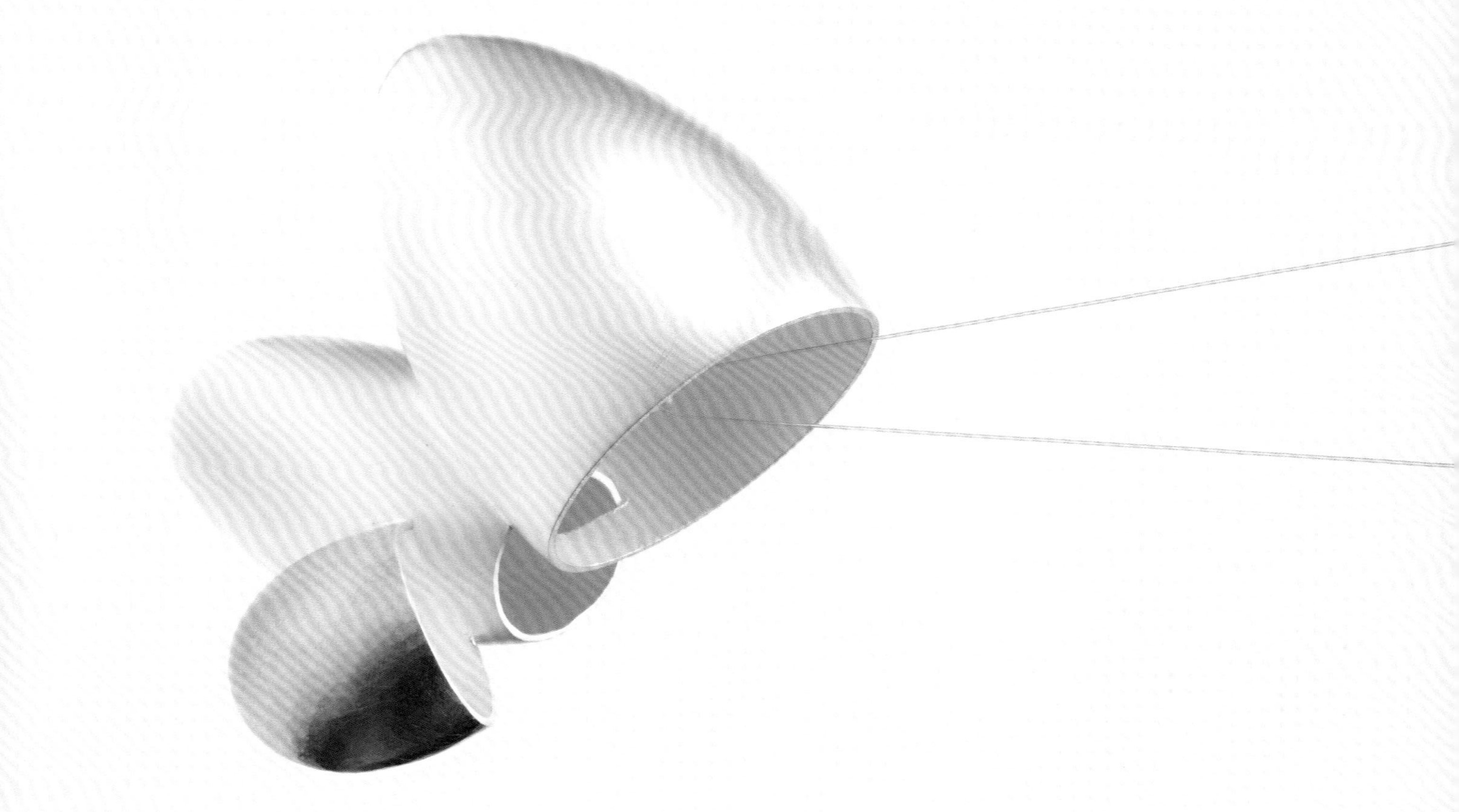

PENDANT 'THE CONDIMENT BAY' STERLING SILVER, STAINLESS STEEL, MONEL

DAEHOON KANG AUSTRALIA

PENDANT/BROOCH 'THE CONDIMENT BAY' FINE SILVER, FINE GOLD, STERLING SILVER

BROOCH/PENDANT 'THE CONDIMENT BAY' FINE SILVER, STERLING SILVER, STAINLESS STEEL

KEPA KARMONA SPAIN

'PARADISE N° 12.3002514/-61.5866106' CREDIT CARDS, SILVER, STEEL WIRE, OPTICAL SCREWS

'PARADISE N° 43.053955/3.043826' CREDIT CARDS, SILVER, STEEL WIRE, OPTICAL SCREWS

MAKI KAWAWA JAPAN

UNTITLED TEXTILE, NYLON CODE

UNTITLED TEXTILE, NYLON CODE

BEPPE KESSLER THE NETHERLANDS

BROOCH 'GRACE' GOLD, SILVER, BALSAWOOD, ACRYLIC FIBRE, RESIN, TEXTILE, COLOUR

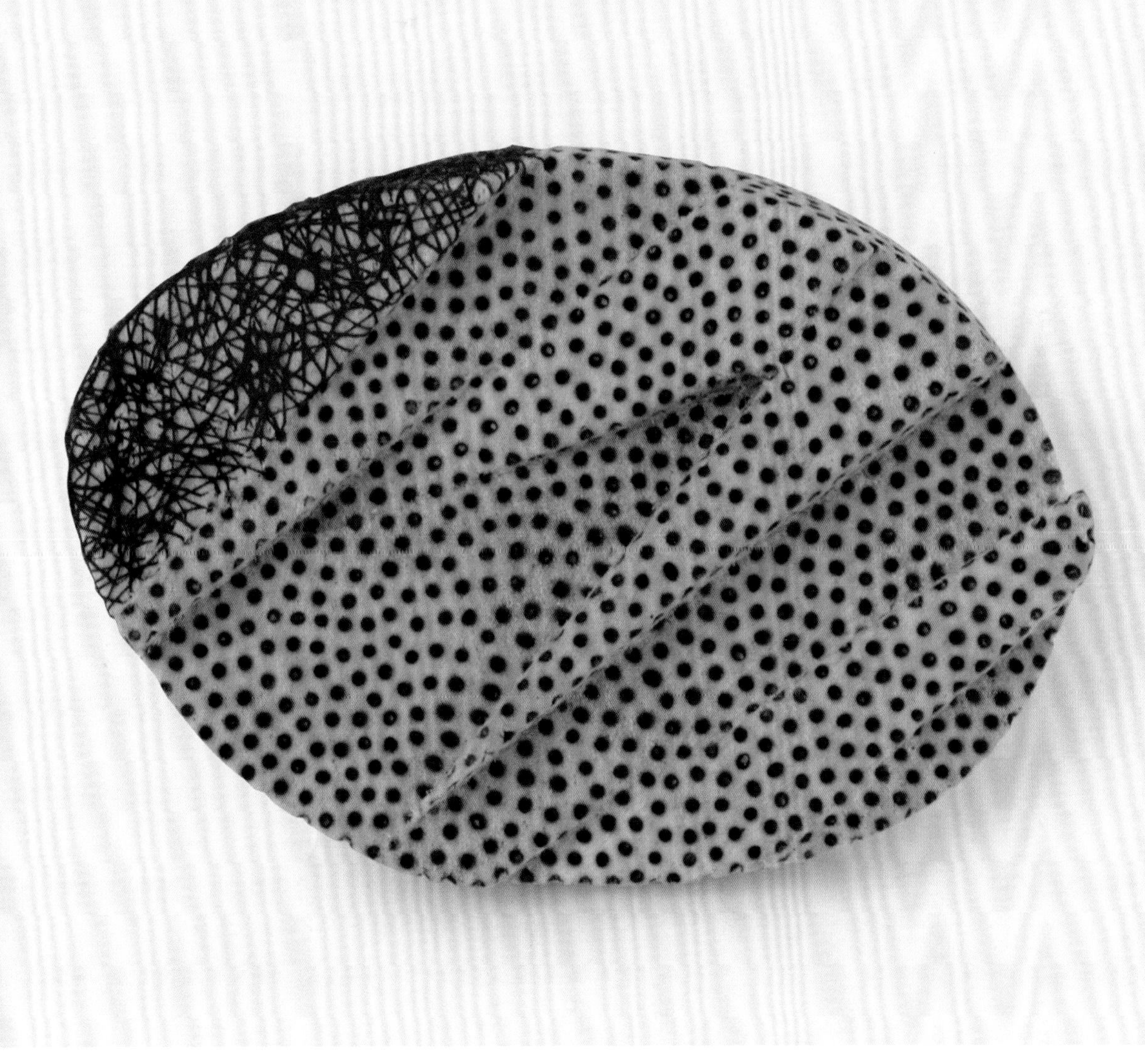

BROOCH 'MIND YOUR STEP 2' BRASS, BALSA WOOD, TEXTILE

CHRISTINE KEYEUX BELGIUM

NECKLACE 'ÉTOILE' FOLDED AND PLAITED PAPER

YONG JOO KIM USA

BRACELET VELCRO

UNTITLED VELCRO, THREAD

YONG JOO KIM USA

INARI KIURU AUSTRALIA

BROOCH FROM THE SERIE 'A LAS CINCO DE LA TARDE' STEEL, CRYSTAL, RESIN, GLUE, PAINT

RING FROM 'WINTER THOUGTHS' (BETWEEN TWO SUMMERS)-SERIES BRASS, ENCAUSTIC WAX, ETCHED, WELDED

'LES SOLEILS' GOLD

BEATE KLOCKMANN THE NETHERLANDS

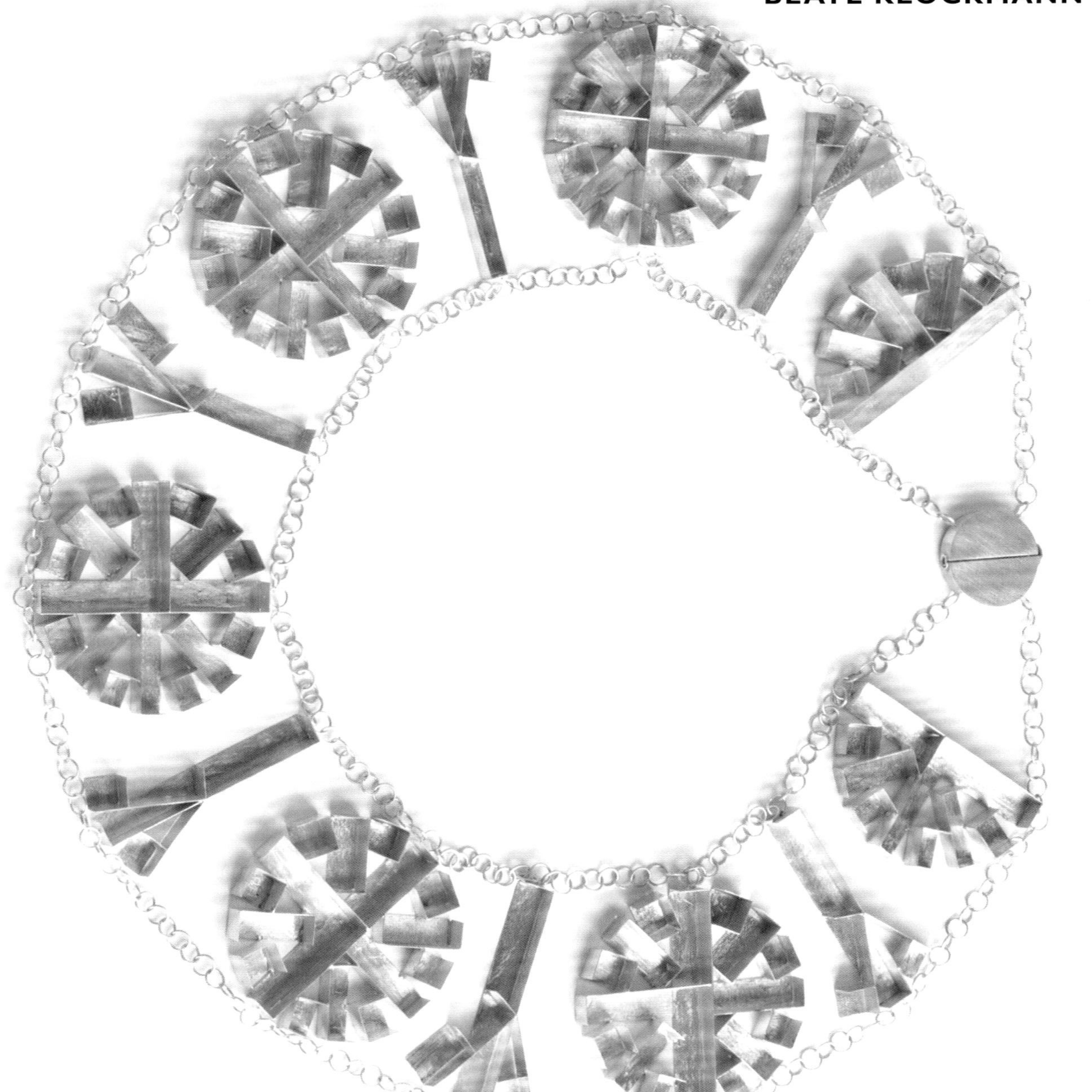

'2 SWIRLS RECTO' ENAMEL ON IRON, GOLD

BRACELET PAPE OF PARCHMENT USE FOR INVITATION, DIAMOND, PURE SILVER

ANETTE KRAEN DENMARK

BRACELET WOOL, SILVER, SILICON, GLASS BEADS, THREAD

YAEL KRAKOWSKI CANADA

JANTINE KROEZE THE NETHERLANDS

BRACELET COLORED ANODIZED ALUMINIUM

DANIEL KRUGER GERMANY

UNTITLED SILVER, PIGMENT

JULIA MARIA KÜNNAP ESTONIA

'MOLTEN' SMOKE QUARTZ, GOLD

'NUBIS' OBSIDIAN, GOLD

AN-FEN KUO TAIWAN

'OGANISM STUDY NO. 2' RING POLYMER CLAY, COPPER, GILT 24KT PLATING, HAND FABRICATED

'ORGANISM STUDY NO.1' RING POLYMER CLAY, STERLING SILVER, COPPER, SILVER PLATING, HAND FABRICATED

DOMINIQUE LABORDERY GERMANY

'CATCHING THE SUN' SILVER, AGATHE

‘C_C’ SILVER, POWDERCOATED

BIRGIT LAKEN THE NETHERLANDS

NECKLACE 'SUMMER IN THE CITY' FROM THE 'LOVIN SPOONFULL' SERIES MELAMINE, GOLD

PENDANT 'HUPPY' FROM THE 'LOVIN SPOONFULL' SERIES MELAMINE

LORE LANGENDRIES BELGIUM

'LA CHÂTELAINE, LOCKET TO PUT DEAR ONES INSIDE'
VIOLET GLASS FROM A PHARMACY BOTTLE, KNITTED MERINOWOOL, GLASSPEARLS, WAXED COTTON THREAD, SILVER

'XLARGE-PONSBAL' BROOCH
SILVER, AHDA WOODEN BEAD TO PUT BEHIND THE CLOTIHING

AGNES LARSSON SWEDEN

UNTITLLED MIXED MEDIA

CLAIRE LAVENDHOMME BELGIUM

'VÉNUS' ACCORDING CRANACH PENDANT SILVER, PICTURE, RESINE, LEMON

EINAT LEADER ISRAEL

'FENCES AND CAMERAS' PENDANT: SILVER 999(OXIDIZED), GOLD 18K
CHAINS: READYMADE SILVER CHAINS (GOLD PLATED)

ELISABETH LEENKNEGT BELGIUM

UNTITLED 3D PRINT IN SYNTHETIC MATERIAL WITH A FLOCK FINISH

UNTITLED HAND FORGED SILVER AND MOUTH BLOWN GLASS

ANNAMARIA LEISTE GERMANY

'TRAUMGEFANGEN' MAHAGONI WOOD, FISHLINE

'SPLIT SHADOW' PEARWOOD

'FINGER 1' ENAMEL, COPPER, BRASS

GUANLAN LIANG GERMANY

'FINGER 2' ENAMEL, COPPER, BRASS

COLLIER 'EPICES INTIMES' SILVER 925 OXIDIZED, PEPER

PATRICIA LEMAIRE FRANCE

SARI LIIMATTA FINLAND

'KINGDOM' GLASS BEADS, A BRASS CHAIN (SELF-MADE), PINS, SILVER, A RUBBER TOY

FELIX LINDER GERMANY

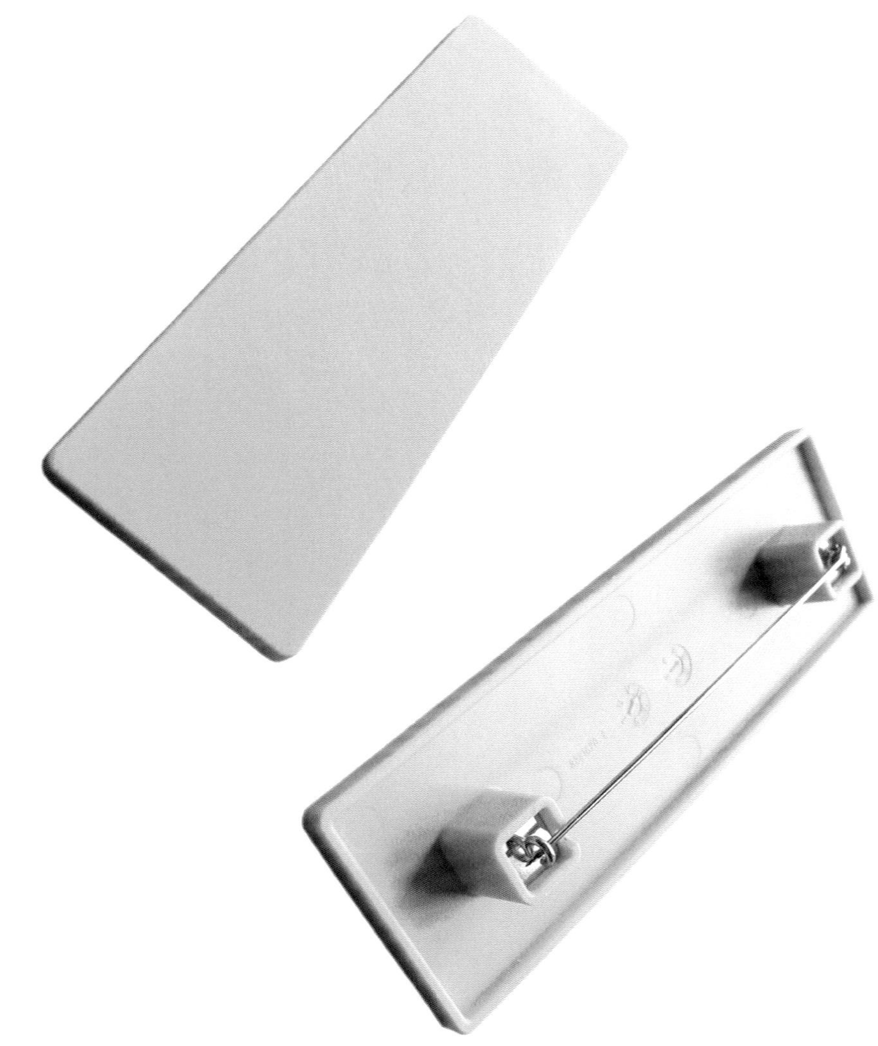

'RECHTECK GRÜN' BROOCH, PLASTIC, GOLD 18 K, STAINLESS STEEL

YU-PING LIN UK

'MUSHROOM' SPRAY & HAND PAINTED FABRIC AND MIXED MEDIA

RIA LINS BELGIUM

'I WILL CARRY YOU' SILVER, THREAD

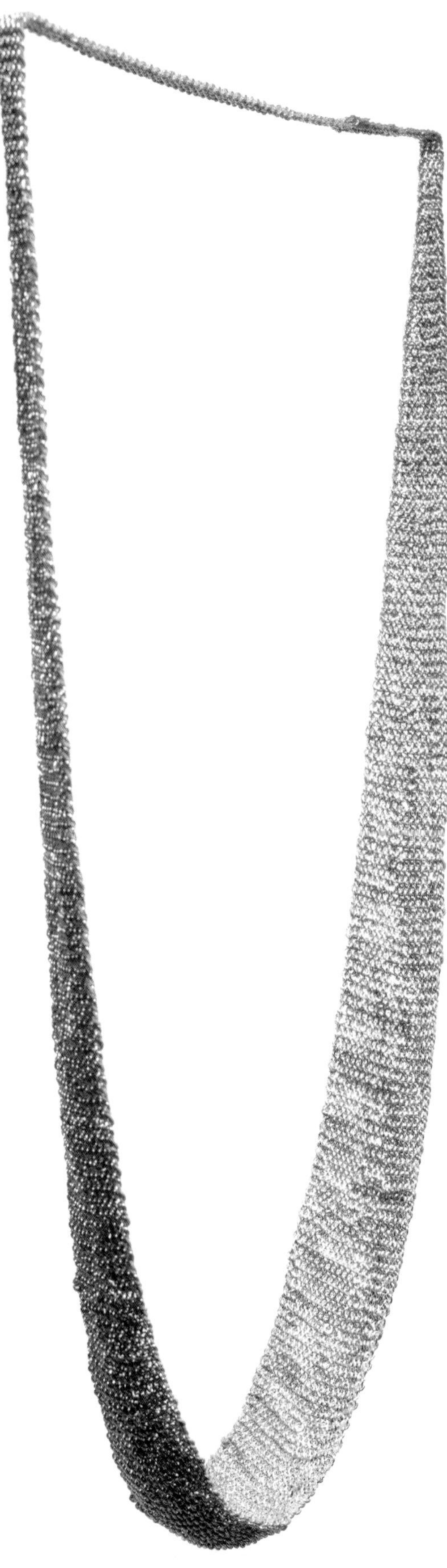

'ROCK ME BABY' GOLD, THREAD

BLANDINE LUCE FRANCE

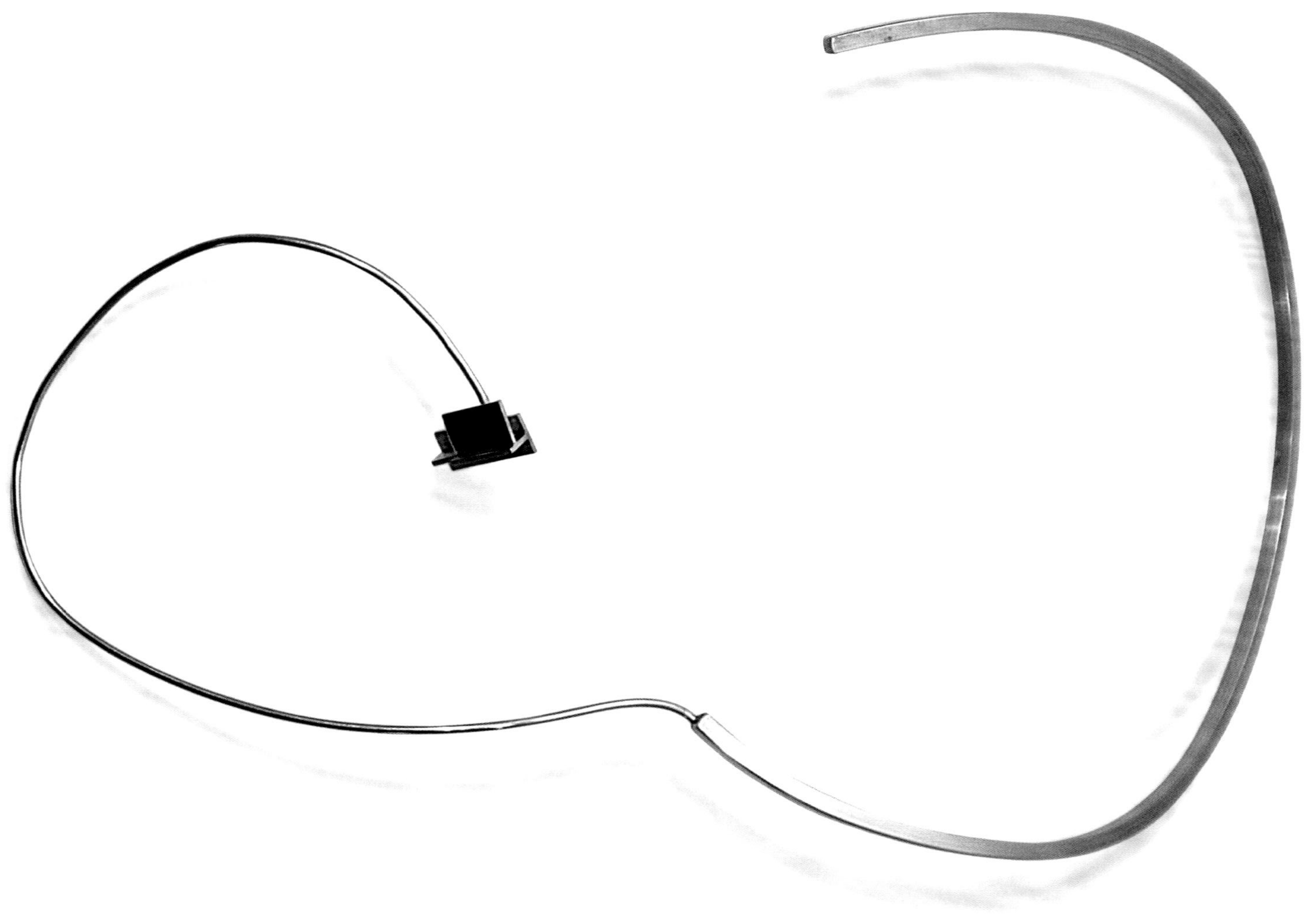

NECKLACE FROM 'THE URBANITY SERIES' SILVER

RING FROM 'THE RECONSTRUCTION SERIES' WOOD, SEPHORA

JANA MACHATOVÁ SLOVAKIA

BROOCH 'LOVE IS LOVE' SILVER, PEARLS, POSTCARDS IN LAMINATED PLASTIC

BROOCH 'LOVE IS LOVE III.' SILVER, PEARLS, POSTCARDS IN LAMINATED PLASTICS

ALISON MACLEOD UK

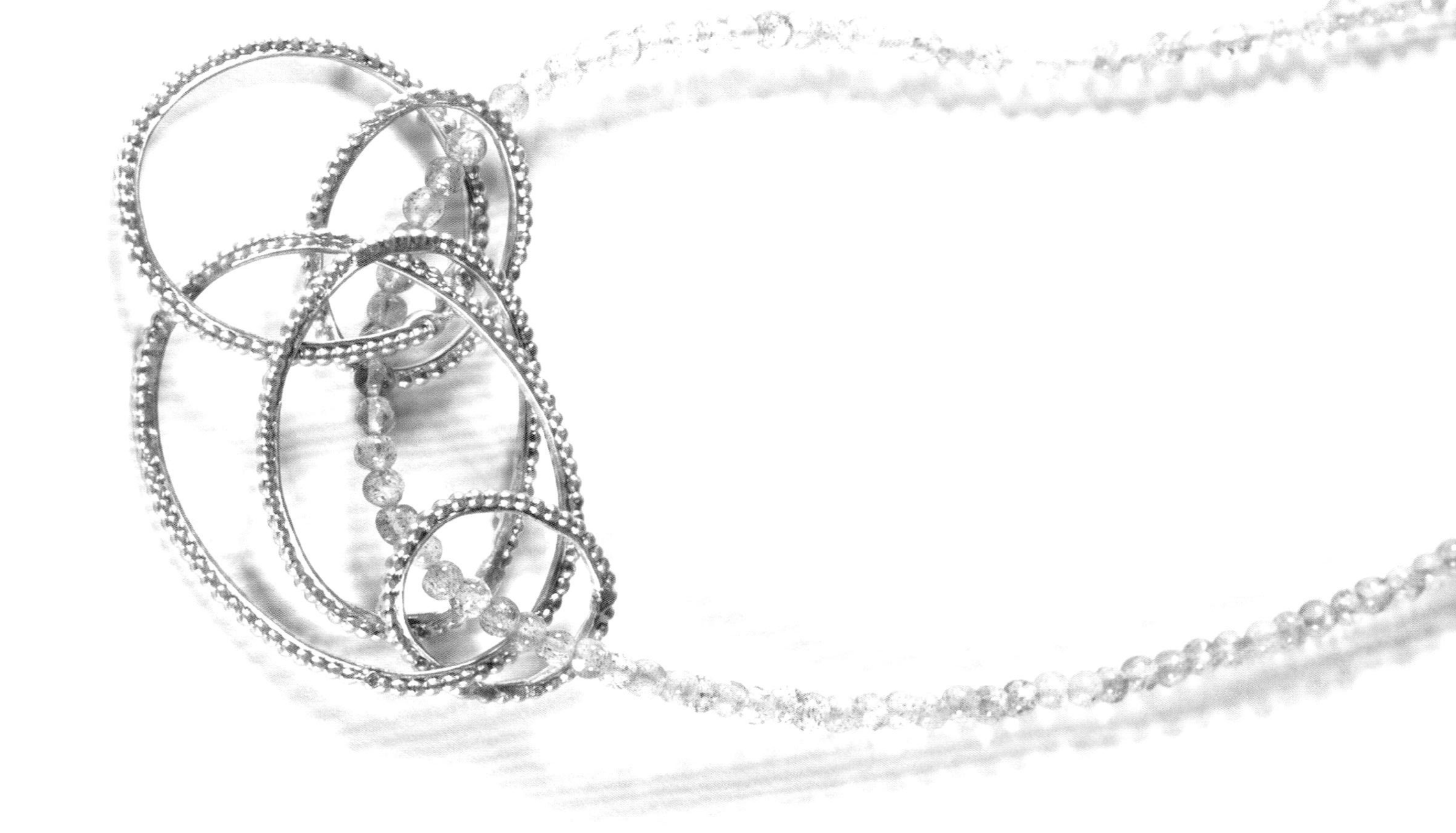

'KNOT NECKLACE' GOLD 18 K, DIAMONDS, LABRADORITE

MIRCA MAFFI SWITZERLAND

'WHITE DEER' PEARLS, LACE, PLASTIC, FABRIC, STERLING SILVER

MIA MALJOJOKI FINLAND

NECKLACE 'AURORA 5' COTTON, PAINT

NECKLACE 'AURORA 2' COTTON, PAINT

'SOLITARITY' STAINLESS STEEL, PLEXIGLASS, NÉOPRIME

PATRICK MARCHAL BELGIUM

'BESAME_MUCHO_MACHO' STAINLESS STEEL, IRON, SILVER, TITANE, SILICONE

PATRICK MARCHAL BELGIUM

'INNOCENS' IRON, STAINLESS STEEL, WOOD, BRASS, ALUMINIUM, TITANE, PHOTOGRAPH

GIGI MARIANI ITALY

'STONEHENGE BRACELET' SILVER, YELLOWGOLD 18 K, NIELLO, PATINA, HANDFABRICATED

'CRACKS-RING' SILVER, YELLOWGOLD 18 K, NIELLO, PATINA, HANDFABRICATED

TUIJA HELENA MARKONSALO FINLAND
'MR VITIL GO' TEXTILE, PLASTIC BEADS, PLASTIC HAND, SHOES, THREAD

'1+1' READYMADE OBJECTS, COPPER, ENAMEL, BEADS, CRYSTAL, PLASTIC

CAROLINA MARTINEZ LINARES GERMANY

BROOCH '(X1,Y-2)' POLYURETHANE, SILVER, STAINLESS STEEL

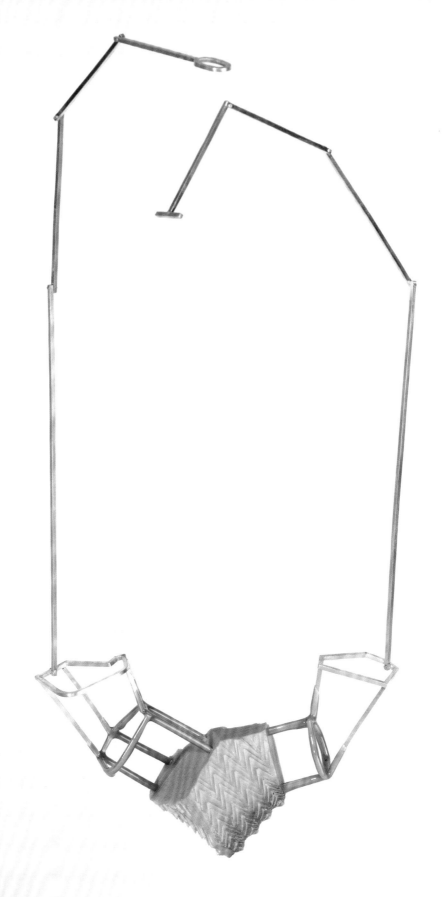

NECKLACE '(X-2, Y-14)' POLYURETHANE, SILVER

MÄRTA MATTSSON SWEDEN

BROOCH 'CAMOUFLAGE' RESIN, BEETLE, GOLD DUST, SILVER

BROOCH 'FOSSIL BLUE' CICADA, CRUSHED PYRITE AND AZURITE, RESIN, SILVER

JUDY MCCAIG SPAIN

'LIGHT OF STONE' TIN, SILVER, PERSPEX, GOLDLEAF, ROCK CRISTAL, TOMBOC

'PETRIFIED ICE' WEATHERED, STEEL, SILVER, PERSPEX, PAINT, WOOD, SHELL, FEATHER, ROCK CR STAL

‘A TAG IN TIME SAVES NINE’ GRAFFITI, COPPER, WHITE METAL, ENAMEL, CERAMIC, DECAL, THREAD

EMMA MCFARLINE UK

TIMOTHY MCMAHON USA

'LUMP ObB' COPPER, BRASS, ALUMINIUM, VITREOUS ENAMEL, RESIN, TOPAZ, AQUAMARINE, AGATE, POWDER COATING

TERESA MILHEIRO PORTUGAL

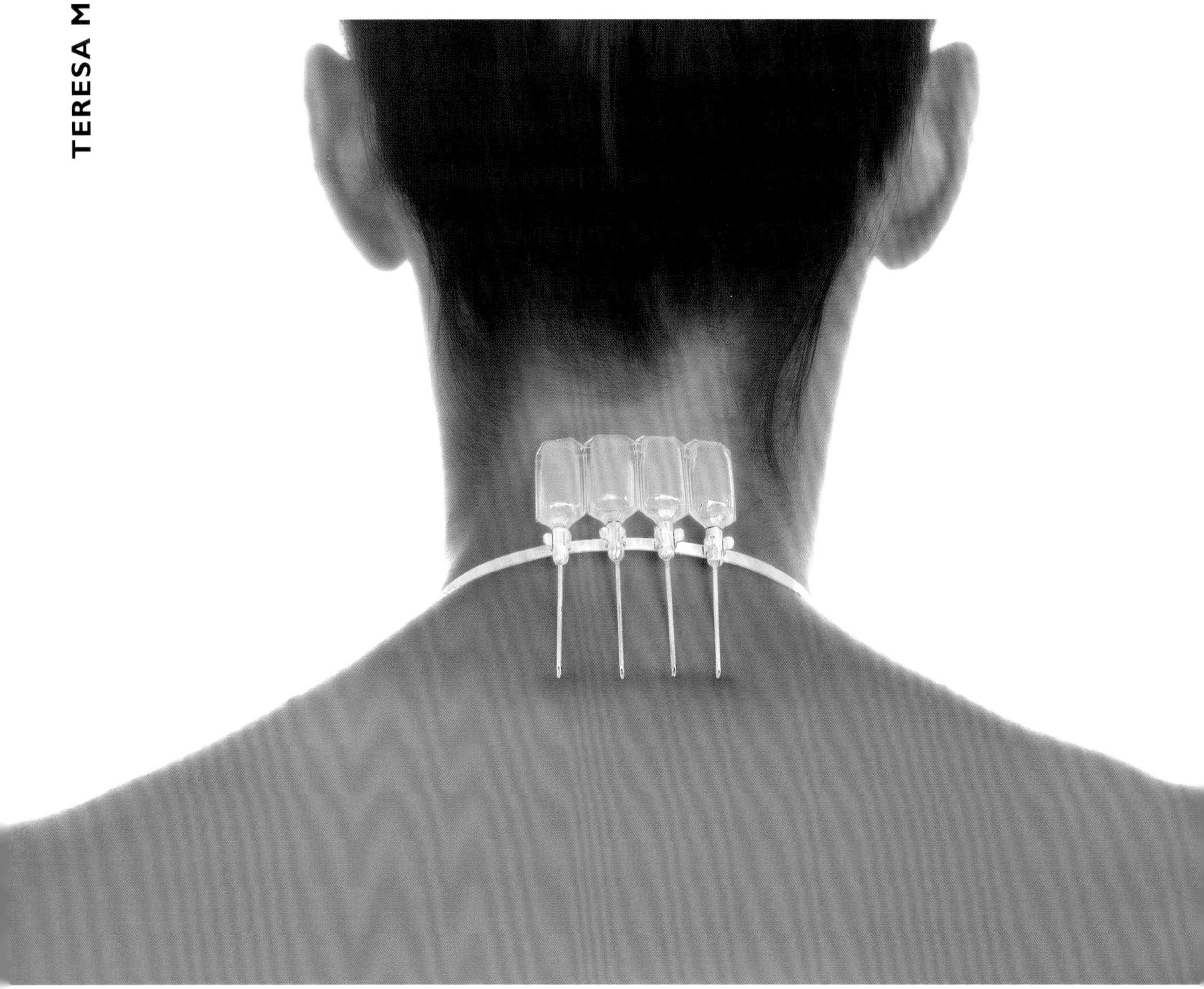

UNTITLED SILVER, PLASTIC

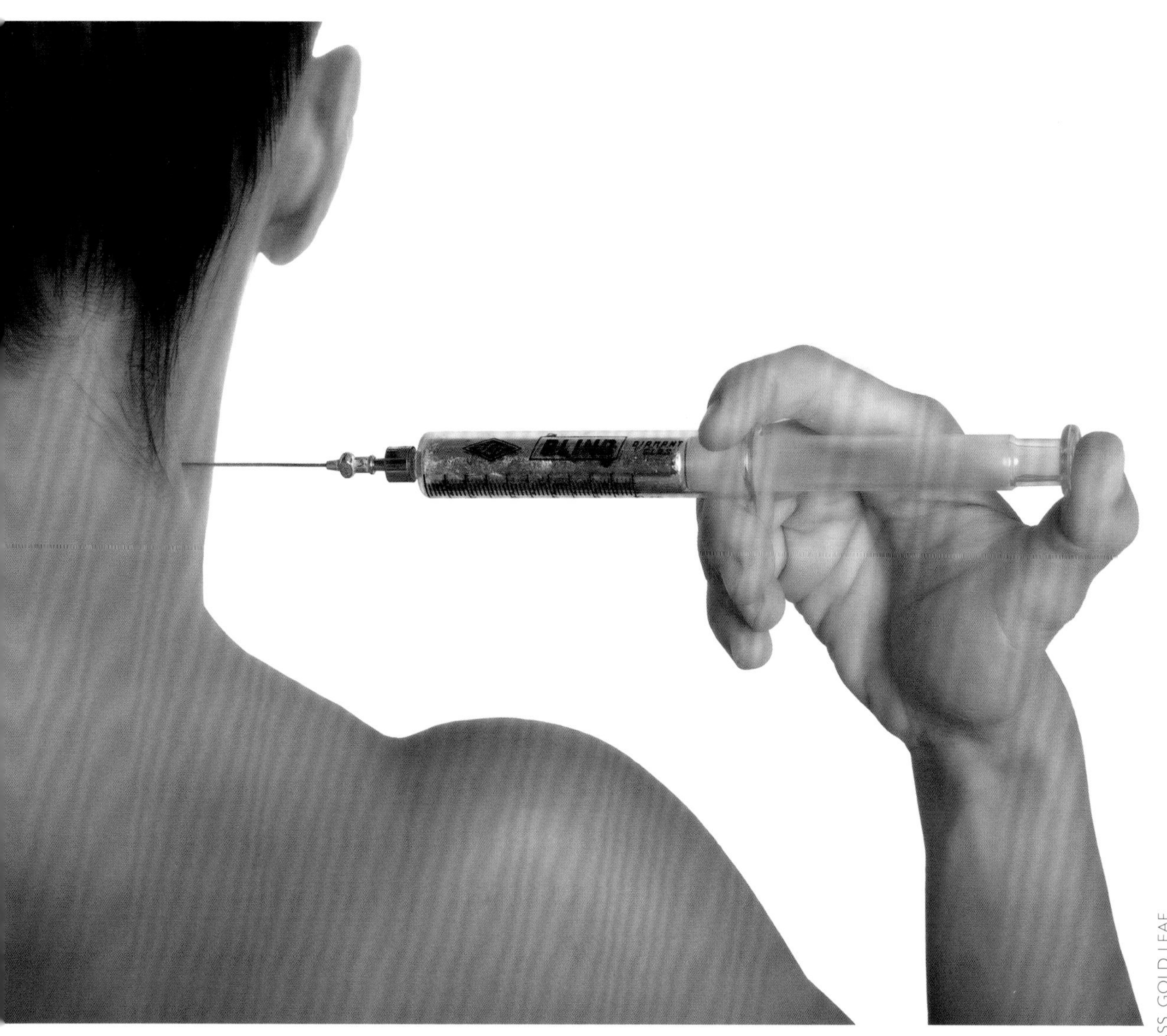

UNTITLED OLD GLASS SYRINGE, BRASS, GOLD LEAF

MARILIA MARIA MIRA PORTUGAL

PIN 'HERE WILL BE THERE' FABRIC, SILVER

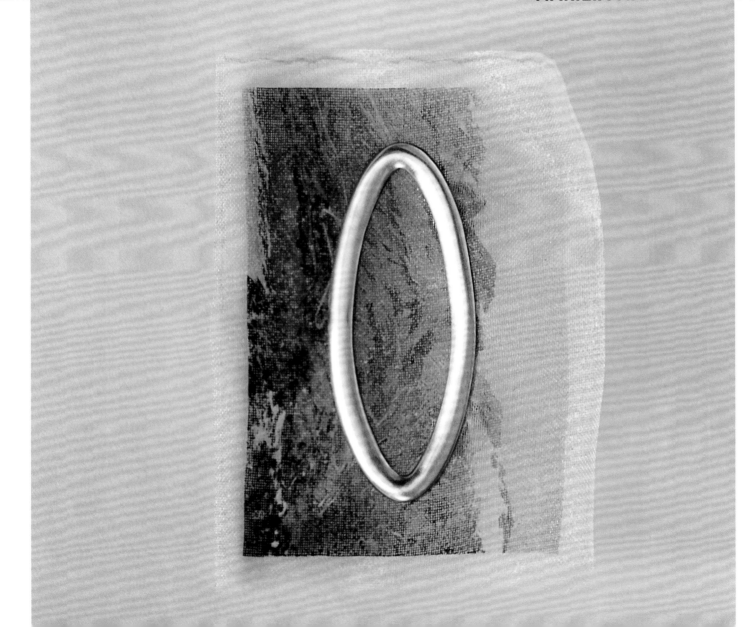

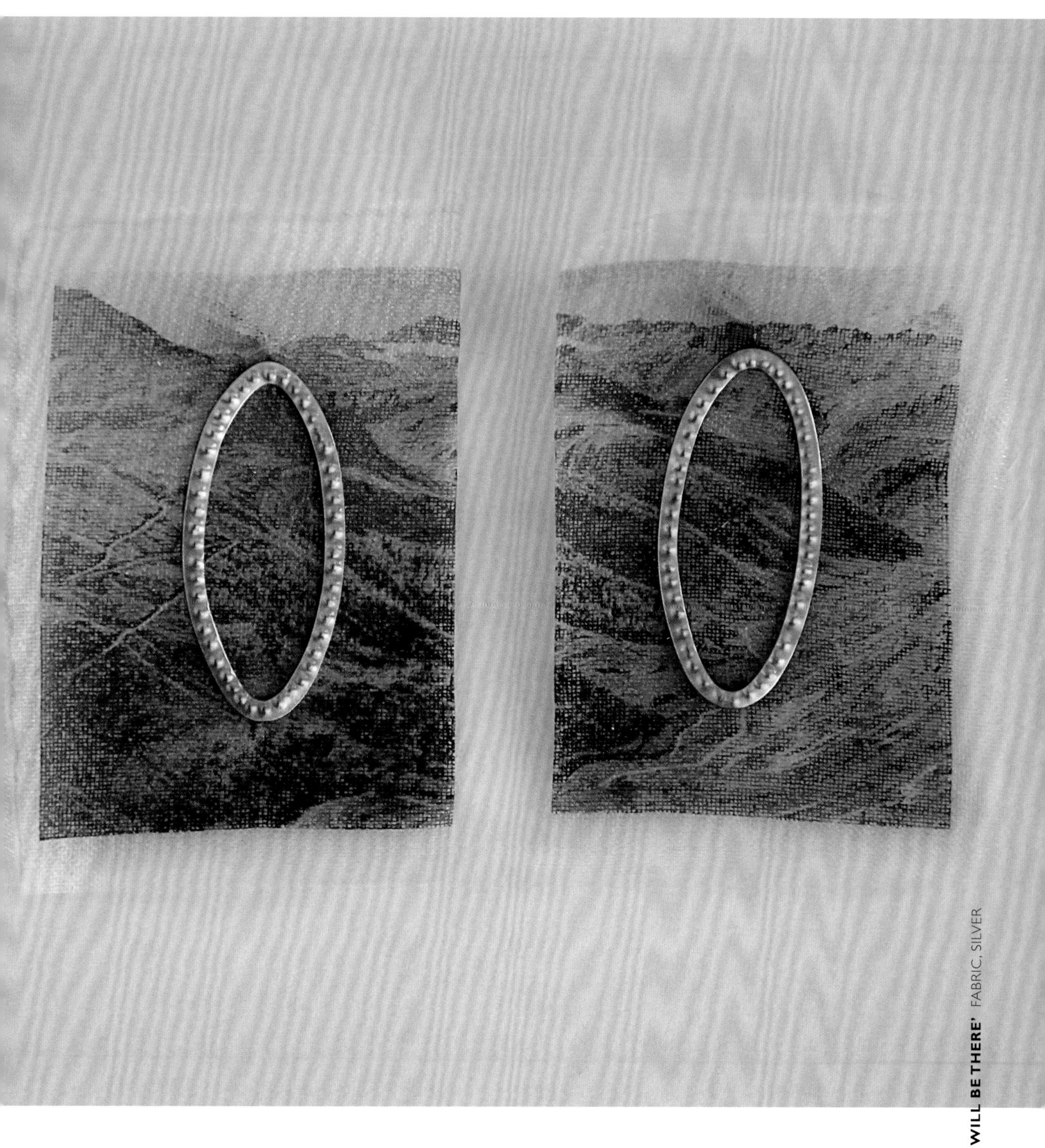

EARRINGS 'HERE WILL BE THERE' FABRIC, SILVER

MARILIA MARIA MIRA PORTUGAL

'A DROP IN THE OCEAN' FABRIC, SILVER

NECKLACE 'HERE WILL BE THERE' FABRIC, SILVER

DARCY MIRO USA

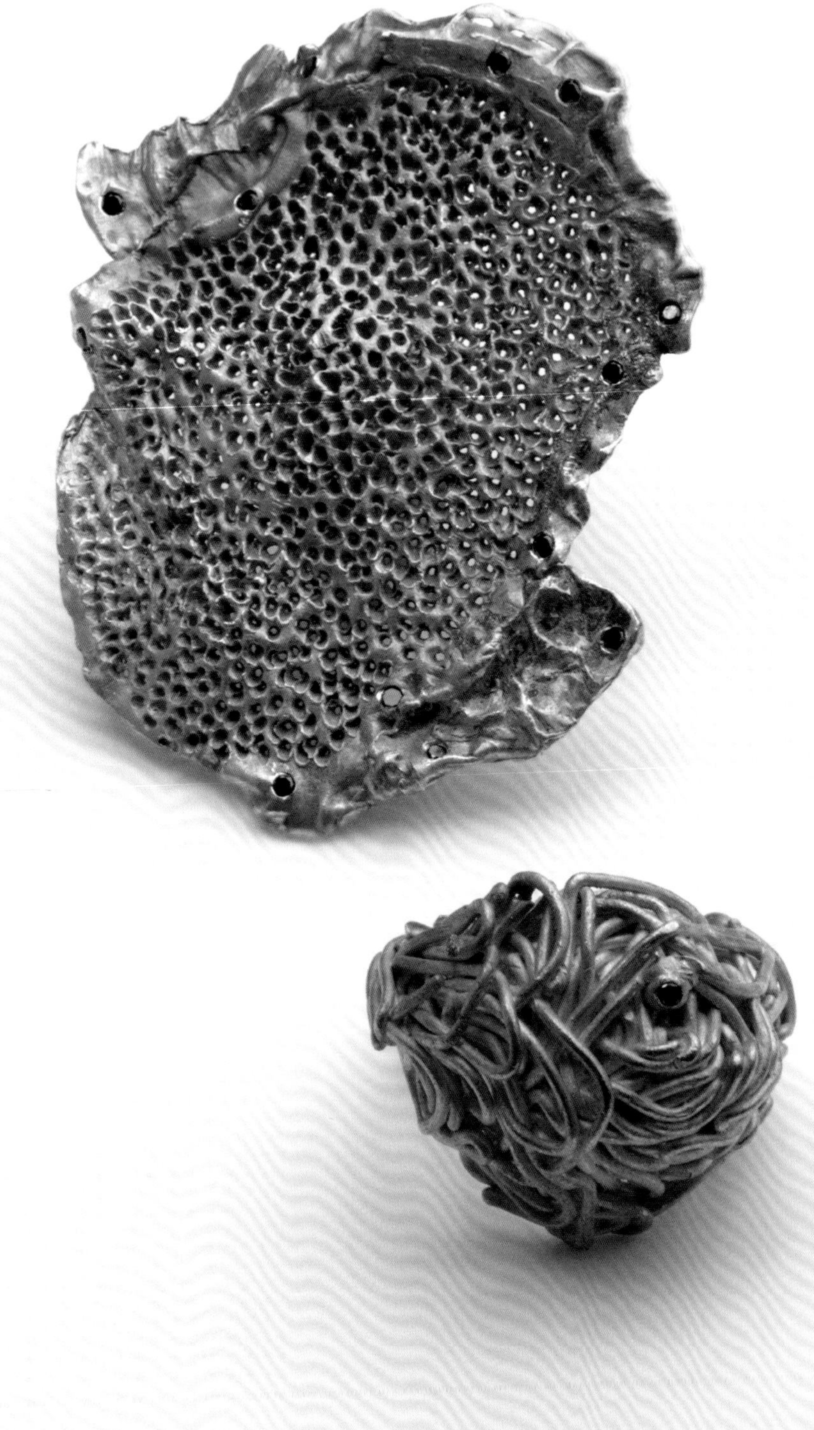

RINGS FOR PRINT 'SHIELD AND MUMMY' SILVER WITH BLACK DIAMONDS

RINGS RAW AND OXIDIZED STERLING SILVER, BLACK DIAMONDS

KATHARINA MOCH GERMANY

UNTITLED
PLASTIC, ENAMEL,
COPPER, AMETHYST

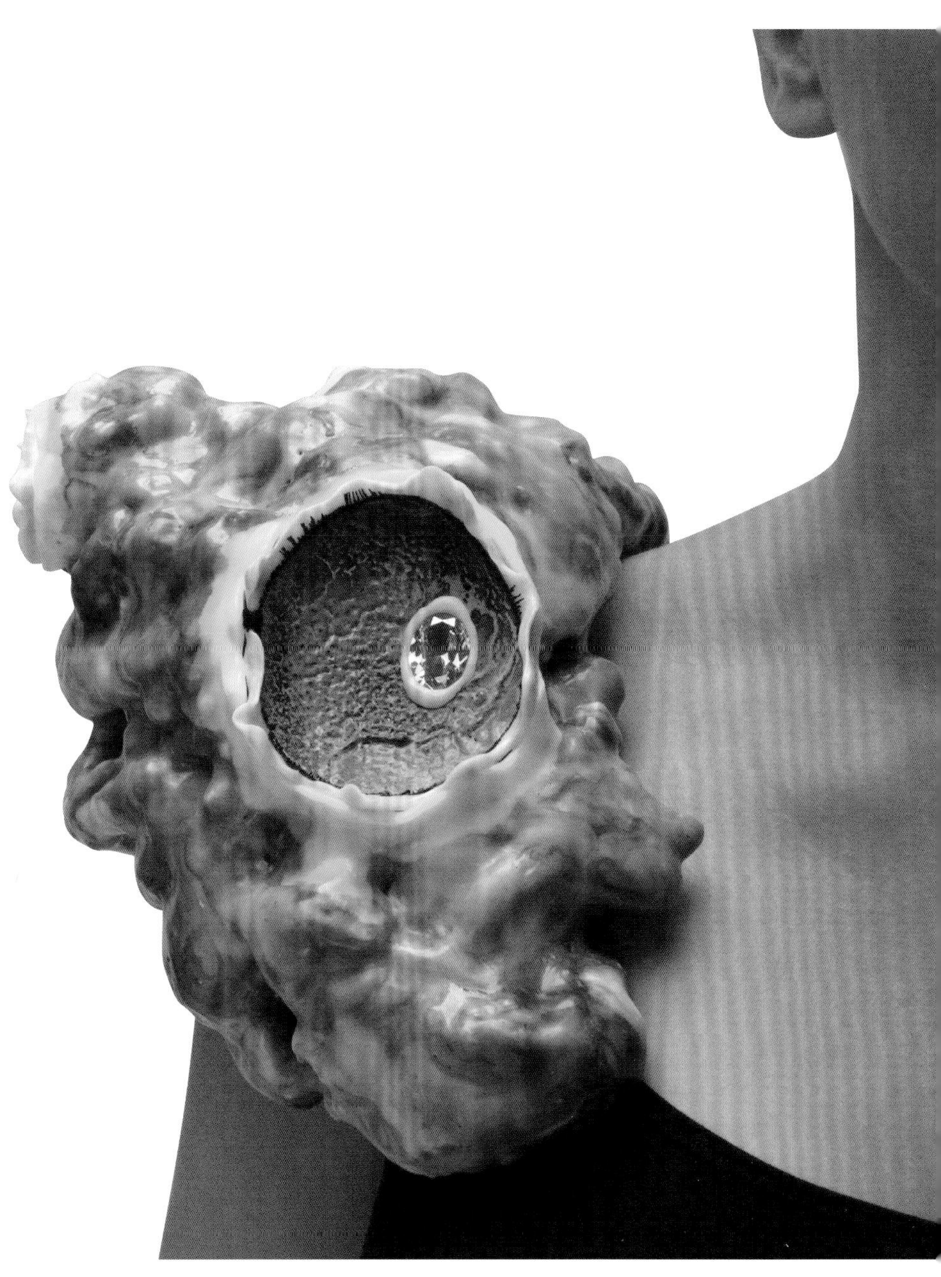

UNTITLED
PLASTIC, ENAMEL, COPPER, CZ

IRENE MORET ITALY

'MEDUSA' FVC, PIERCING IN STEEL

'ARMADILLO' STERLING OR GOLD OR BRASS

EDGAR MOSA USA

'THE HOURS' WOOD

'ALISSA LAMARRE WITH THE MOUNTAIN 4' WOOD, PLASTIC, HAIR, SILVER

ROSA NOGUÉS FREIXAS SPAIN

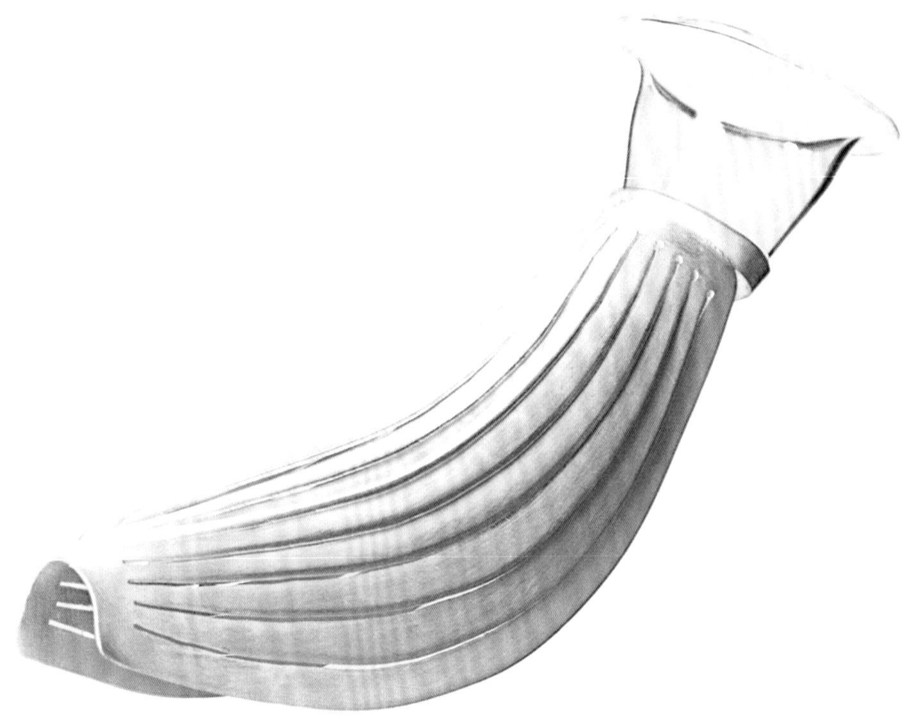

UNTITLED SILVER, GLASS, STEEL

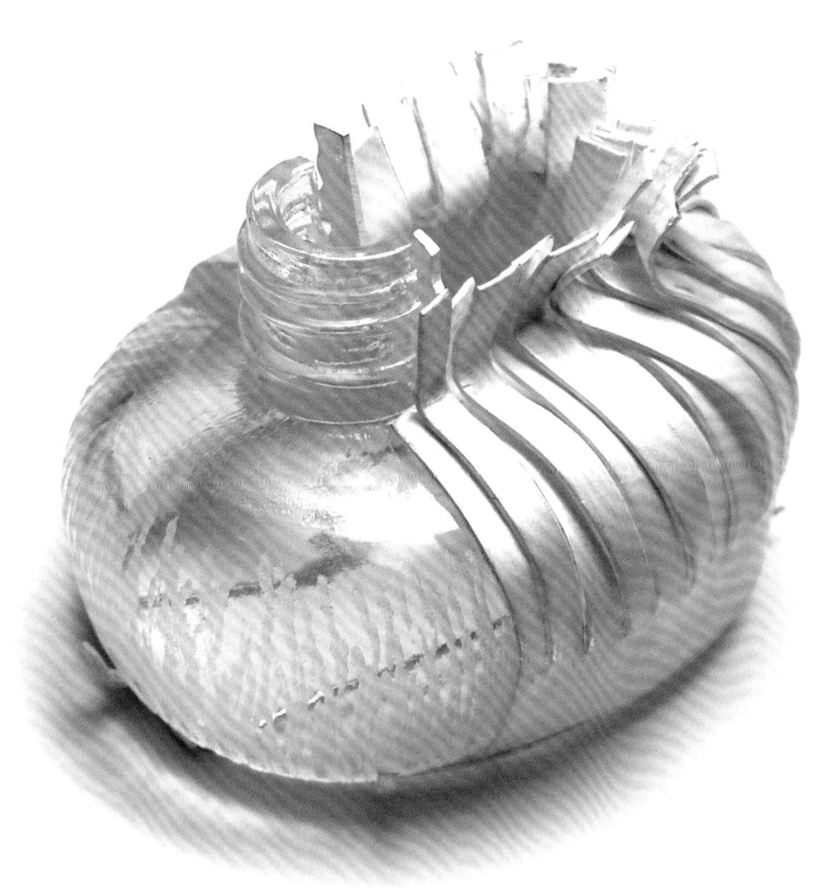

UNTITLED SILVER, GLASS, STEEL

ROSA NOGUÉS FREIXAS SPAIN

UNTITLED SILVER, GLASS

UNTITLED GERMAN SILVER, GLASS, STEEL

UNTITLED
BINCHOTAN STAINLESS STEEL, SILVER

GITTE NYGAARD THE NETHERLANDS

UNTITLED
BINCHOTAN, SILVER

KRISTI PAAP ESTONIA

BROOCH 'FIRST VIEW IN RED' LILAC WOOD, CHERRY WOOD, CORALS, COPPER, SILVER

BROOCH 'TWELVES VIEW' CHERRY WOOD, THREAD, SILVER

UNTITLED MIXED MEDIA

TATIANA PAGES USA

GUSTAVO PARADISO SPAIN

'THOUSANDFLOWERSRING' DEER HORN, CABLE, SILVER 925

'THOUSANDFLOWERSRING' DEER HORN, CABLE, SILVER 925

'COLLIER BOULES DE VERRES 2' SILVER 925, HI-MACS, GLASS, QUARTZ, DYNEEMA

FONT-SALA SAMANTHA AS PE/AH GERMANY

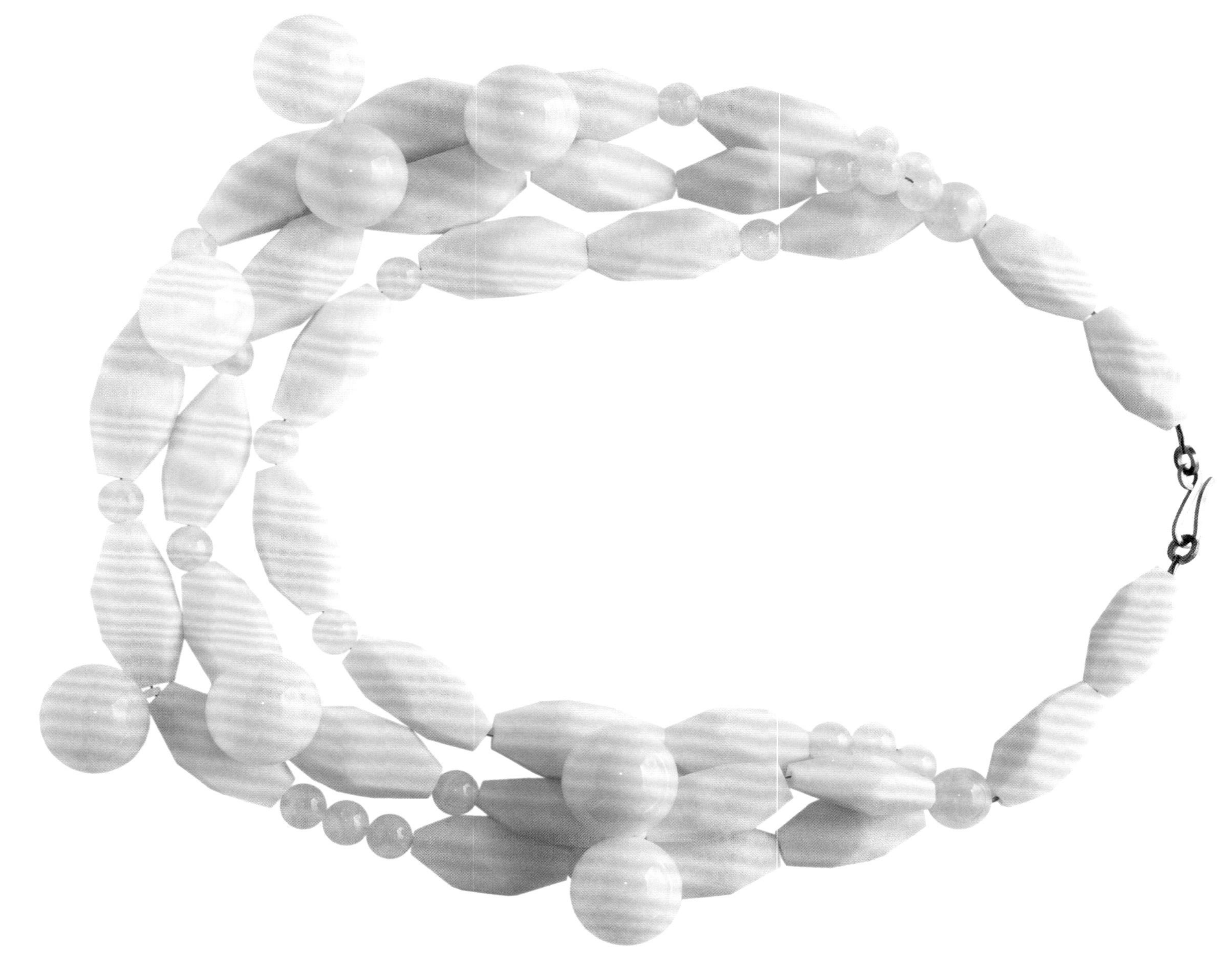

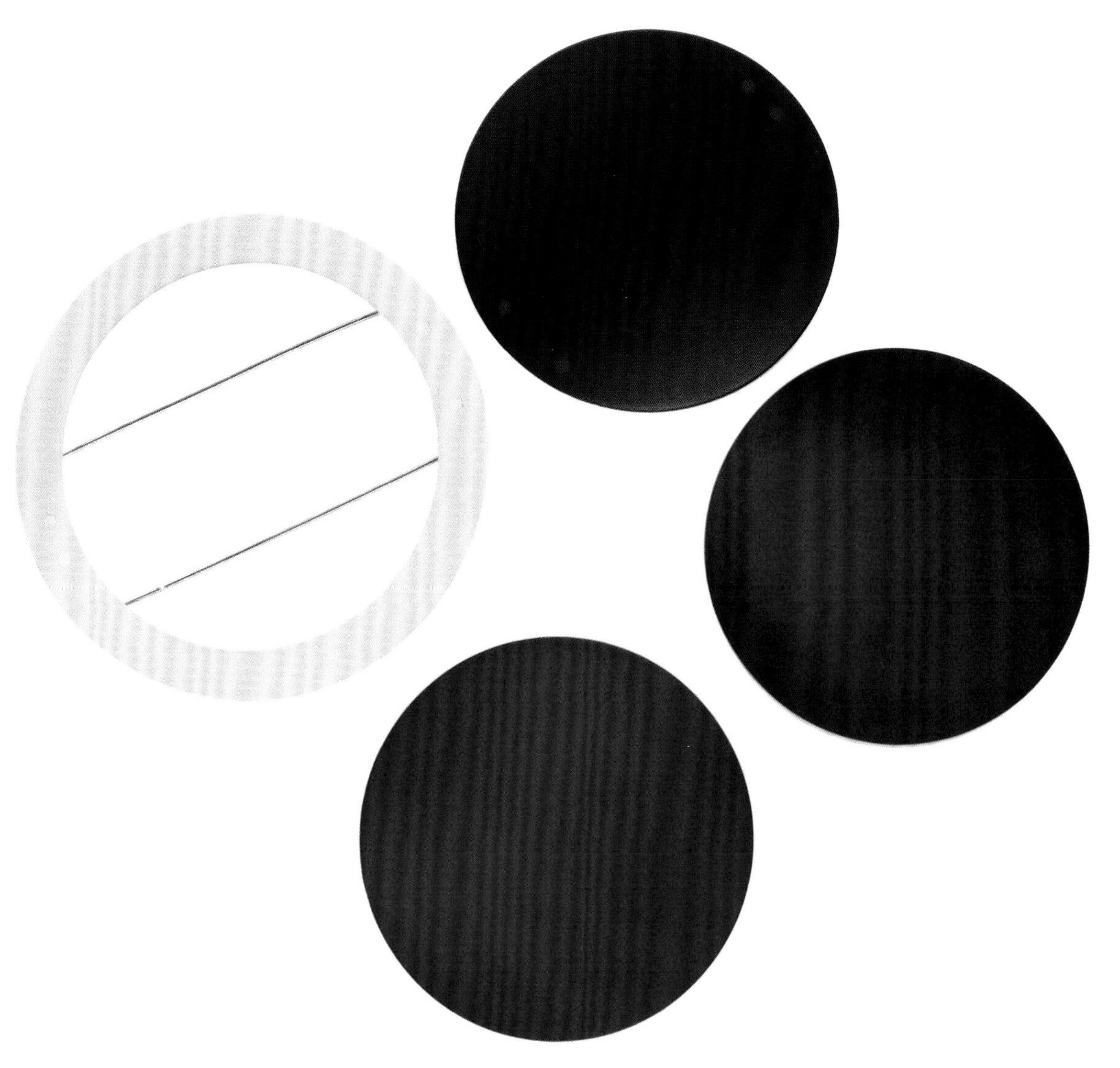

BROOCH 'CERCLE' ALUMINIUM ANODIZED, STAINLESS STEEL

PENDANT 'CORPUS FEMUR' POLYURETHANE, RUBBER

RUUDT PETERS THE NETHERLANDS

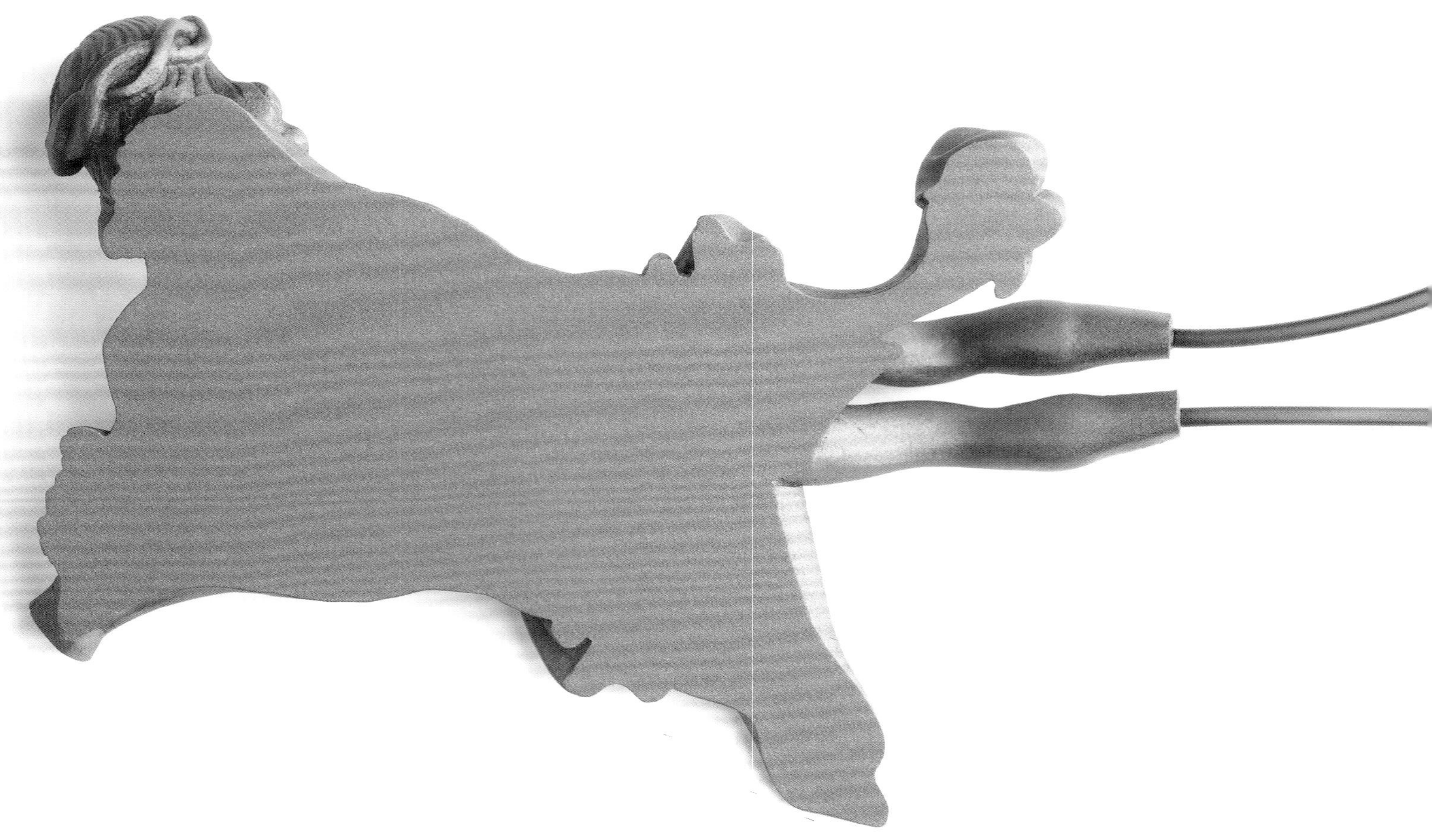

BROOCH 'CORPUS CRUS' POLYURETHANE, SILVER

RUUDT PETERS THE NETHERLANDS

COLLAR 'CORPUS LUMBUS' POLYURETHANE, NYLON

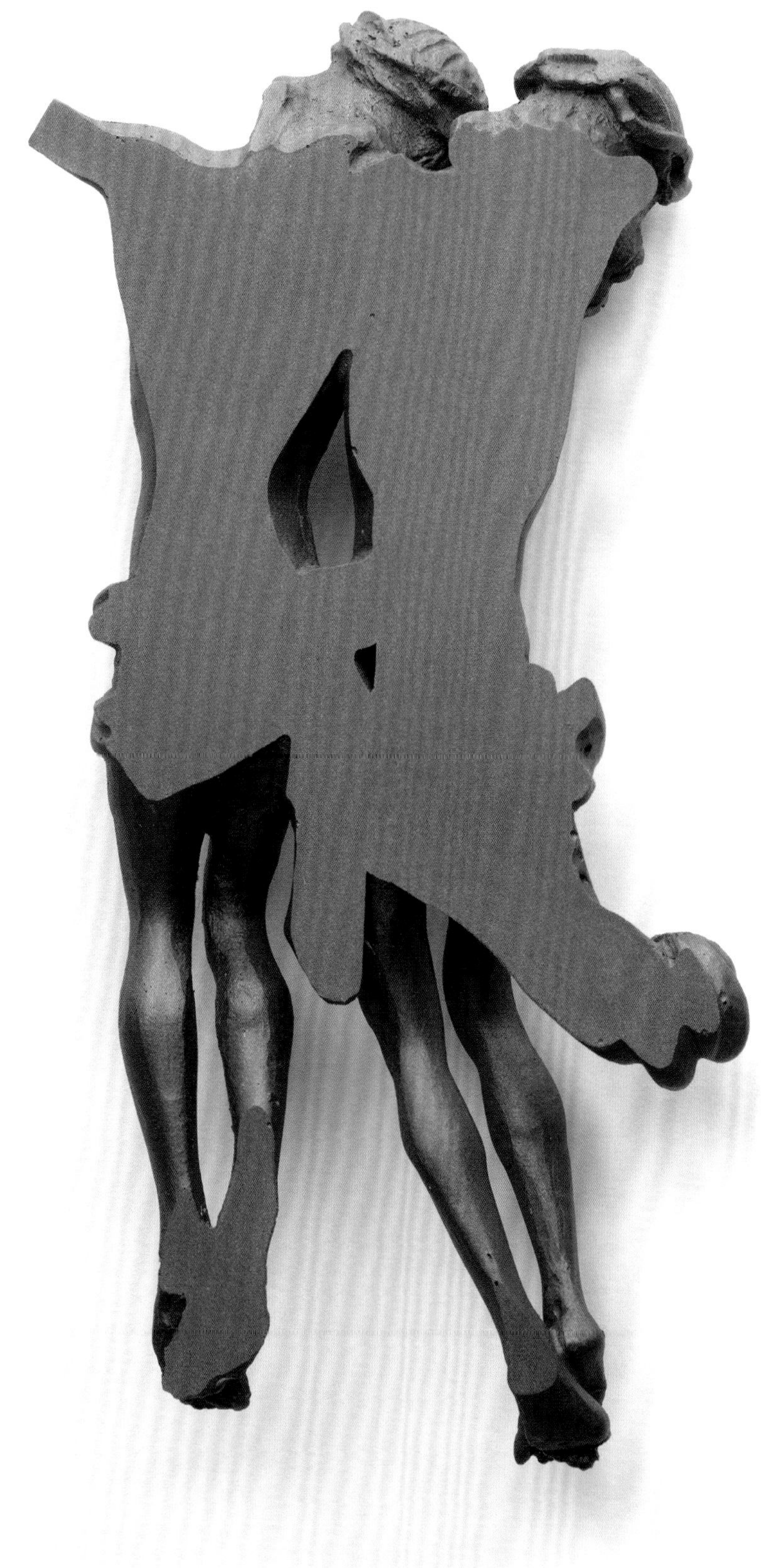

BROOCH 'CORPUS COAX' POLYURETHANE, SILVER

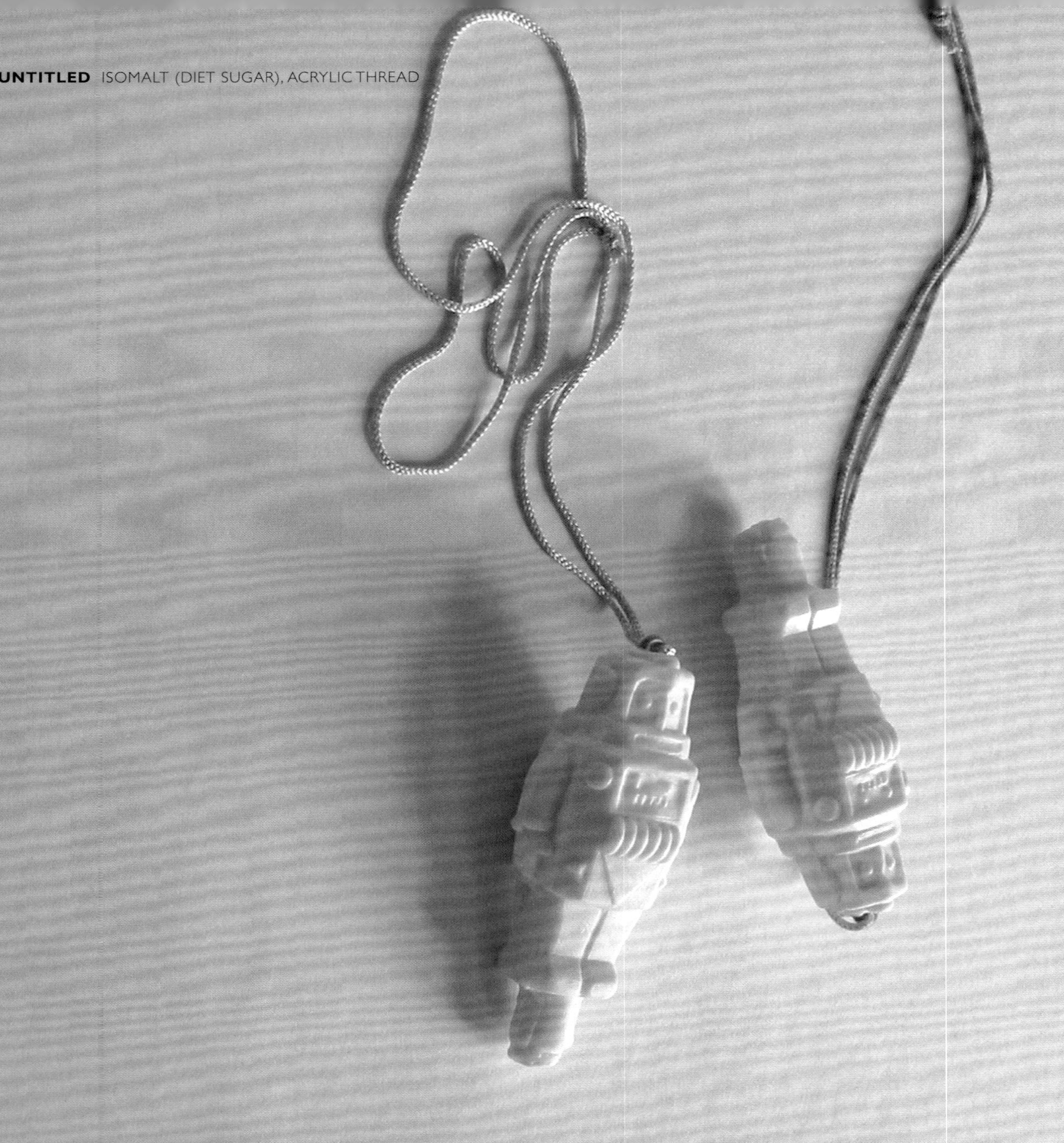

UNTITLED ISOMALT (DIET SUGAR), ACRYLIC THREAD

SUSAN PIETZSCH JAPAN

ANDREA PIÑEIRO SPAIN

'AMOR INTRAVENUSO' STERLIN SILVER, THERMAL ACETATO, DRUGG/PILLS

PENDANT 'ENSEMBLES' SILVER 925, NYLON WIRE

ANDREA PINEROS FRANCE

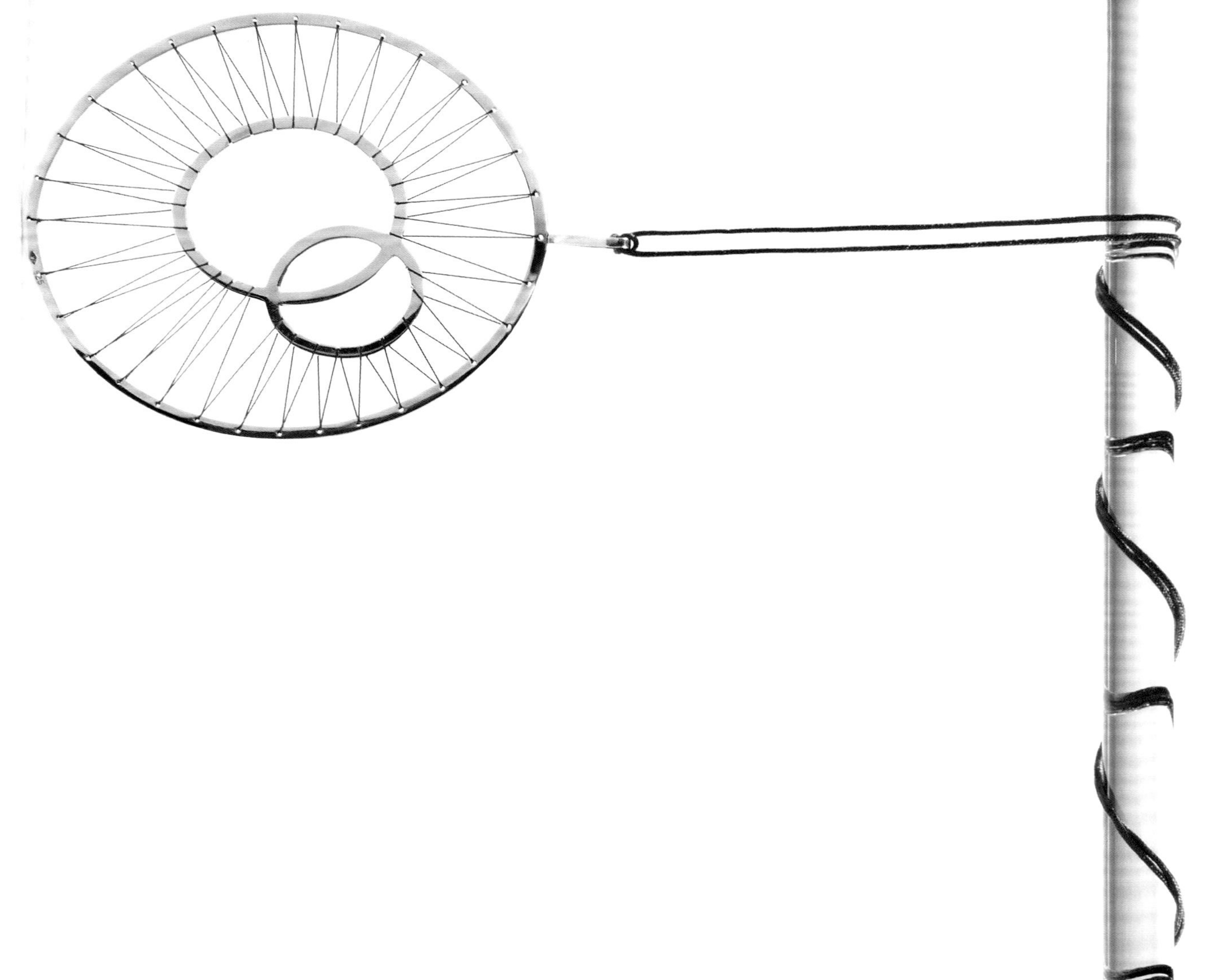

RINGS 'DESTINS CROISÉS' SILVER 925, NYLON WIRE

ALICE POTTER AUSTRALIA

NECKPIECE 'RIDICULOUS CHAIR' WOOD, SILVER 925, PAINT, GLASS, PLASTIC, FABRIC, CZ'S

RENATA PORTO BRAZIL

HYBRID PIN FISH SILVER 950, RUBBER

BEVERLEY PRICE SOUTH AFRICA

UNTITLED HOLOGRAPHIC POSTCARD, SWAROVSKI CRYSTALS, COPPER, THREAD, PLEXIGLASS, PLASTIC, FINE GOLD, SILVER, CZECH SAUSAGE PAPER, SILK THREAD

UNTITLED LAMINATED FINE GOLD LEAF, BRASS, JAPANESE DELICA SEED BEADS

KATJA PRINS THE NETHERLANDS

'7 INTER-ACT' NECKLACE SILVER, LABORATORY GLASS, SILICON RUBBER, STEEL

'4 INTER-ACT' NECKLACE SILVER, RECONSTRUCTED ONYX, STEEL

KATJA PRINS THE NETHERLANDS

'15 INTER-ACT' BROOCH SILVER, RECONSTRUCTED RED CORALS, GLASS

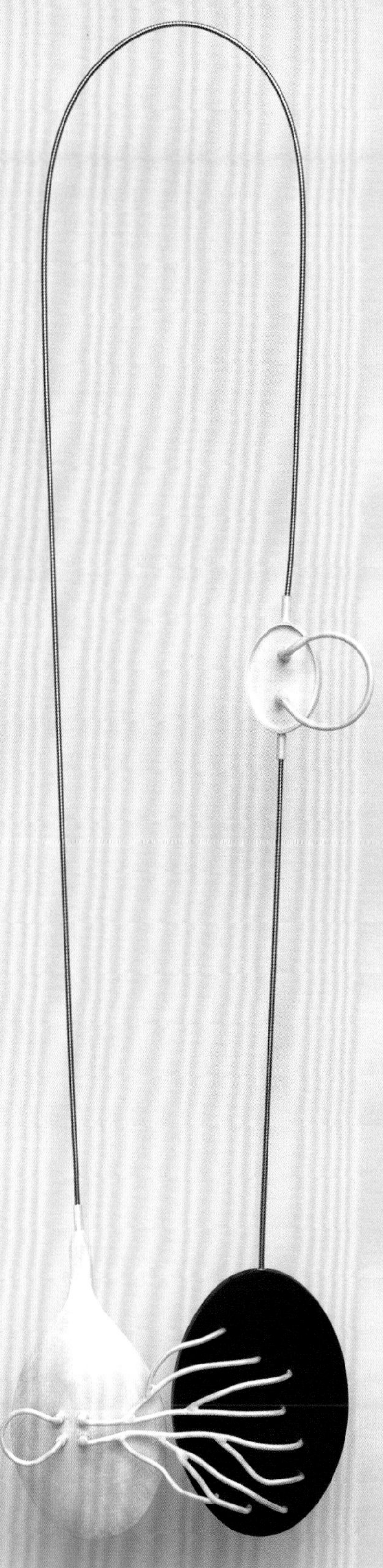

'12 INTER-ACT' NECKLACE SILVER, RECONSTRUCTED RED CORAL, STEEL

'PARTICULAS ALEATORIAS N° 1' SILVER, HORN, ONYX, SILK, STEEL **WALKA STUDIO, NANO PULGAR / CLAUDIA BETANCOURT** CHILI

TIINA RAJAKALLIO FINLAND

UNTITLED BARK OF CORK, COTTON, YARN, SEALING, WAX, PAINT

KAIRE RANNIK ESTONIA

BROOCH 'INONOTUS-OBLIQUUS III' SILVER, COPPER, RUBBER, WOOD, STEEL

BROOCH 'INONOTUS-OBLIQUUS V' SILVER, COPPER, MIRROR, STEEL

ULI RAPP THE NETHERLANDS

'PEARLRE' TEXTILE, SILICONE RUBBER, SCREENPRINTING TECHNIQUES, METAL FOIL

DAVE RENPERMETER NORWAY

'COSMIC NOISE BROOCH N°6' ALUMINIUM, SILVER, RUTILE, QUARTZ

JORDAN REMBRANDT BELGIUM

BROOCH 'ROTAR N°4'
SILVER, OLD GLASS STOP, SPIRNG STEEL, PARTLY PAINTED

'FLOATING RING'
SILVER, BELLOW CONSTRUCTED

'SNAPSHOT' SILICONE, SILVER

DENISE JULIA REYTAN GERMANY

UNTITLED SMOKEY QUARTZ, HETEROSIT, RECONSTRUCTED CORAL, ONYX, SILVER, PLASTIC, CABLE

DENISE JULIA REYTAN GERMANY

UNTITLED SILVER, FINEGOLD 24 K, STEEL

'VERREAUXII' CARNEOL, CORAL, CAIRINGORM, ROSE QUARTZ, GARNET, SILVER, STAINLESS STEEL, SILICONE, PLASTIC, ROPE

JOANA DA SILVA RIBEIRO PORTUGAL

RING SILVER, PAINTED WITH METALLIC INKT

RING SILVER AND ROCKS

TERESA RICHTER GERMANY

'BECOPEGI' ROCK-CRYSTAL, GLASS, BEADS, CORAL, NYLON, STAINLESS STEEL

'SETTINGWOR' COLOURED GLASS, ANDEANOPAL, PLEXIGLASS, NYLON, STEEL

CORINA RIETVELD THE NETHERLANDS

UNTITLED SILVER, EMBROIDERY THREADS

UNTITLED SILVER, EMBROIDERY THREADS

ZOE ROBERTSON UK

BROOCH 'DOUBLE BUBBLE' HIGH DENSITY FOAM, FLOCK FIBRE, PLASTIC, SUBLIMATION DYE, STEEL, MAGNET

BROOCH 'DOUBLE BUBBLE' HIGH DENSITY FOAM, FLOCK FIBRE, PLASTIC, SUBLIMATION DYE, STEEL, MAGNET

NORA ROCHEL GERMANY

'HERBALISM' ALUMINIUM, BRONZE, SILVER BLACKENED (FAIRTRADE)

CRISTINA ROQUE PORTUGAL

BROOCH 'PSICOTHERAPY' THREAD, CROCHETED

REBECCA ROSE USA

'HIRING' 4.128 TROY OZ. CAST. 925 STERLING SILVER, FERRIS WAX, FOUND OBJECTS, ORGANIC MATERIALS

'SUGARING' 2.630 TROY OZ. CAST. 925 STERLING SILVER, FERRIS WAX, FOUND OBLECTS, ORGANIC MATERIALS

DEBORAH RUDOLP GERMANY

'FELDER' JASPER, SILVER, CORD STRING

'ACHATMAFF' AGATE, SILVER, KEVLAR

'BROKEN' PORCELAIN, HEMATITE, SILK CORD, STERLING SILVER

ELENA RUEBEL GERMANY

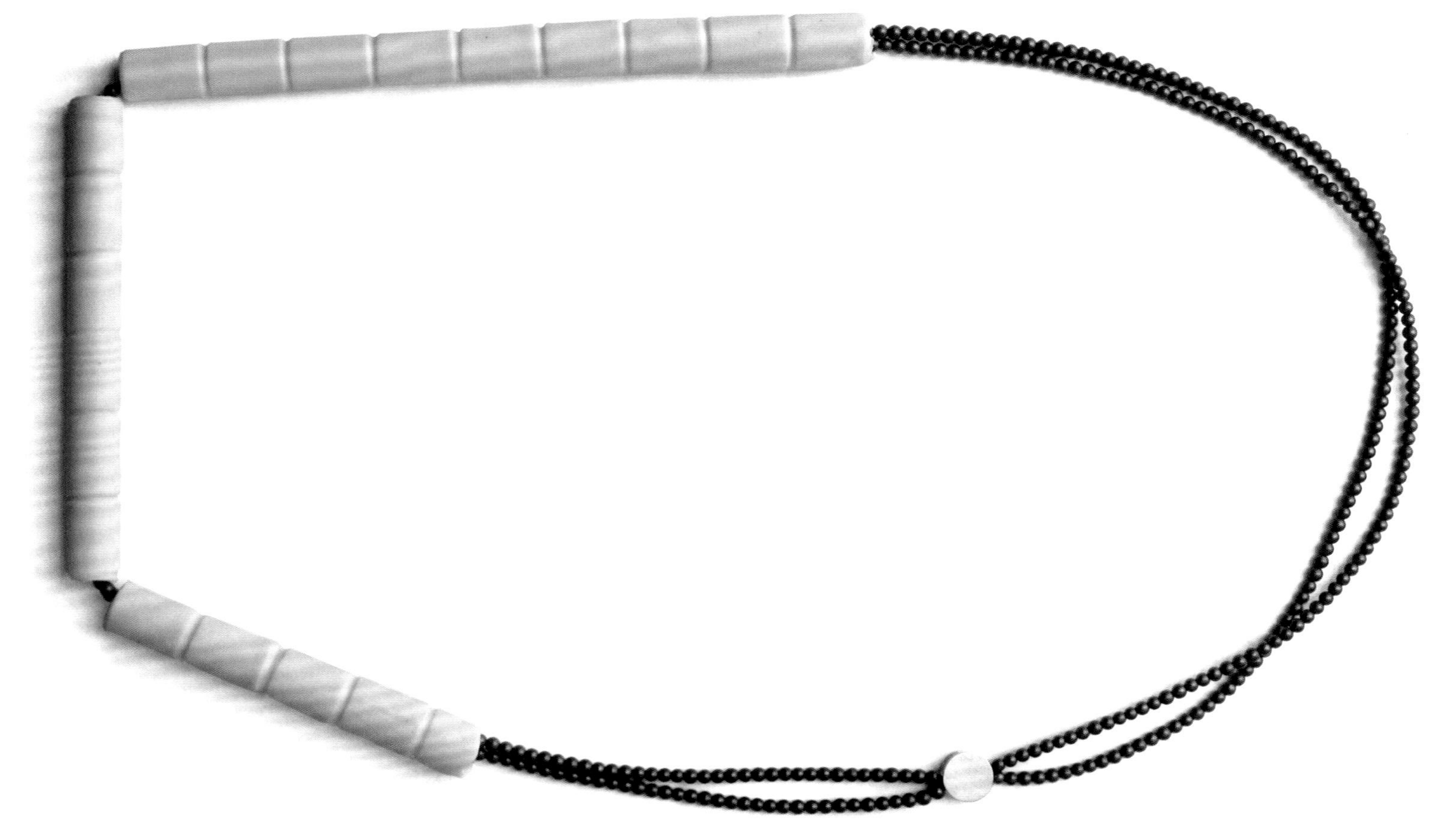

'BROKEN' STAINED PORCELAIN, GLASS BEADS, SILK CORD, STERLING SILVER

CARMEN AMADOR RUIZ SPAIN

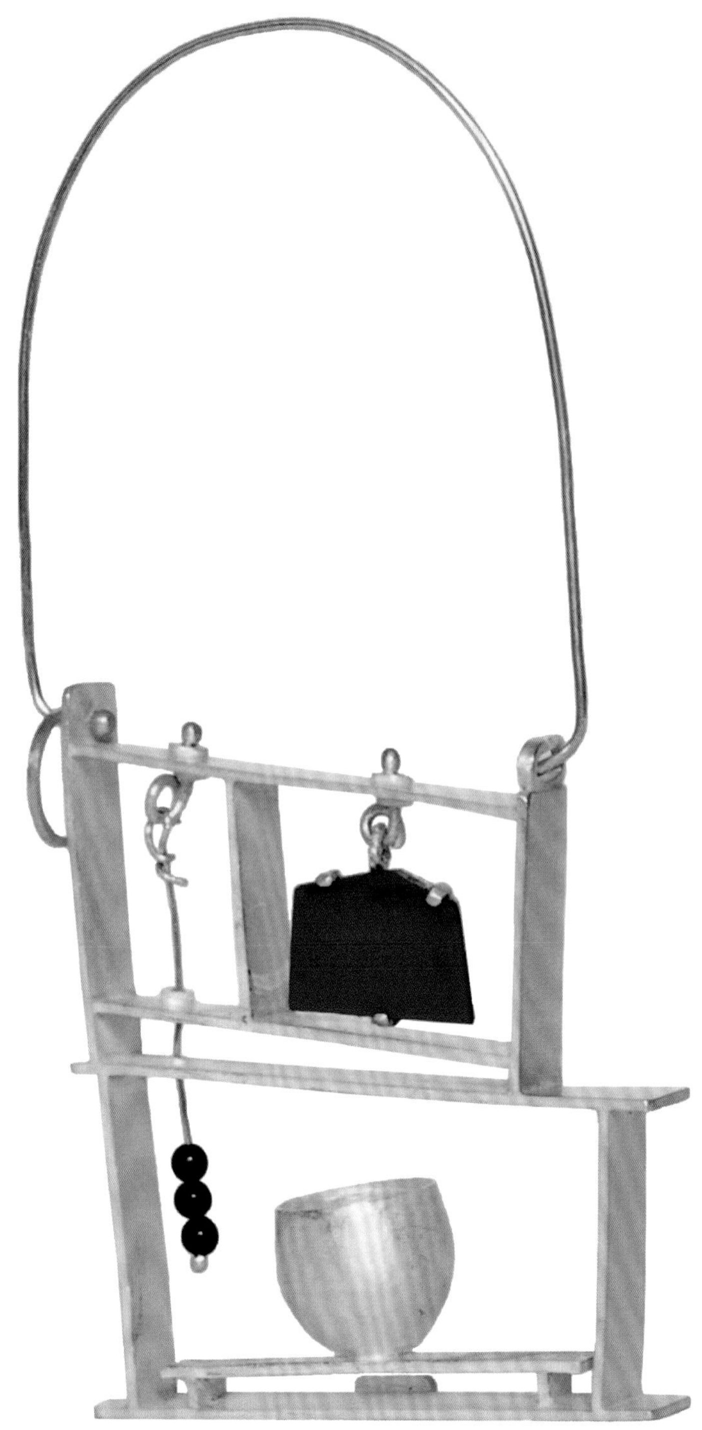

BROOCH/PENDANT 'ESPACIOS' SILVER, RECONSTRUCTED CORAL, ONIX, GOLD

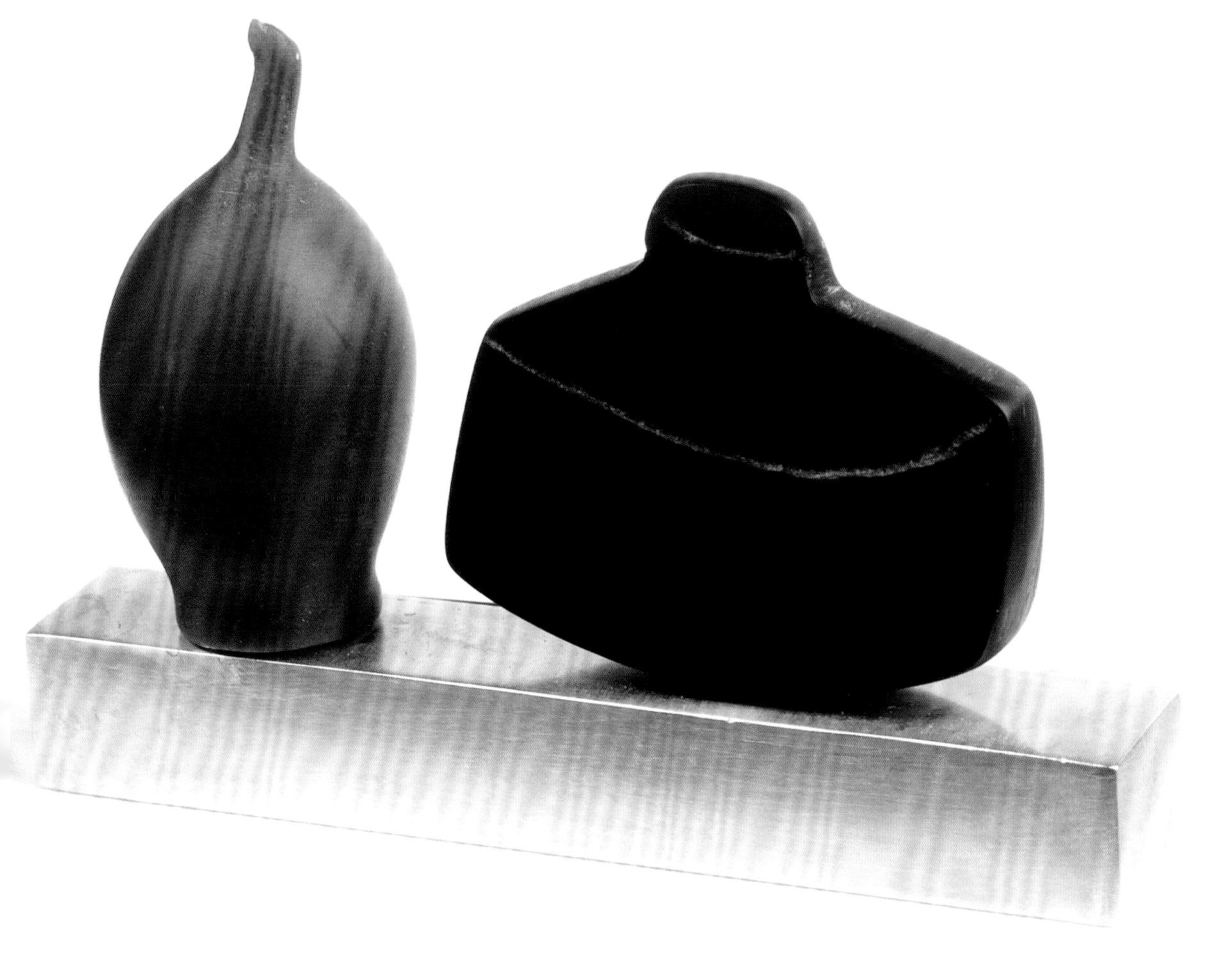

BROOCH 'DIALOGO I' SILVER, CRYSTAL, RESIN

VANIA RUIZ CHILI

RING 'PIMPED PICOROCO' PICOROCO SHELL, COLOURED RESIN, SILVER

RING 'CURAHUILLA SUNRISE' CURAHUILLA, COLOURED RESIN, SILVER

JILL RYCKAERT BELGIUM

'ZIRCONIAINSIDE' SILVER, ZIRCONIA

ESTELA SAEZ THE NETHERLANDS

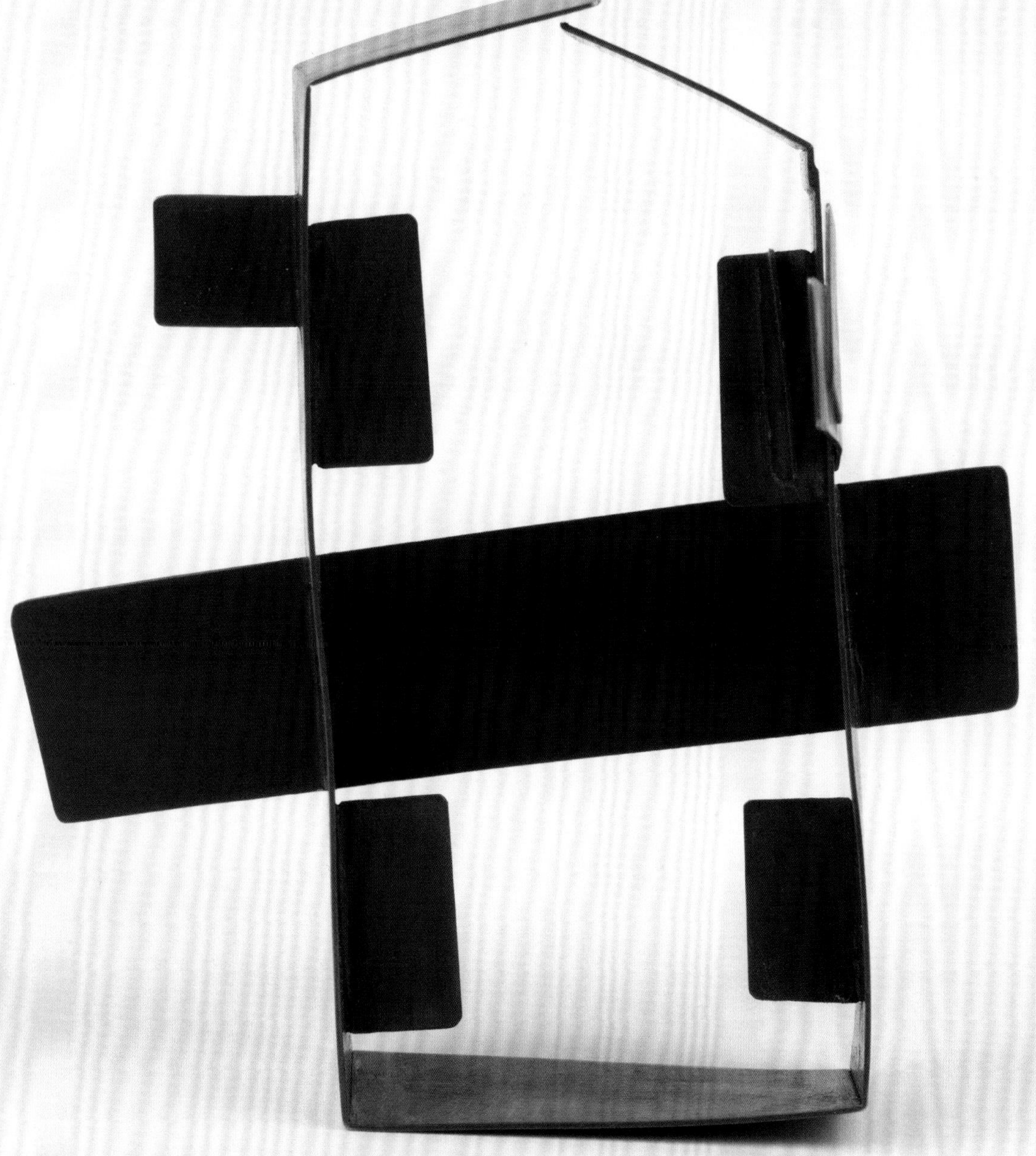

UNTITLED SILVER

PHILIP SAJET THE NETHERLANDS

'GLUE RING' JADE, ROSE QUARTZ

'A LA RECHERCHE DU JOYAU PERDU 2' AMETRHYST, ENAMEL ON SILVER, GOLD

GABRIELA SÀNCHEZ Y SANCHEZ DE LA BARQUERA
THE NETHERLANDS

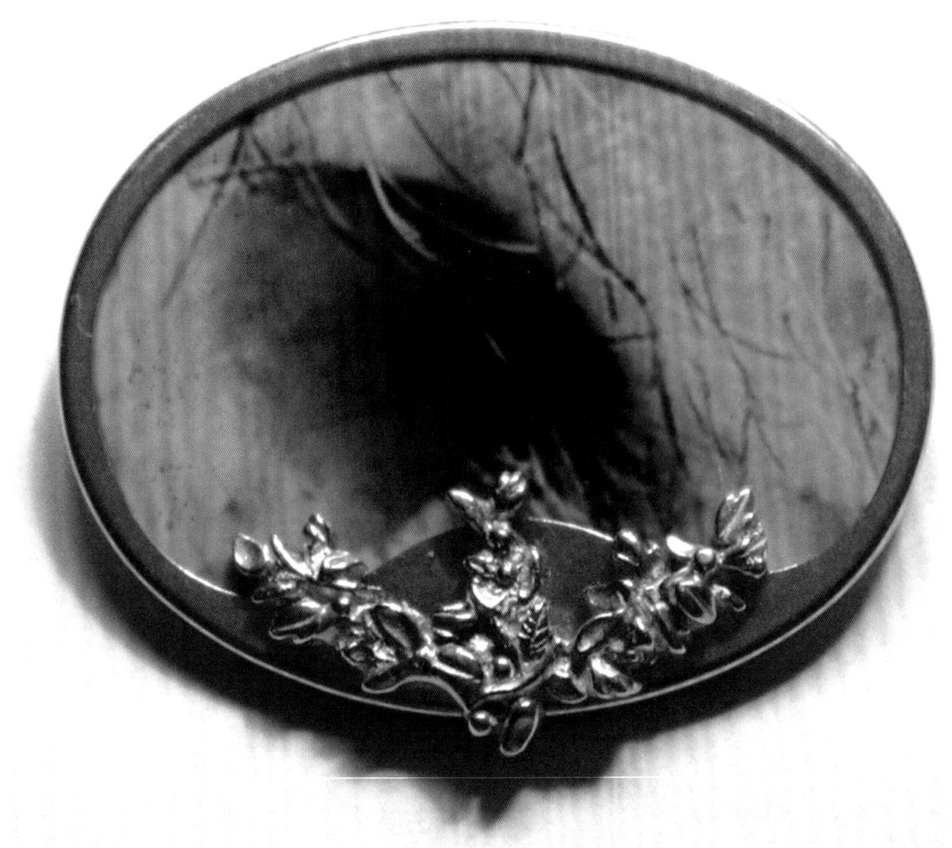

BROOCH 'NORMALCAMEO'
GOLD PLATED BRASS, EPOXY, PHOTO PAPER

BROOCH 'AB NORMALCAMEO'
GOLD PLATED BRASS, EPOXY PHOTO PAPER

BROOCH 'ANIMALWISH'
LEATHER, NK, THREADS

GABRIELA SÀNCHEZ Y SANCHEZ DE LA BARQUERA
THE NETHERLANDS

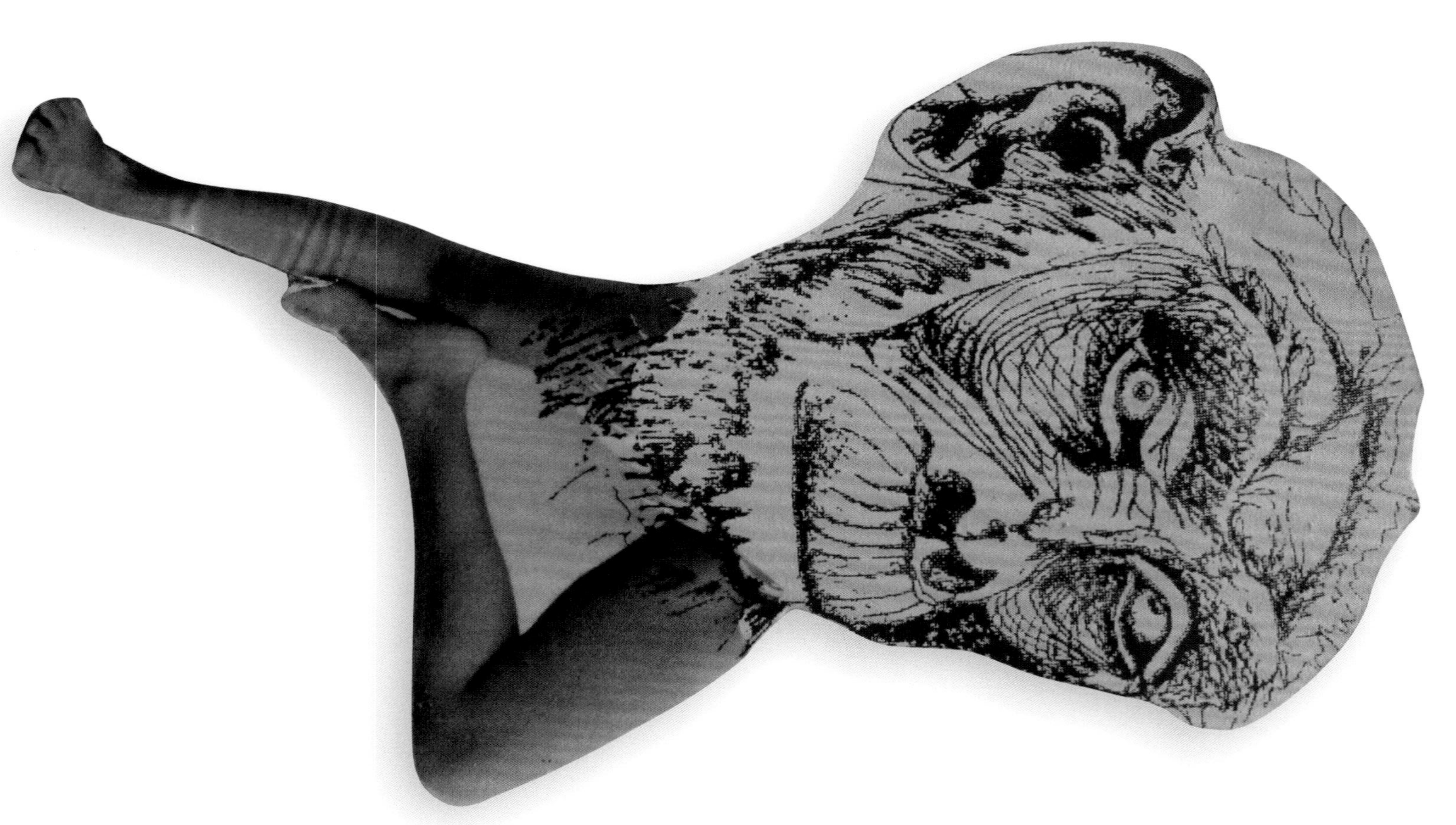

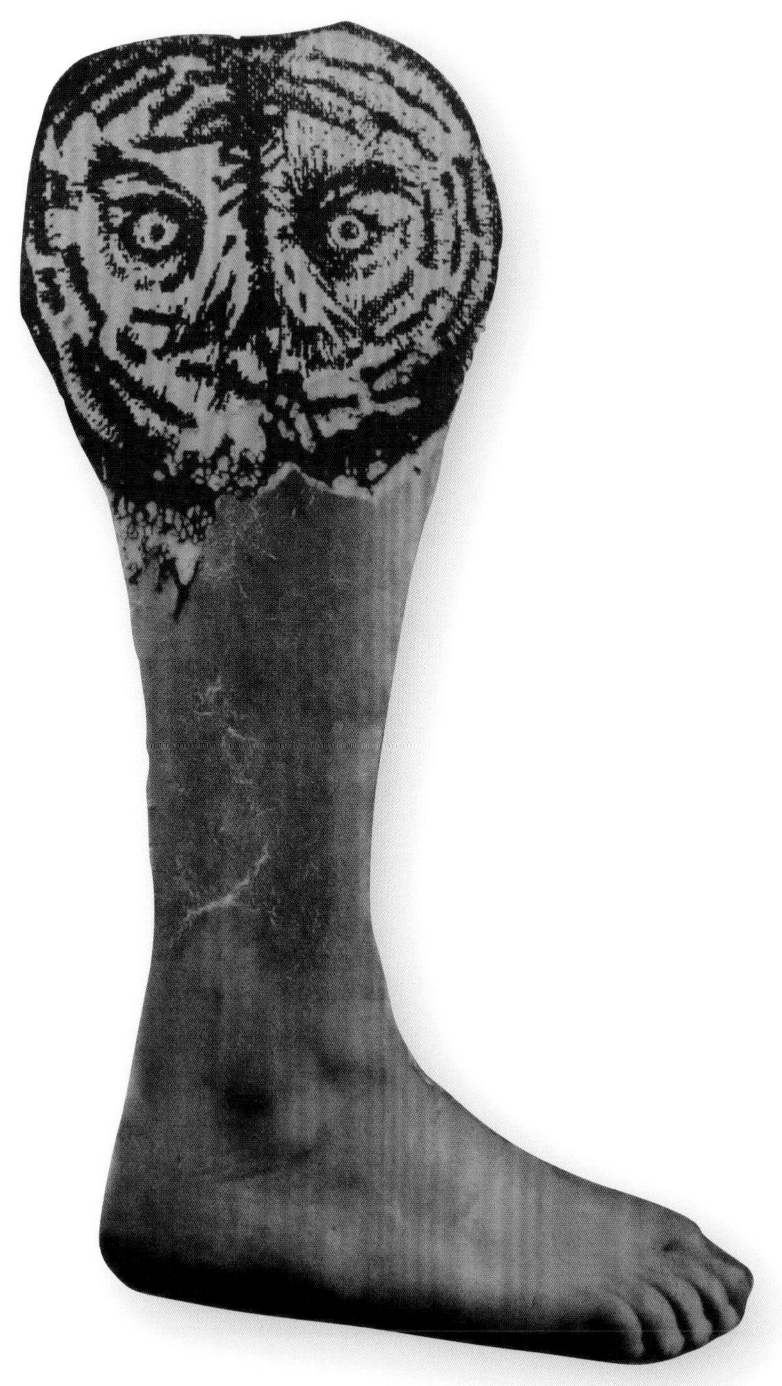

BROOCH 'ANIMALWISH'
LEATHER, INK, THREADS

LUCY SARNEEL THE NETHERLANDS

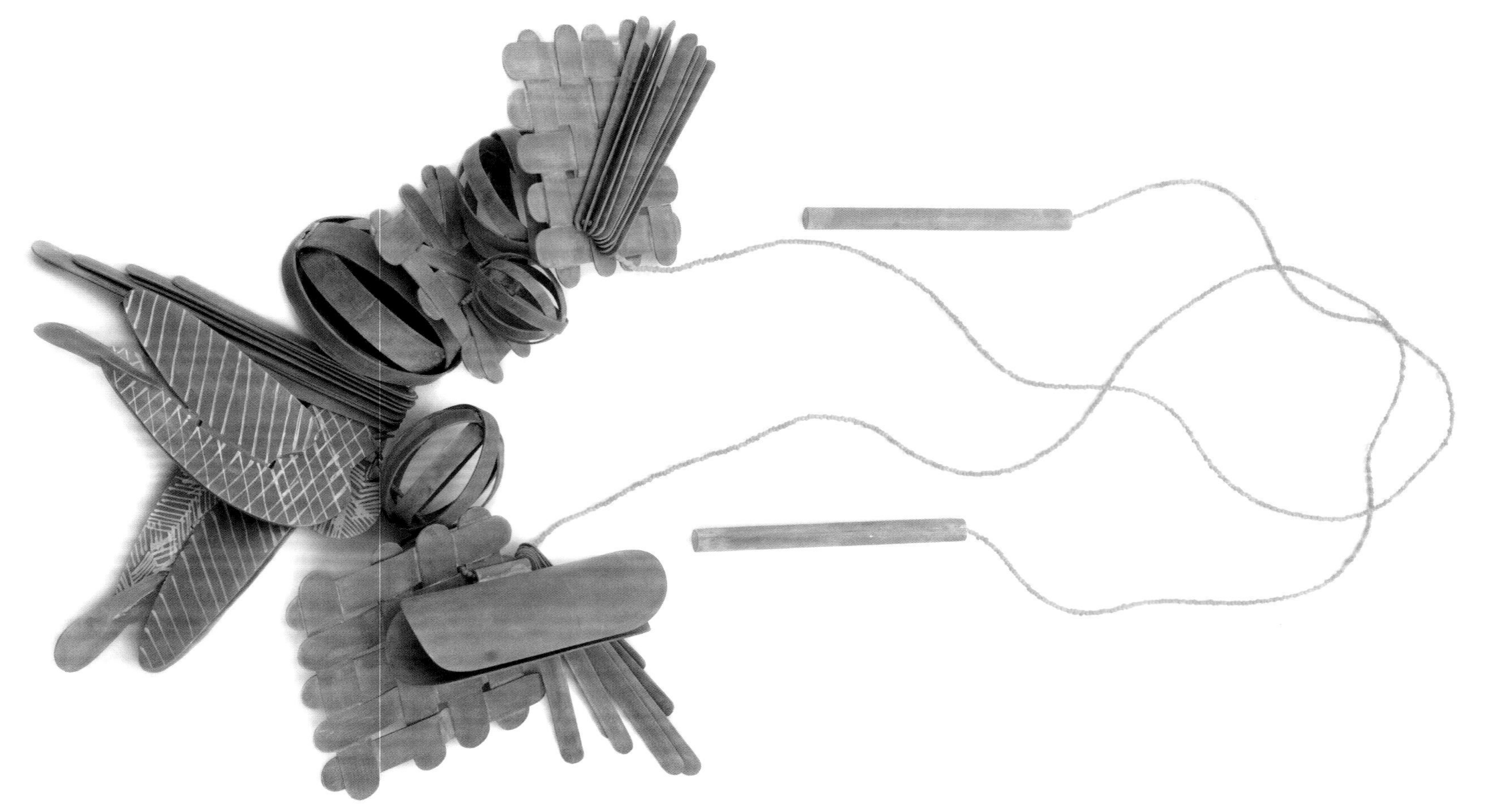

NECKLACE 'LOVEPOWER' ZINC, ANTIQUE VENETIAN GLASS BEADS, NYLON THREAD, PERMANENT INK

BROOCH 'SHELTER SPELL' ZINC, PERSPEX, PERMANENT INK

BROOCH 'PRIVATE TERRITORY I' ZINC, WOOD, VARNISH, EPOXY, DRIED SEED

LUCY SARNEEL THE NETHERLANDS

NECKLACE 'STARRY SKY DRIVE YEAR' ZINC, WOOD, PAINT, VARNISH, NYLON THREAD, LAPIS LAZULI BEADS

GIULIA SAVINO ITALY

BROOCH RUBBER FOAM, ACRYLIC PAINT, RESIN, MAGNET

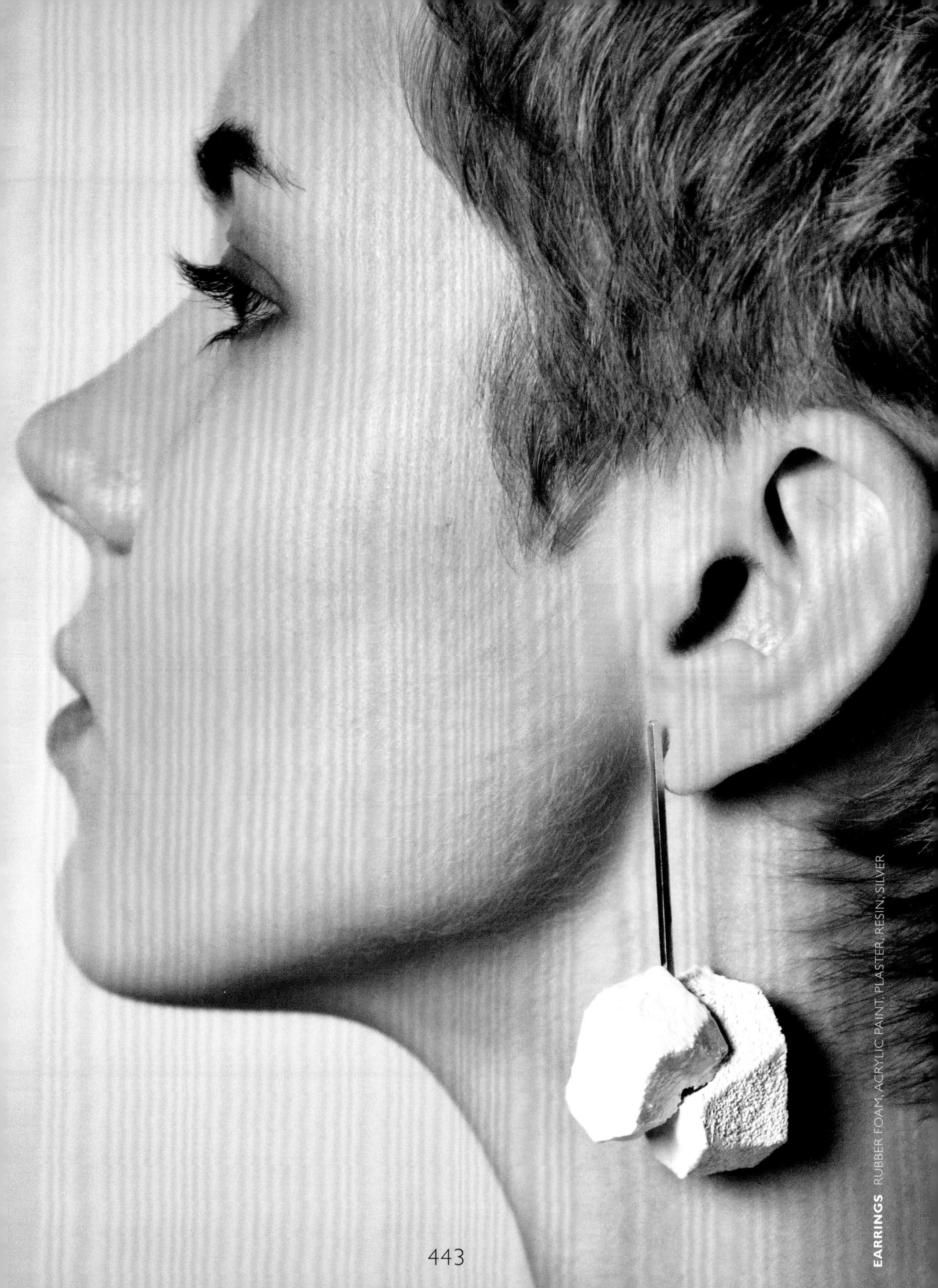

EARRINGS RUBBER FOAM, ACRYLIC PAINT, PLASTER, RESIN, SILVER

FABRICE SCHAEFER SWITZERLAND

RING TITANIUM, AMETHYSTE

RING TITANIUM, GOLD 750/000, DIAMONDS

NICOLE SCHUSTER GERMANY

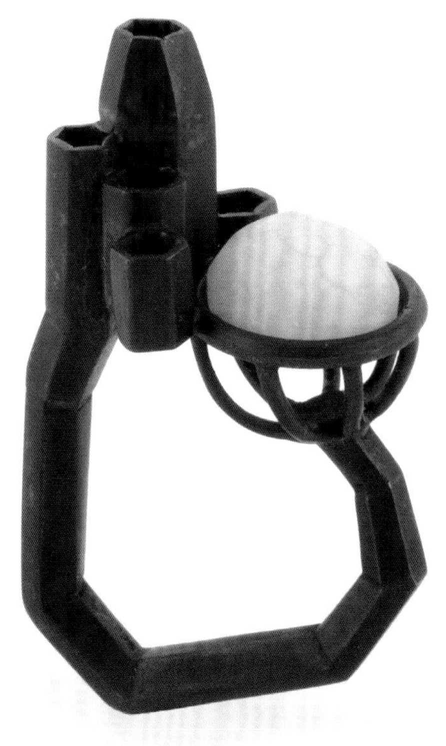

RING THE SPRING SILVER 925, OXIDISED, RESIN, PIGMENT

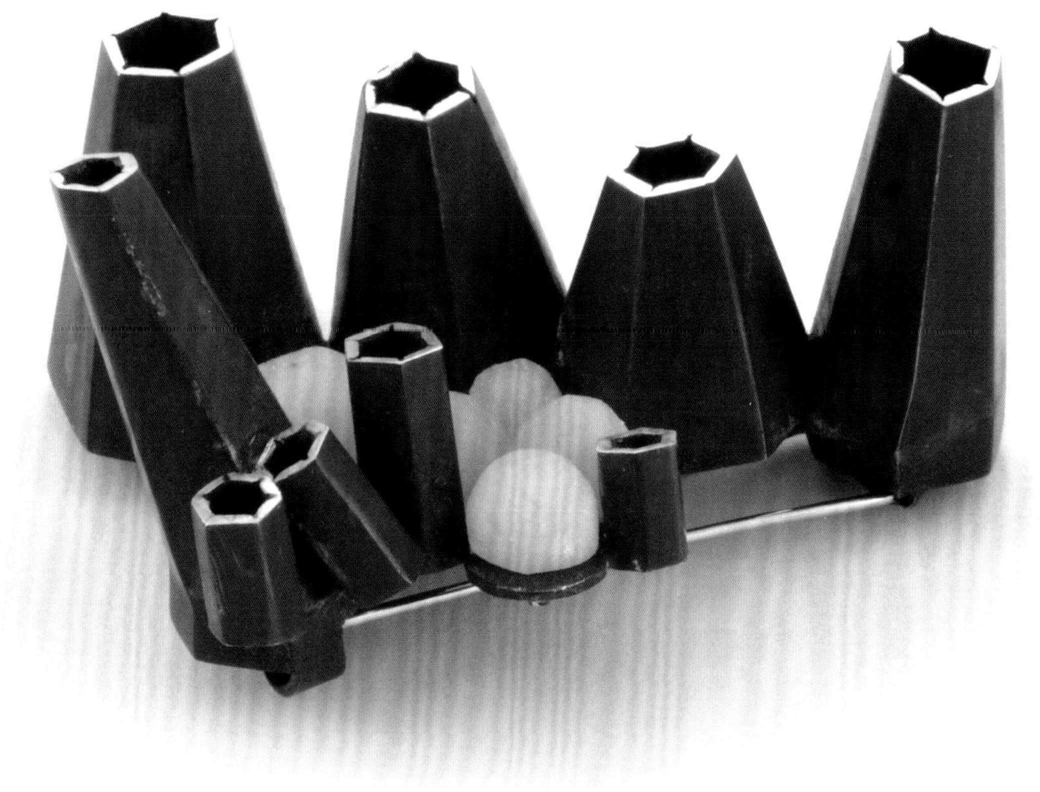

'CRYSTALCITY' SILVER 925, OXIDISED, RESIN, PIGMENT

CLAUDE SCHMITZ LUXEMBOURG

BROOCH 'RED LEAVES' SILVER, LACQUER

BROOCH 'UNDERTOW' SILVER, LAQUER, GLASS

BROOCH 'NIGHTFRUIT' SILVER, LACQUER, HEMATITE

CLAUDE SCHMITZ LUXEMBOURG

BROOCH 'WHATREMAINS' SILVER (PATINA), PEARLS

DANNI SCHWAAG GERMANY

BBROOCH 'MIRROR' MOTHER OF PEARL, ENAMEL ON COPPER, GOLD

BROOCH 'O.T.' MOTHER OF PEARL, EBONY, ENAMEL ON COPPER, GOLD

PAOLO SCURA UK

'CONSTRUCTION IN GREEN AND YELLOW' SILVER, OXIDANT SOLUTION, ENAMEL PAINT, SILK, CURBIC ZIRCON

REGINE SCHWARZER AUSTRALIA

UNTITLED STERLING SILVER, PATINA, FLUORITE CRYSTALS

KARIN SEUFERT GERMANY

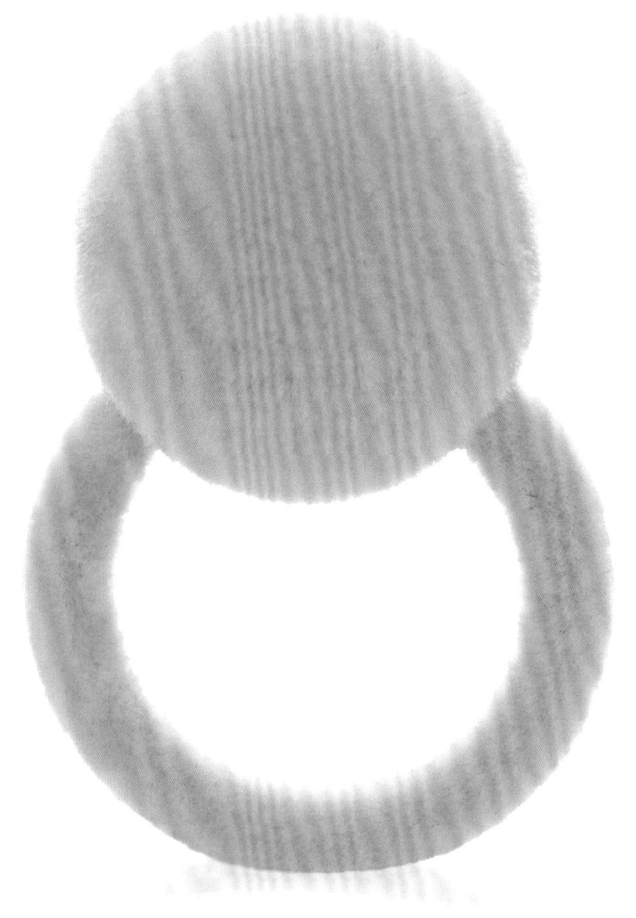

RING SILVER, FLOCK

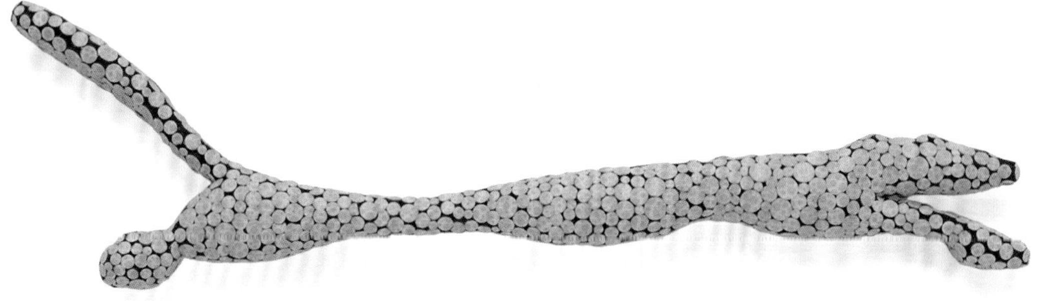

BROOCH PVC, PAPER, STEEL

MARINA SHEETIKOFF BRAZIL

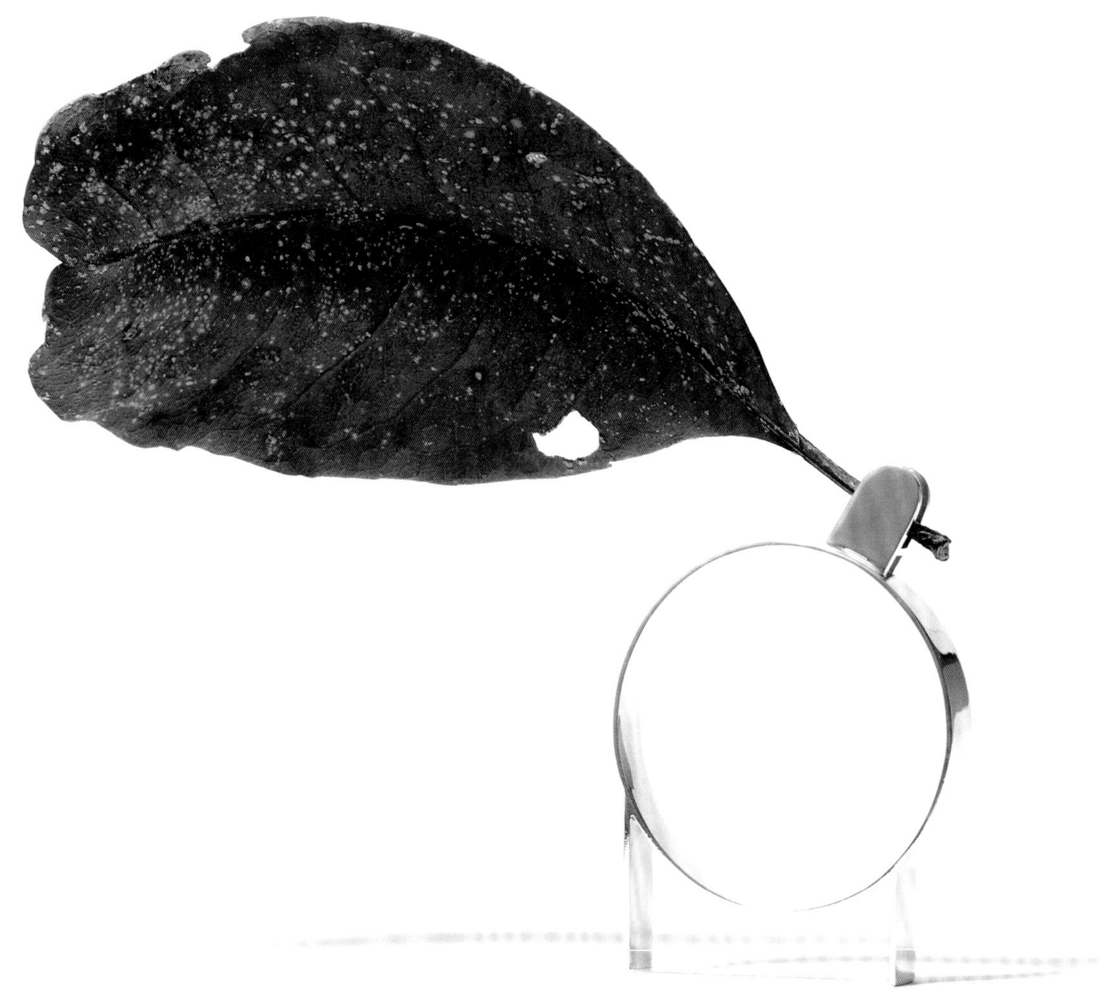

BRACELET 'STILL LIFE' SILVER, LEAF

ALEXANDER SOLAR LUXEMBOURG

UNTITLED PHOTO TRANSFER IN POLYURETHANE, NYLON STRING

NATALIE SMITH UK

RING 'NCW WAKE THE SEA' PLASTIC, TEXTILES, STEEL, SUGAR

BROOCH 'FRAGMENTS' PLASTIC, SUGAR, STEEL

NECKLACE STEEL, ELASTIC, SILVER

MANUELA SOUSA PORTUGAL

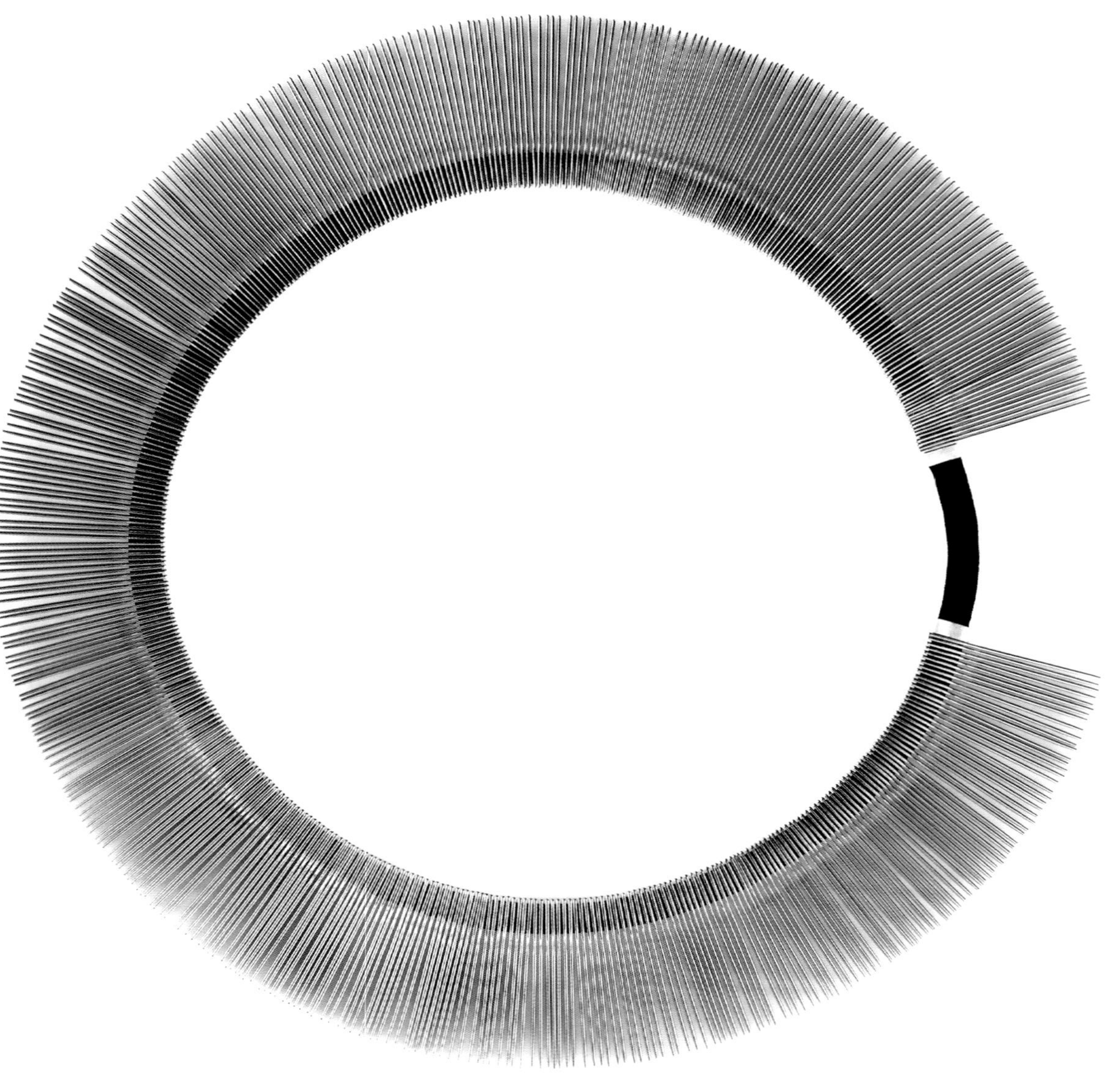

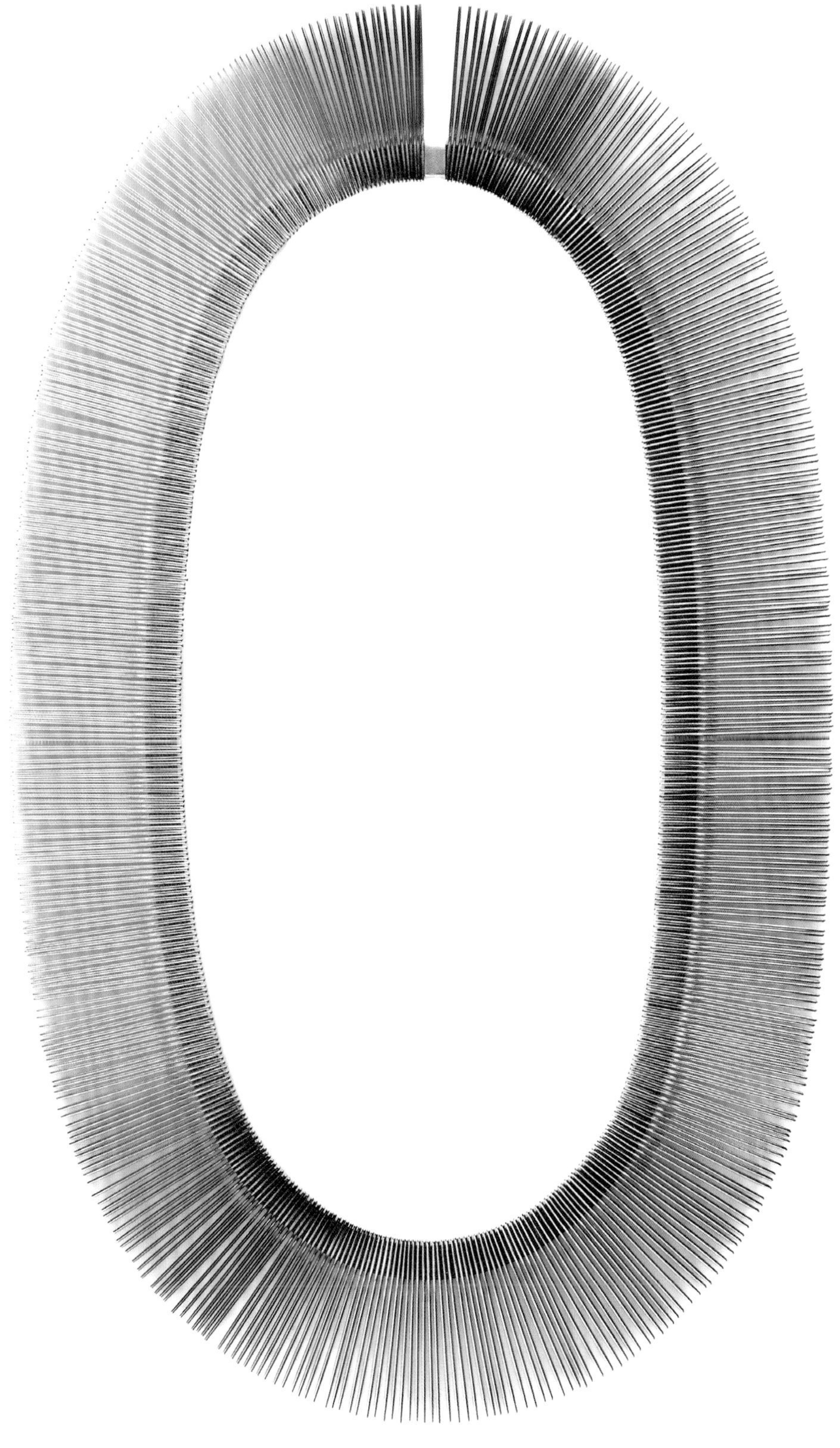

NECKLACE STEEL, ELASTIC, SILVER

KATRIN SPRANGER GERMANY

SKELETON OF A NECKLACE 'BEST BEFORE' CRUDE OIL LEAVINGS, SILVER, GOLD

NECKLACE 'BEST BEFORE' CRUDE OIL AND ITS PRODUCTS, SILVER, GOLD

ALIKI MARGARITA STROUMPOULI GREECE

ROBOT RING SILVER, PLASTIC DOLL'S EYE

GISBERT STACH GERMANY
RÉKA LÖRINCZ HUNGARY

BRACELET 'JEEP' BRASS, TOMBAK, PLASTICS, GLASS STONES

NIKI STYLIANOU
GREECE

NECKPIECE
HAND CUT RUBBER, OXIDIZED SILVER

ETHNICCOLLAR
HAND CUT RUBBER, HAND CUT LEATHER

JIE SUN CHINA

BROOCH 'BIG FISH' PINK CHERRY WOOD, SILVER, STEEL PAINT

BROOCH 'HAPPINESS' CHERRY WOOD, SILVER, STEEL, PAINT

TORE SVENSSON SWEDEN

BROOCH STEEL, PAINT

RING STEEL, PAINT

NELLI TANNER FINLAND

'EMPTY III' SIBATOOL, SILVER

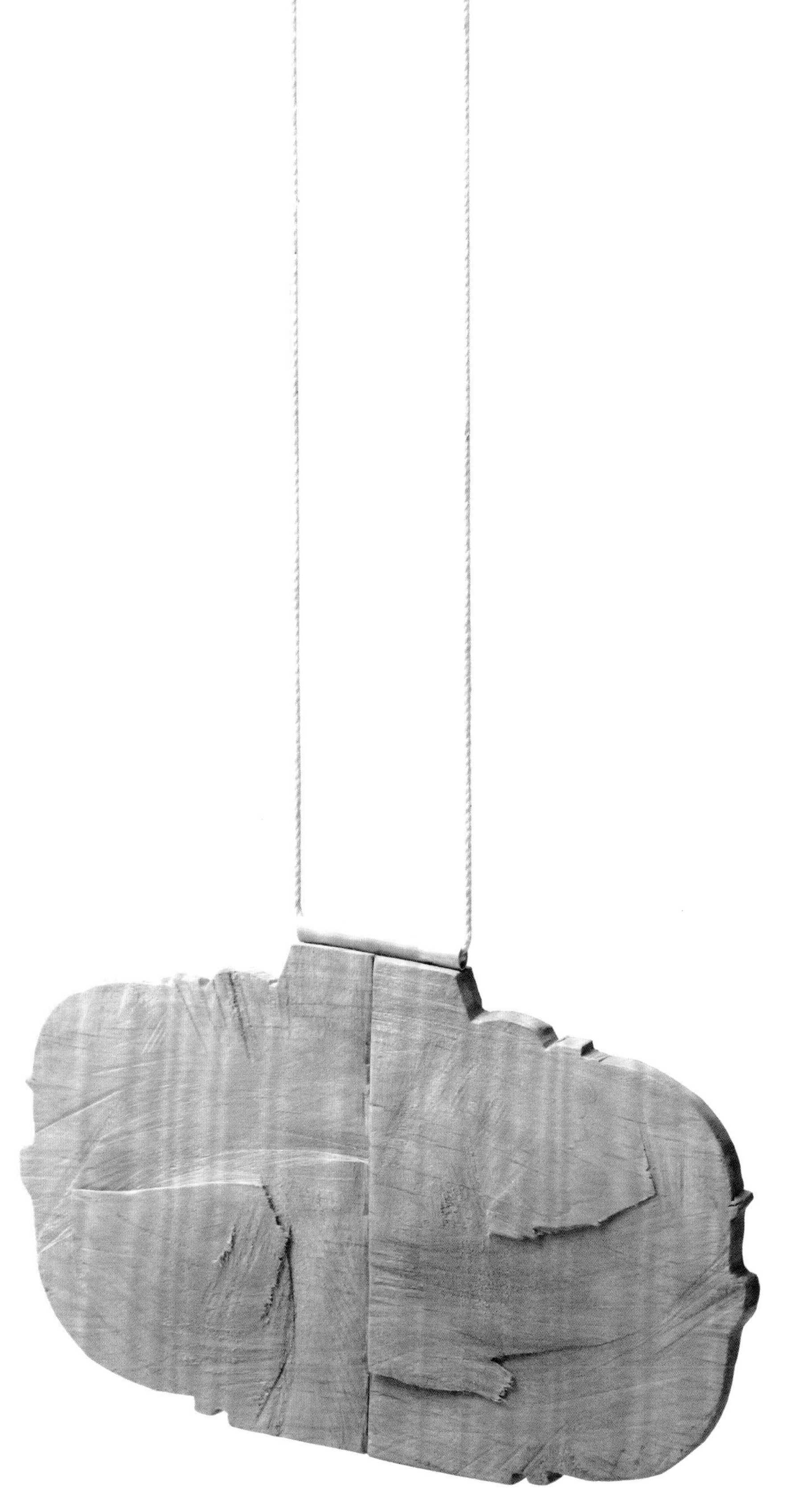

'EMPTY I' JUNIPER, SILVER, COTTON

SALIMA THAKKER BELGIUM

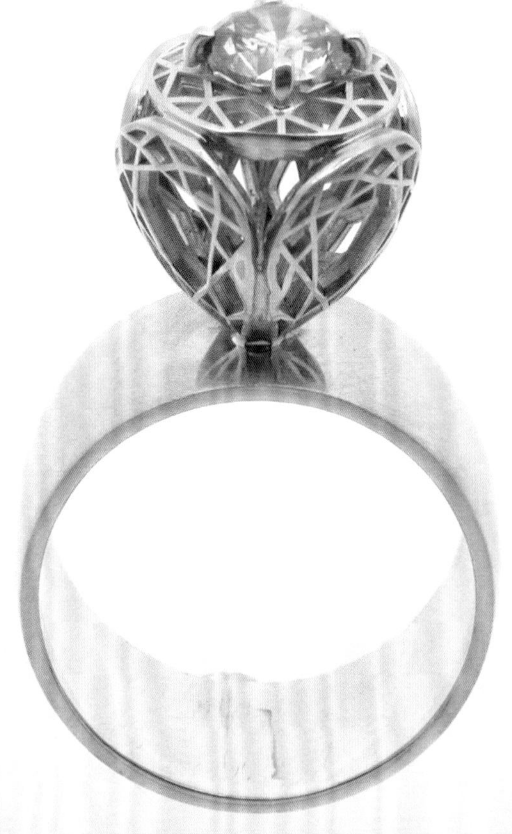

RING FROM THE 'FACET' COLLECTION 18 K YELLOW GOLD, GREEN DIAMOND

SABINE THULER SWITZERLAND

RING 18 K GOLD

KETLI TIITSAR ESTONIA

BROOCH 'HOMESICKNESS II' BIRCHBARK, SILVER, ENAMEL, WOOD, COTTON

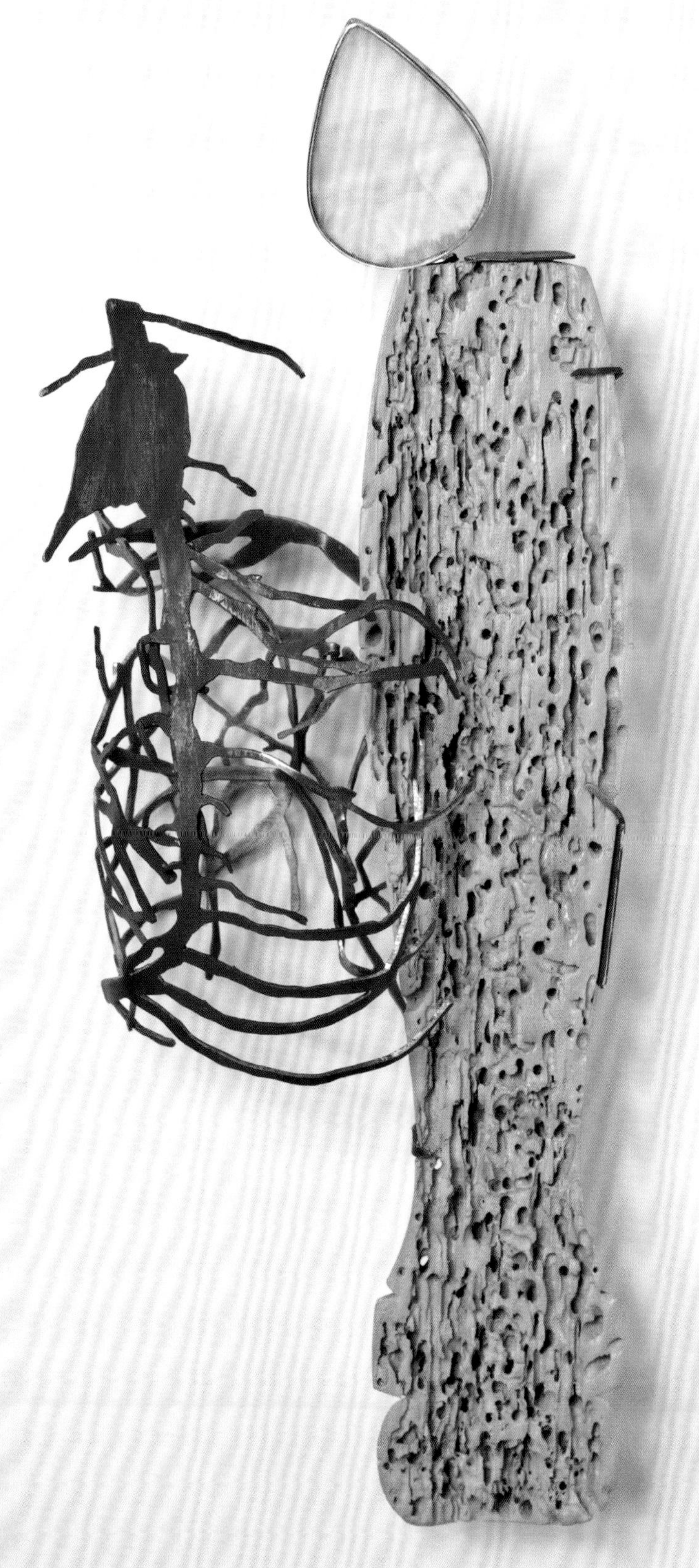

BROOCH 'HALFWAY' WOOD, SILVER, GERMAN SILVER, FLUORITE

BROOCH 'STEMS III' WOOD, SILVER, COPPER, ENAMEL, POWDER COATING

KETLI TIITSAR ESTONIA

BROOCH 'STEMS I' WOOD, SILVER, COPPER, PAINT

RACHEL TIMMINS USA

UNTITLED SPANDEX, THREAD, BRASS, STAINLESS STEEL, POWDER COATING, STERLING SILVER HARDWARE

UNTITLED SPANDEX, THREAD, POLYESTER STUFFING, BRASS, STAINLESS STEEL, POWDER COATING, STERLING SILVER HARDWARE

JOHANNA TÔRNQVIST
SWEDEN

'CERCLAGE DE NOCE'
RECYCLED MATERIAL: TEXTILE

'EN SKÖNHET KLÄR I ALLT'
RECYCLED MATERIAL: TEXTILE, PLASTIC

UNTITLED BRASS, PLASTIC, CORRUGATED CARDBOARD, IRON, ACRYLIC PAINT

FABRIZIO TRIDENTI ITALY

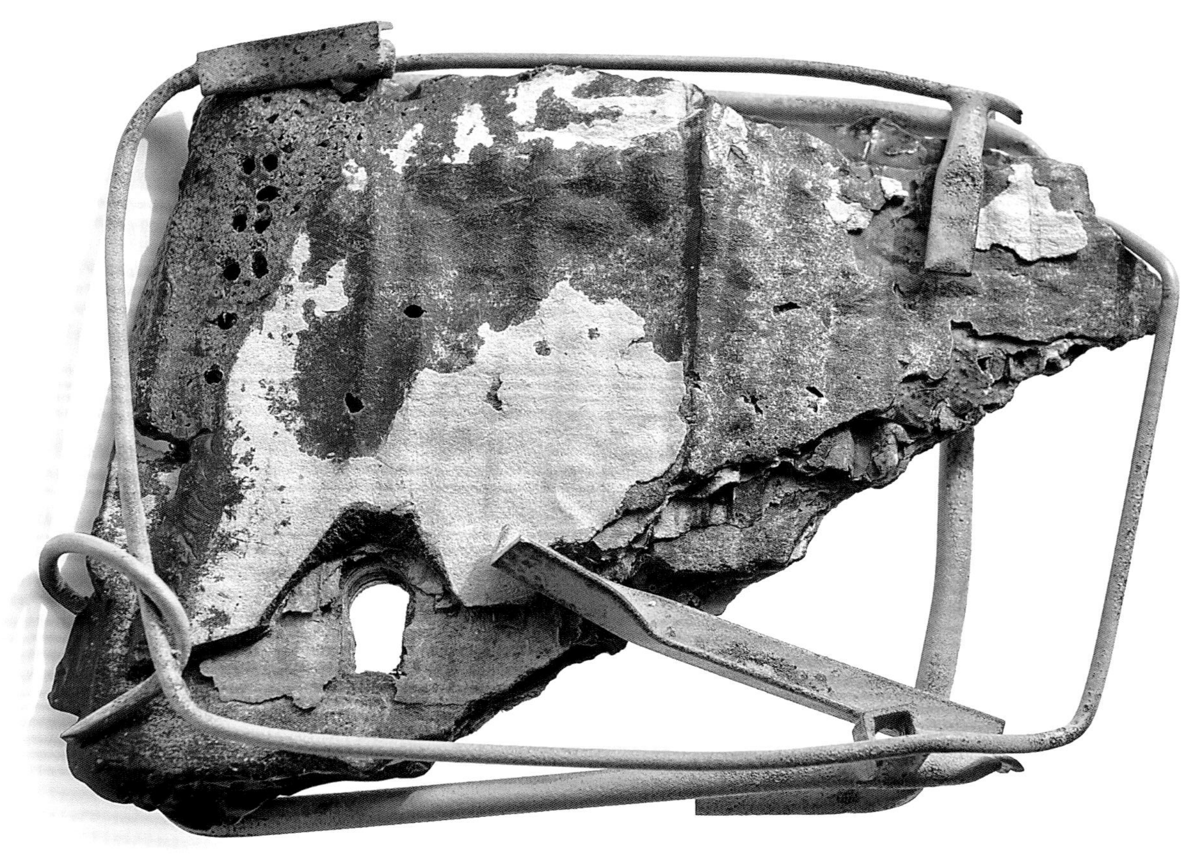

UNTITLED BRASS, ACRYLIC FAINT

BARBARA UDERZO ITALY

BLOB RING INCREDIBLE 'VOLPE ROSA' SILVER 925/1000 (RHODIUM PLATED), RECYCLED AND SPERIMENTAL PLASTIC, PLASTIC, CRYSTAL

BLOB RING INCREDIBLE 'CARPA' SILVER 925/1000 (RHODIUM PLATED), RECYCLED SPERIMENTAL BLU PLASTIC, PLASTIC, CRYSTAL

MARIA VALDMA ESTONIA

'GUESTHOUSE' OLD ROOF PLATE, GOLD, SILVER

'GUESTHOUSE' BLACK OAK, OLD ROOF PLATE, SILVER, GOLD

WIRE N°2 WITH 5 SCULPTURELINGS COTTON THREAD, OLIVE WOOD

MERTE VAN DE PERRE AUSTRALIA

ANNA HELENA VAN DE POL DE DEUS ITALY

'UNIEASHING THE SOUL' BRACELET SILVER, VINTAGE FABRIC, SILK THREAD

WILLY VAN DE VELDE
BELGIUM

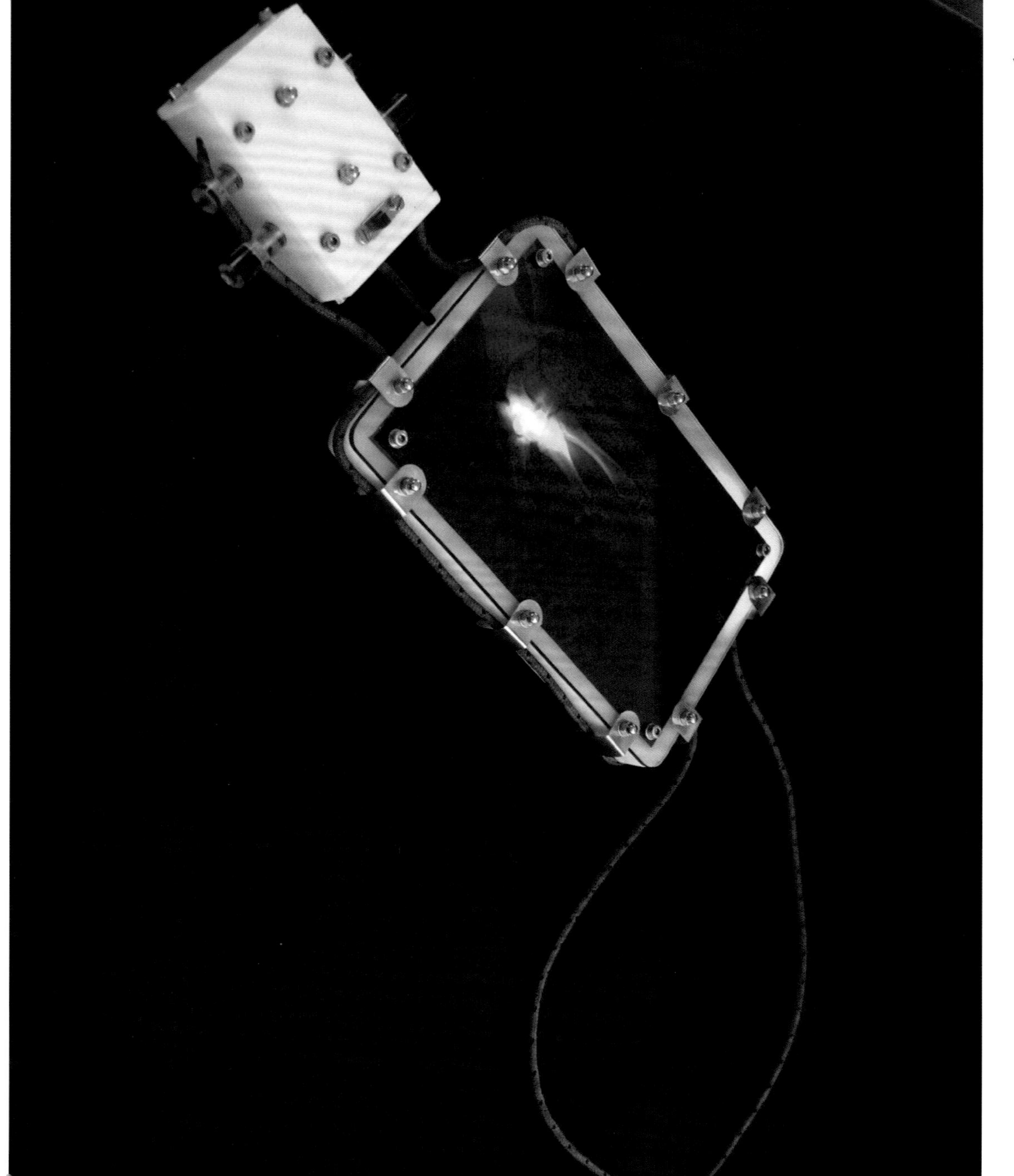

'X RAY'
PLEXIGLASS, XRAY,
LED, INOX THREAD

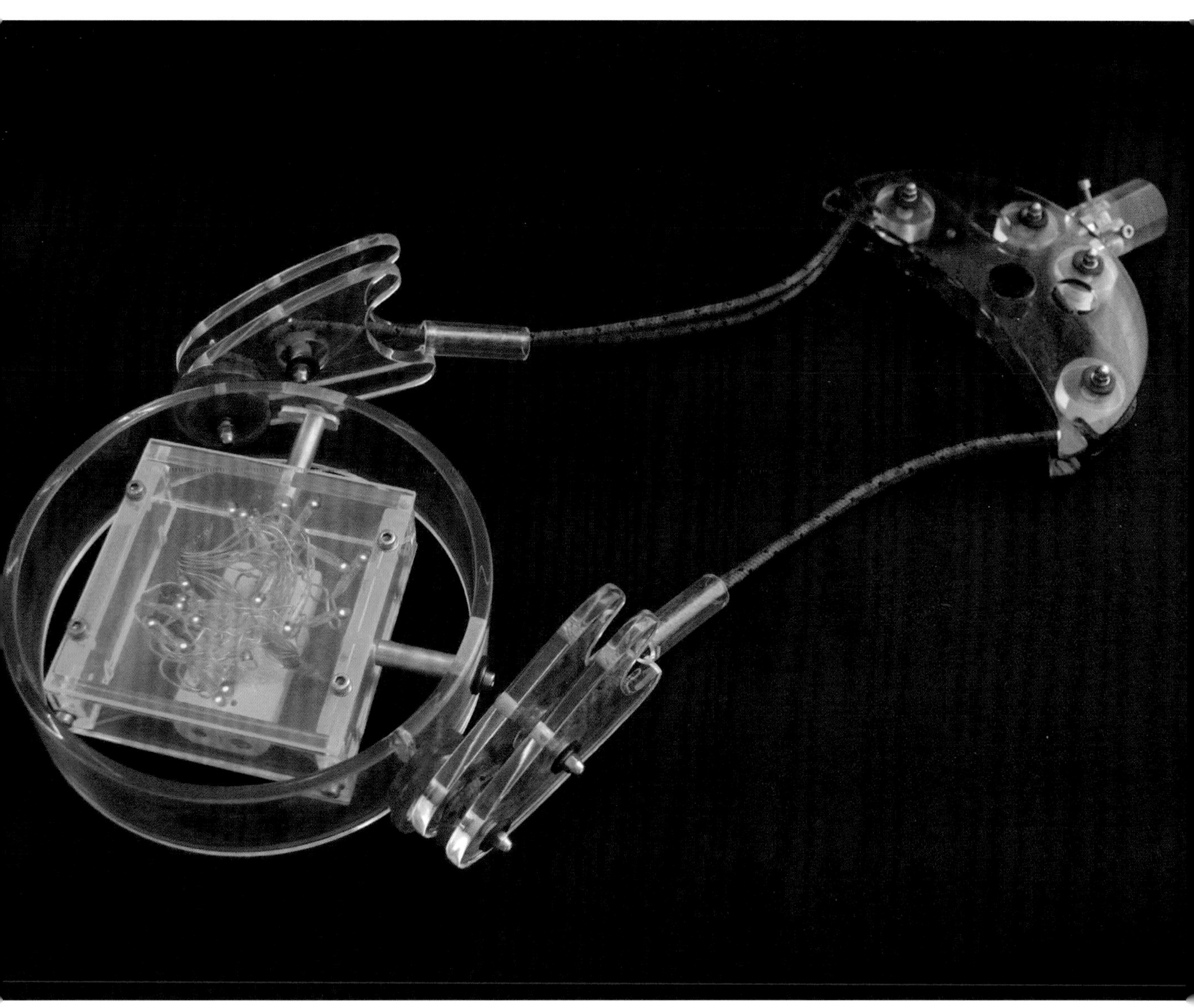

‘ELECTRONICS’
PLEXIGLASS, LED’S,
NOX THREAD

MECKY VAN DEN BRINK THE NETHERLANDS

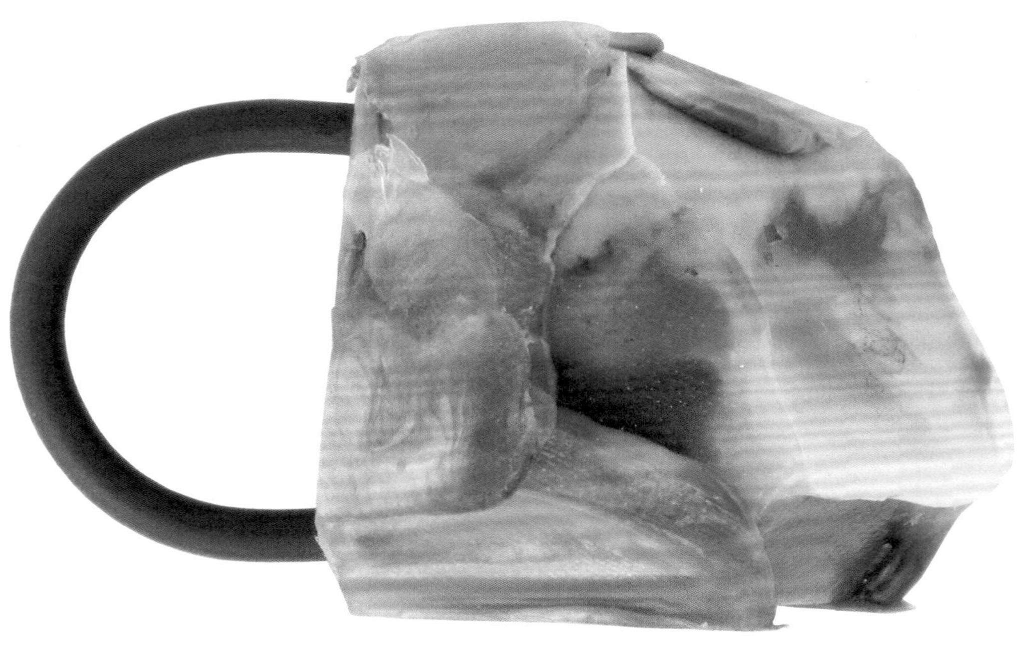

'RING FOR THE FINGER WICH FITS' MELTED AND MODELED PLASTIC

‘RING FOR THE FINGER WICH FITS’ MELTED AND MODELED PLASTIC

MECKY VAN DEN BRINK THE NETHERLANDS

'FLYING LEAVES' MELTED PLASTIC, PARTLY COVERED WITH WHITE AND YELLOW GOLD LEAF

'COLLORED COLLAR' MELTED PLASTIC LINES

BROOCH 'HOLIER THAN THOU' CERAMIC, HONEYCOMB, SILVER, PAINT, MICROGEODES

CHRISTEL VAN DER LAAN AUSTRALIA

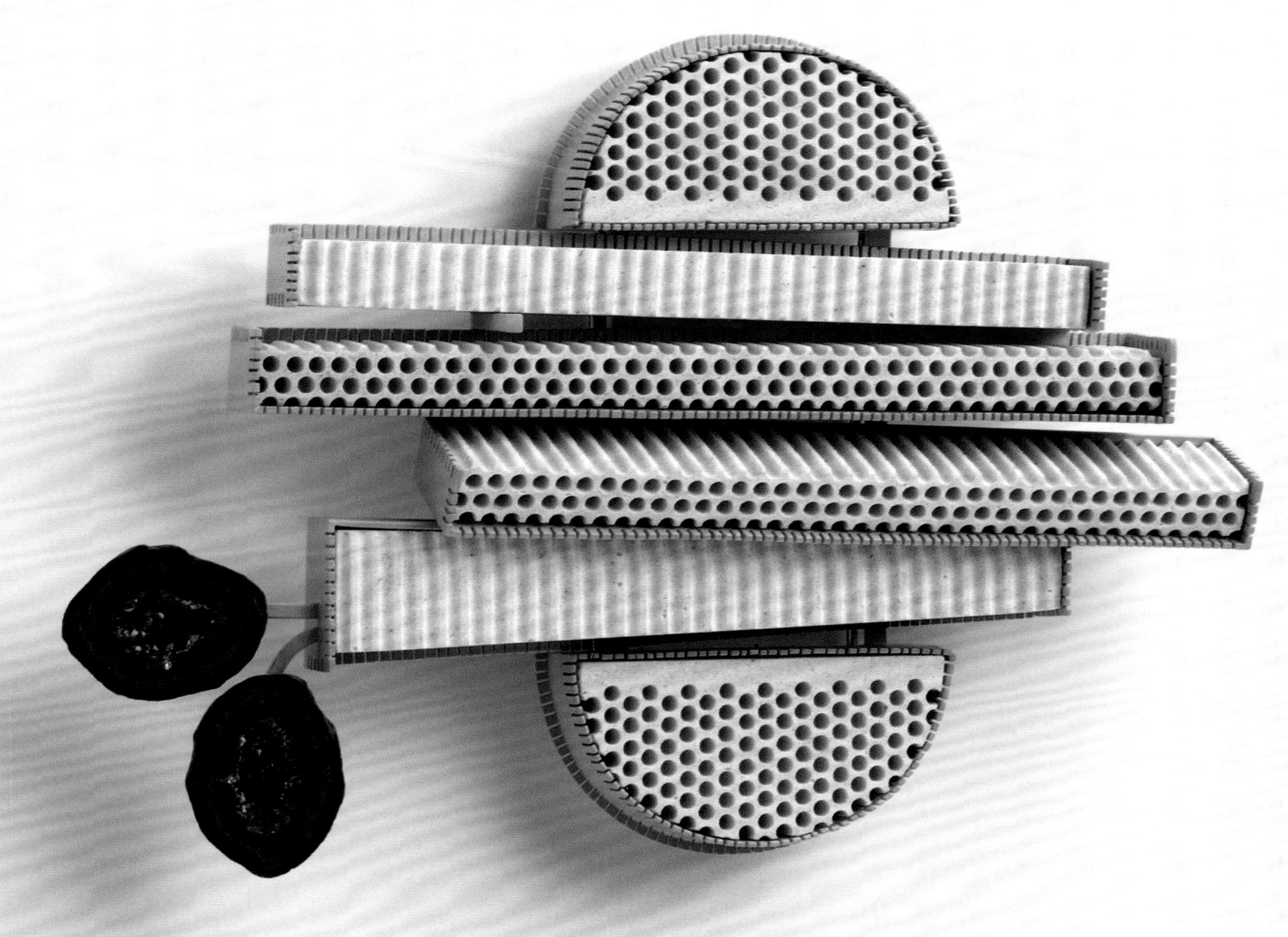

BROOCH 'HOLIER THAN YOU' CERAMIC, HONEYCOMB, SILVER, PAINT, GOLD, VINTAGE BEADS

CHRISTEL VAN DER LAAN AUSTRALIA

'BUG BROOCH' CERAMIC, HONEYCOMB, SILVER, PAINT, MICROGEODES, ELECTRICAL PART

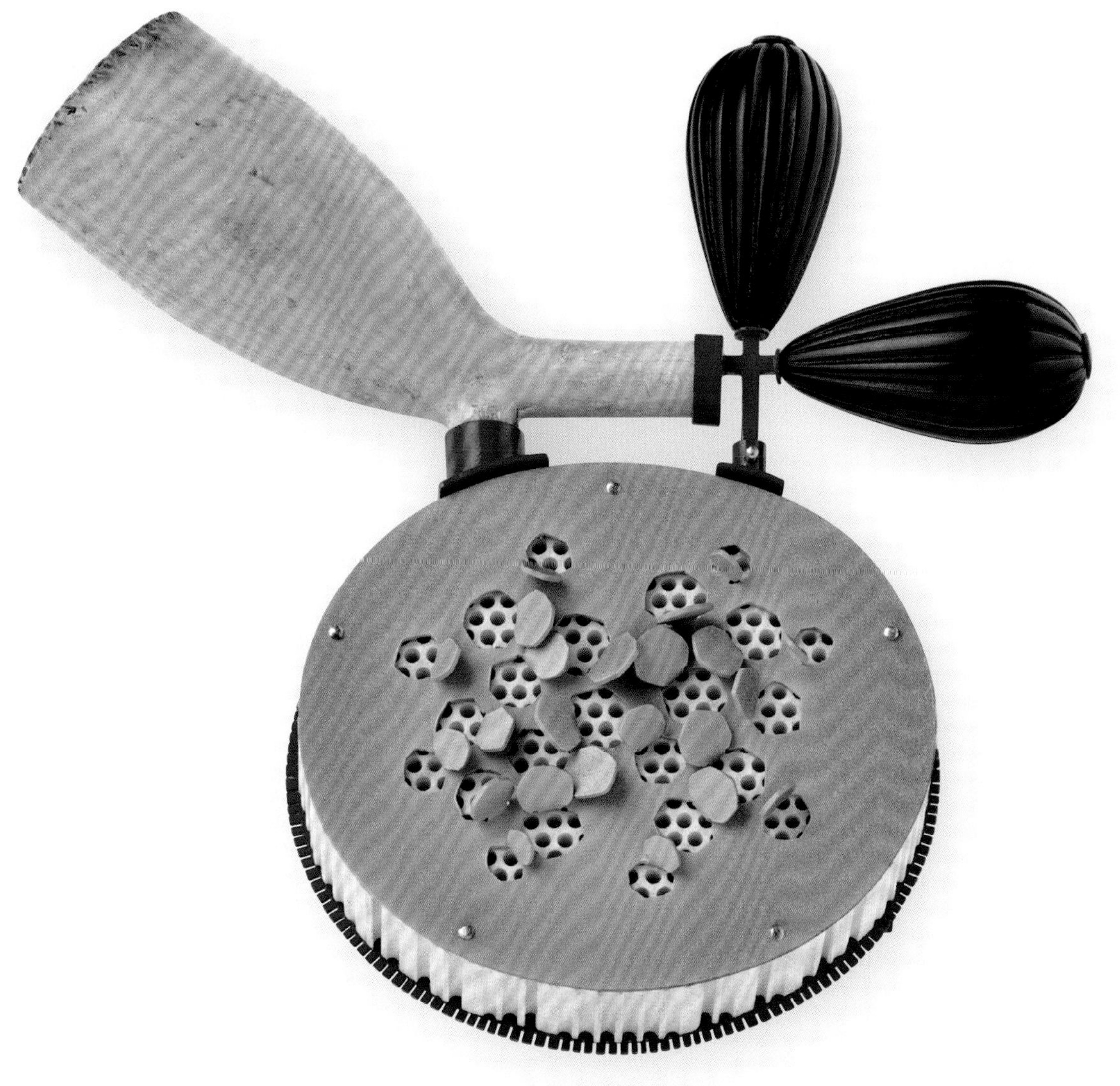

BROOCH 'HOLY SMOKE' CERAMIC, HONEYCOMB, SILVER, PAINT, OLD CLAY PIPE, VINTAGE BEADS

FELIEKE VAN DER LEEST NORWAY

BROOCH 'CRAZY HORSE' TEXTILE, GOLD, SILVER, PLASTIC ANIMAL, GLASS BEADS, TAPAZ

BROOCH 'BILLY THE KIDS' TEXTILE, PLASTIC ANIMALS, SILVER, GLASS BEADS, GOLD, CUBIC ZIRKANIA

FELIEKE VAN DER LEEST NORWAY

OBJECT WITH NECKLACE 'INCOGNITOS ANONYMOUS' PLASTIC ANIMALS, SILVER, GLASS BEADS, TEXTILE

BROOCH 'THE END' GLASS BEADS, PLASTIC ANIMAIL, SILVER, LEATHER

NELLY VAN OOST FRANCE

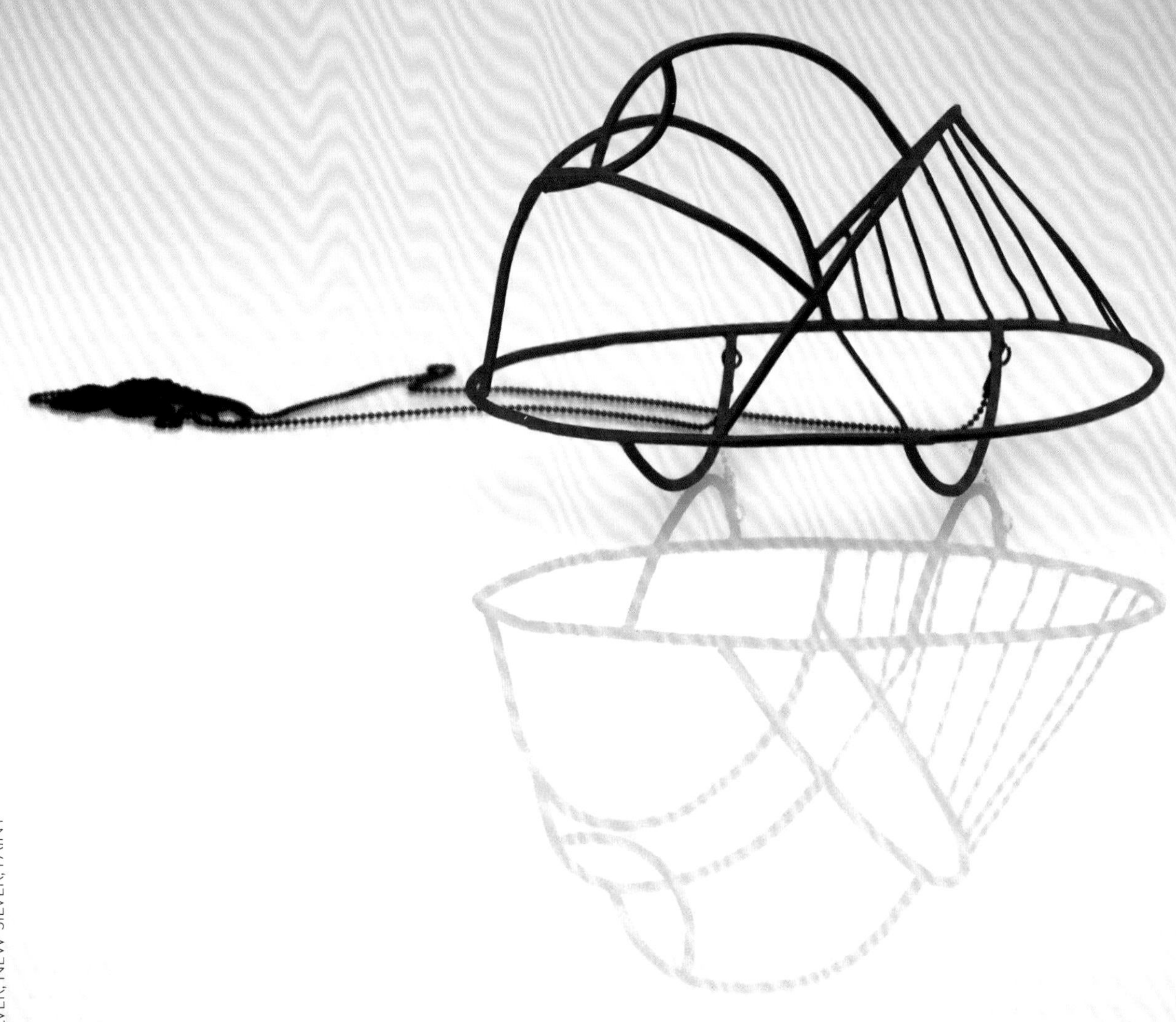

'HÉRITAGE NICOLE' SILVER, NEW SILVER, PAINT

'HÉRITAGE DENYSE' SILVER, NEW SILVER, PAINT

NELLY VAN OOST FRANCE

'LLIO' NEW SILVER, PAINT

'TERES' NEW SILVER, PAINT

UNTITLED SILVER, METAL, STRASS, GLASS, PLASTIC, PAINT

ROOS VAN SOEST THE NETHERLANDS

UNTITLED SILVER, BRASS, PLASTIC, PAINT

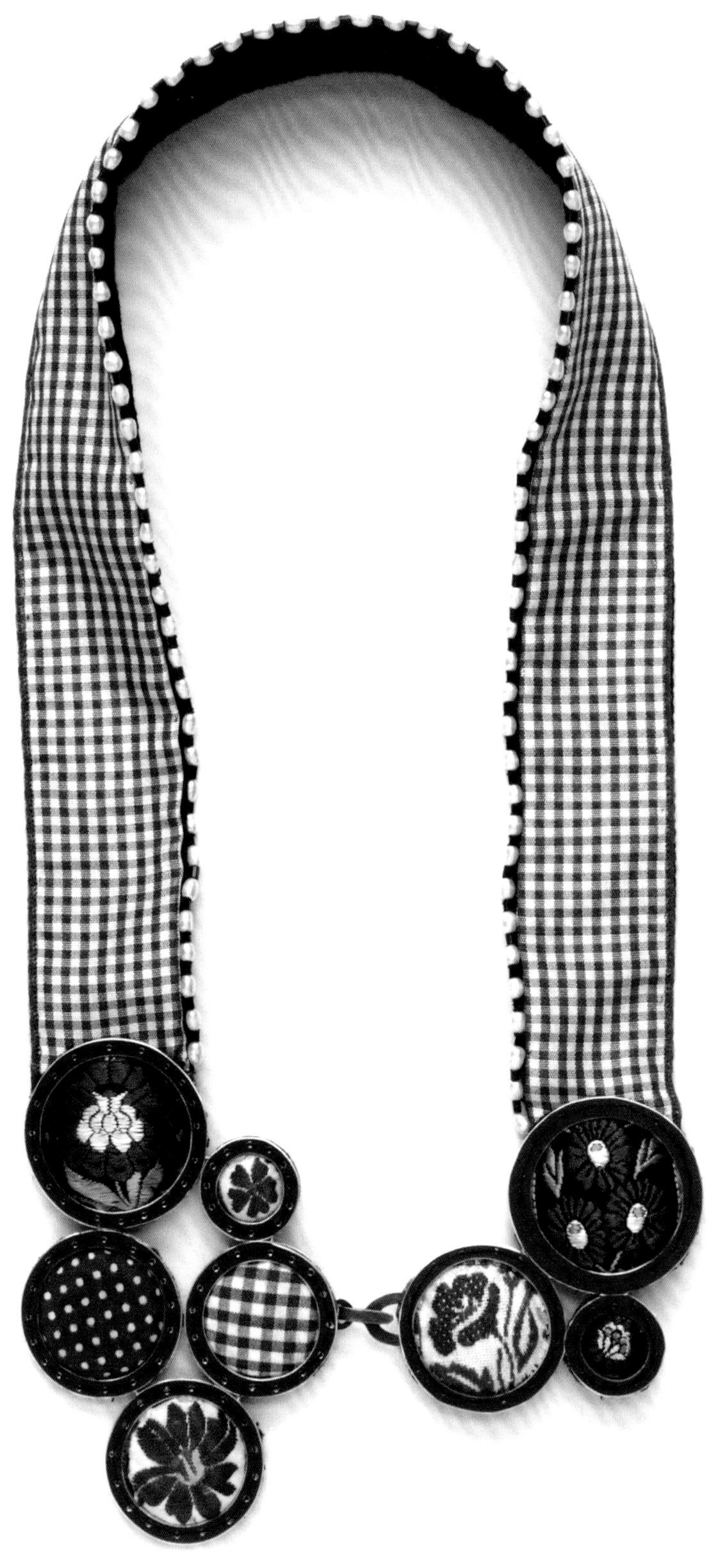

INGEBORG VANDAMME THE NETHERLANDS

'LOOKING FOR MISTER RIGHT' ANODISED ALUMINIUM, SILVER, PEARLS, GLASS, TEXTILE

'SECRETS' ANODISED ALUMINIUM, PAPER, RIBBON

OCTAVE VANDEWEGHE BELGIUM

'WATERPIPE' -PIPE ON STAND BRASS, CERAMIC, IRON WIRE, FOUND OBJECTS: FITTING, TEAPOT, SPOUT

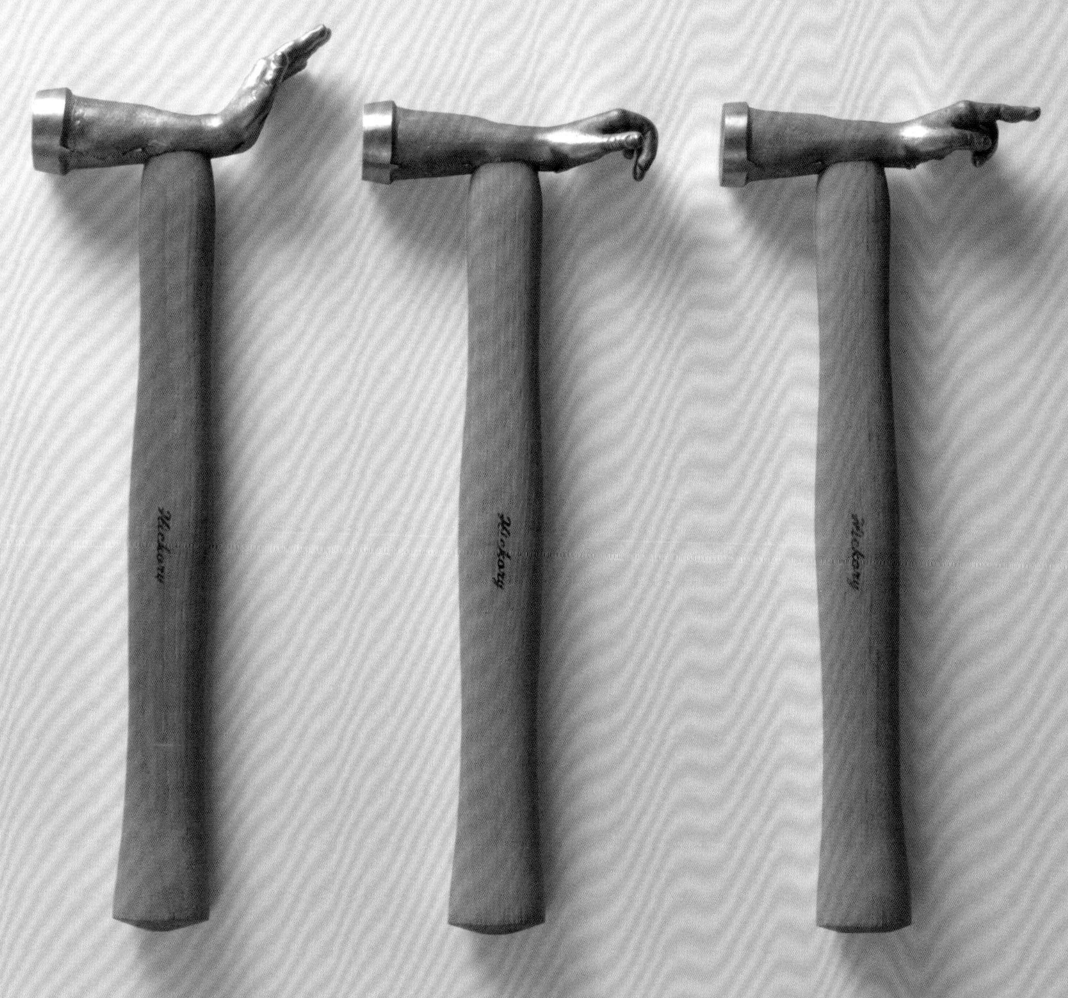

'HAMMERSPRACHE'-HAMMERS TIN, WOOD, FOUND OBJECTS: HAMMER HANDLES

'TIME TO ROLL B' - NECKLACE ON GREY SHIRT BRASS, IRON, PAINT, PLASTIC, FOUND OBJECTS: BEETLE HOOD, CHAIN

OCTAVE VANDEWEGHE BELGIUM

'CHAIRBACK' ON BROWN PULLOVER LEATHER, WOOD, FOUND OBJECTS: CHAIRBACK

KAREN VANMOL BELGIUM

UNTITLED WOOD, ZINC, PAINT, BRASS, GOLF LEAF, STEEL

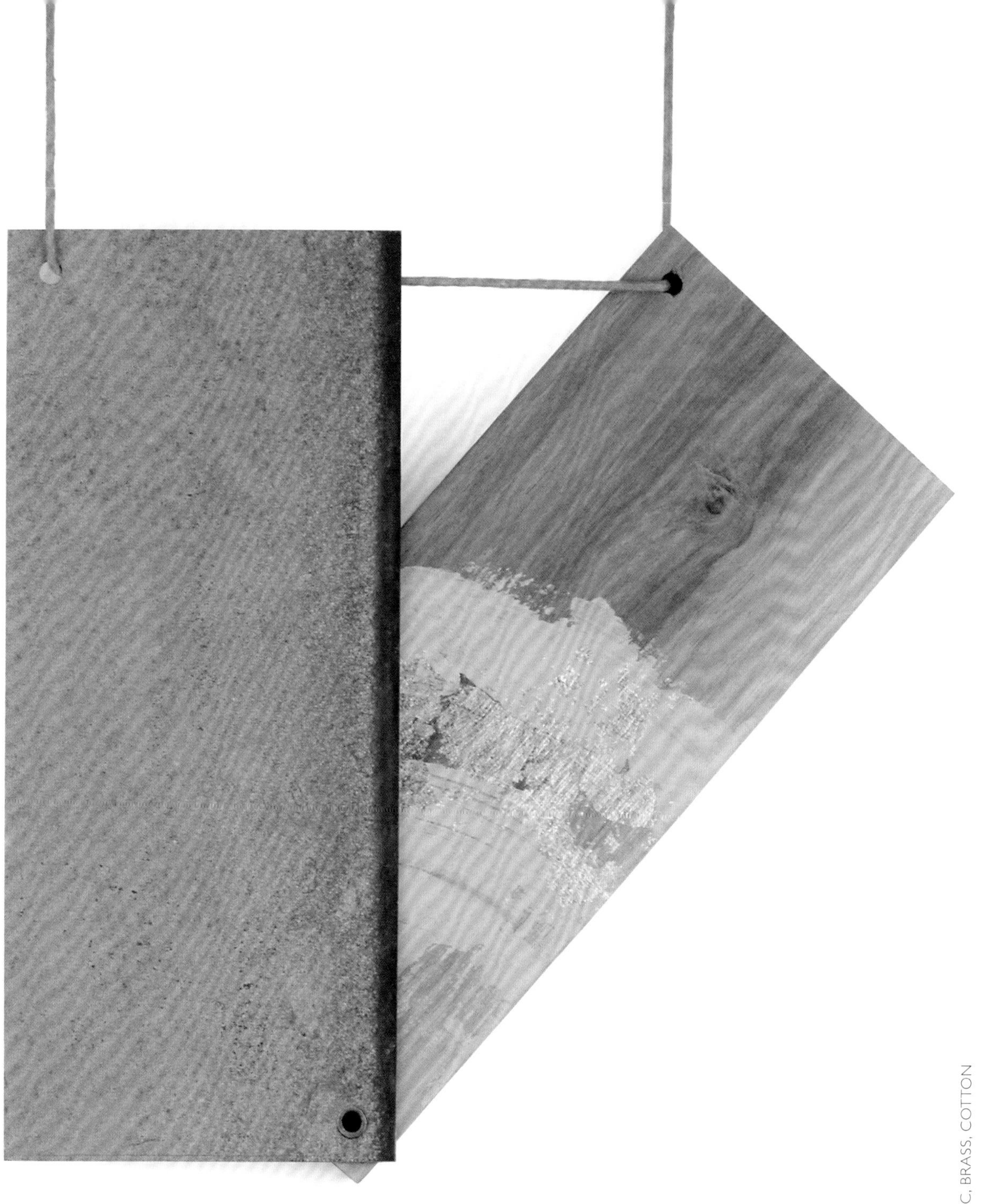

UNTITLED WOOD, PAINT, GOLD LEAF, ZINC, BRASS, COTTON

TANEL VEENRE ESTONIA

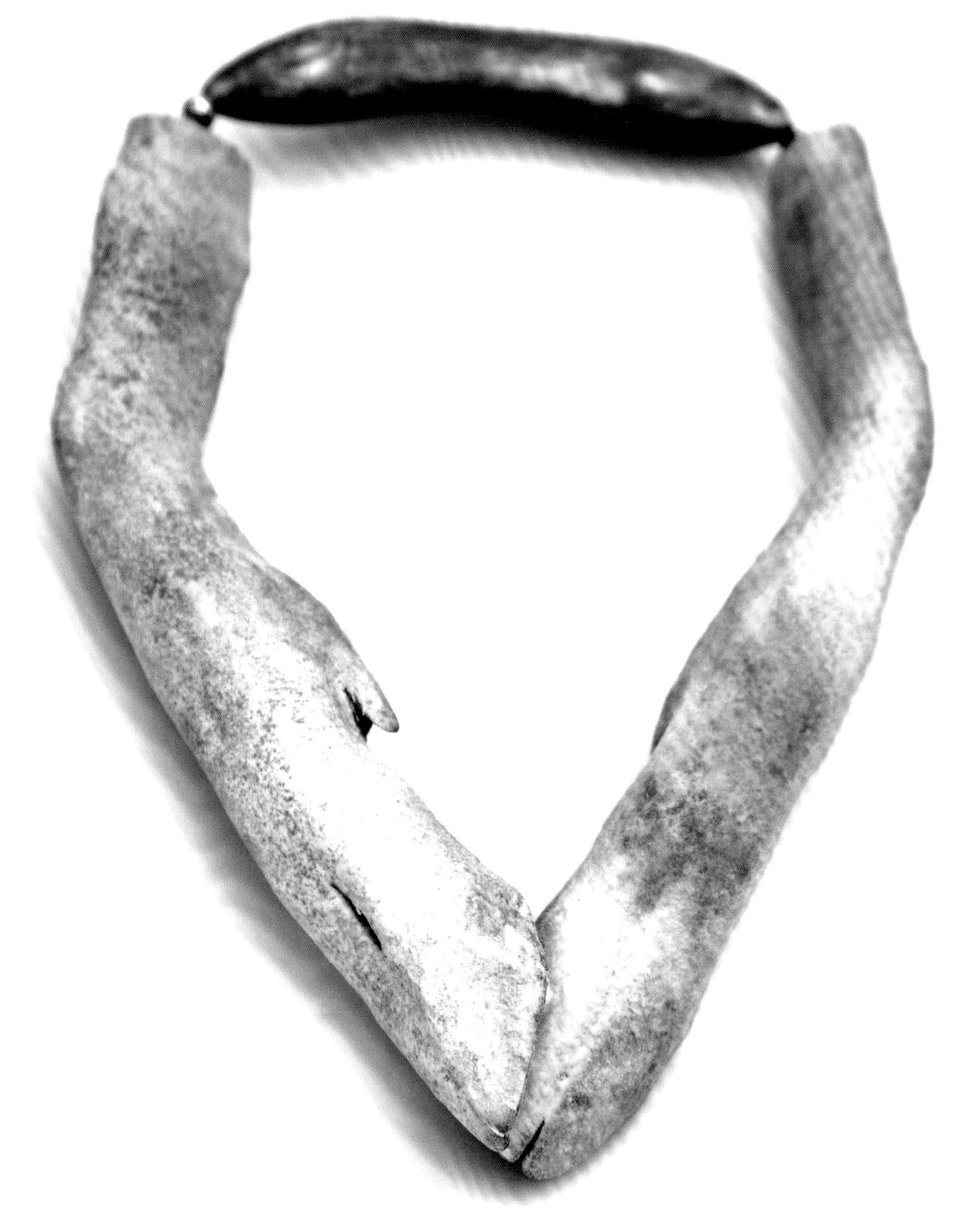

'EVEN PARADISE HAS WINTER' LEGS OF UNICORN, WOOD, SILVER, COSMIC DUST

'LES FLEURS DU MAL' BALSAWOOD, LAPIS LAZULI, RESIN, SMOKY QUARTZ, COSMIC DUST

ROCIO VEGAS SPAIN

'NATURE' PATINATED SILVER, GOLD 18 K

PETER VERMANDERE BELGIUM

'HOTTON WHEELS BROOCH N°4' FOSSIL CORAL, ALUMINIUM

BRECHJE VERMAAT / MAARTEN VERSTEEG THE NETHERLANDS

male ring

female ring

pattern when female ring is placed in male ring

'TWEE-EENHEID' (TWOFOLDNESS) TITANIUM

'CO'DERING/CODE' RING TITANIUM

RING ‘BAAS IN EIGEN BOS’ MADE BY BROKEN DVD

TINE VINDEVOGEL BELGIUM

NECKLACE 'BALLY 1984' MADE WITH OLD SHOE

ANDREA WAGNER THE NETHERLANDS

'MIGRATIONAL PARALLAX' (FROM SERIES SUBSET SYNERGISM-TALES OF MIGRATION)
SILVER 925, SILVER 999, BONE CHINA STAINED, SYNTHETIC RESIN, LACQUER

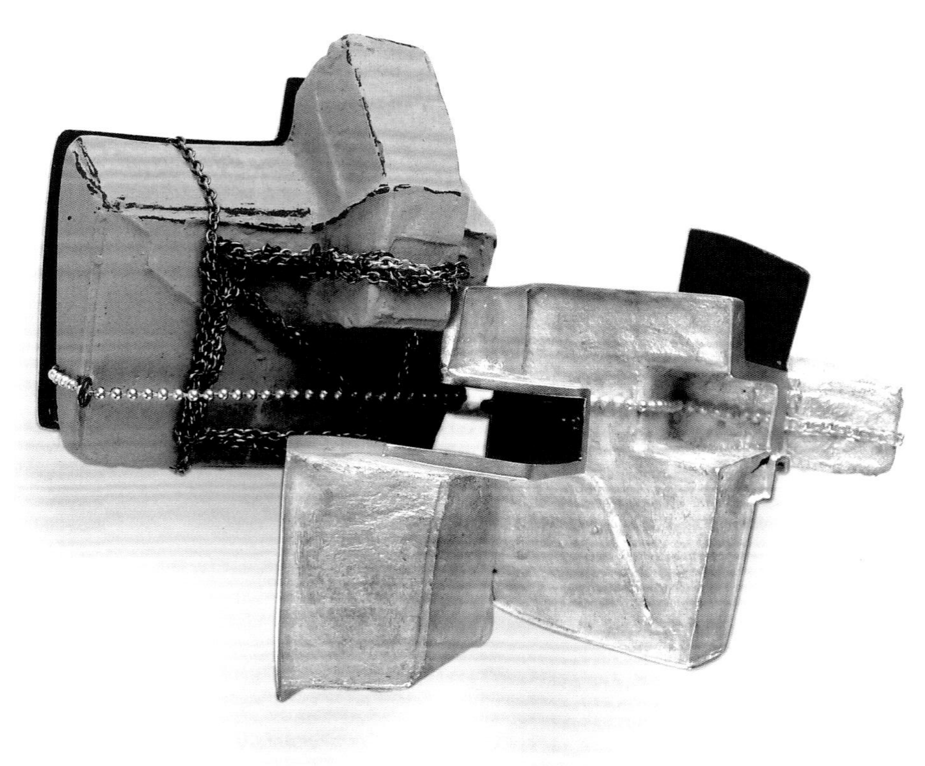

'RE-INVENT' (FROM SERIES SUBSET SYNERGISM-TALES OF MIGRATION)
SILVER 925, SILVER 999, SYNTHETIC RESIN, LACQUER

SILVIA WALZ SPAIN

BROOCH 'TWO LAKES' COPPER, ENAMEL, RESIN

BROOCH COPPER, ENAMEL, RESIN

NORMAN WEBER GERMANY

BROOCH 'AUTO 33' SILVER GILT, DIGITAL PRINT, PLASTIC STOWES, LACQUER

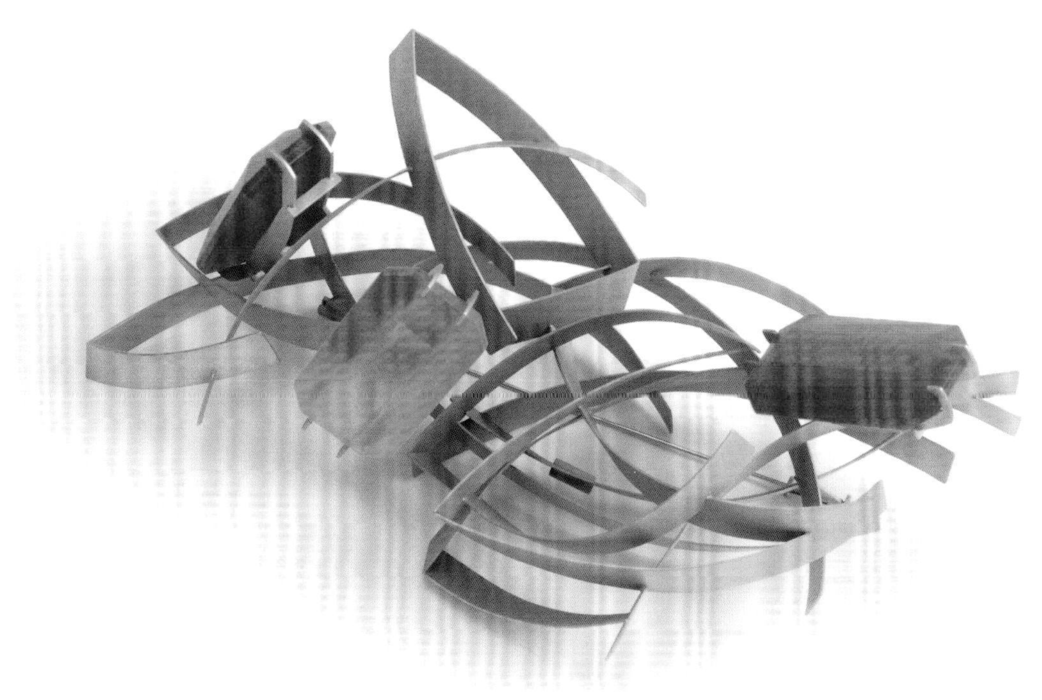

BROOCH 'SCHAUSTÜCK 4' SILVER GILT, PLASTIC STONES, LACQUER

'AROS CUERO COLORES' SILVER, LEATHER

MARINA MOLINELLI WELLS ARGENTINA

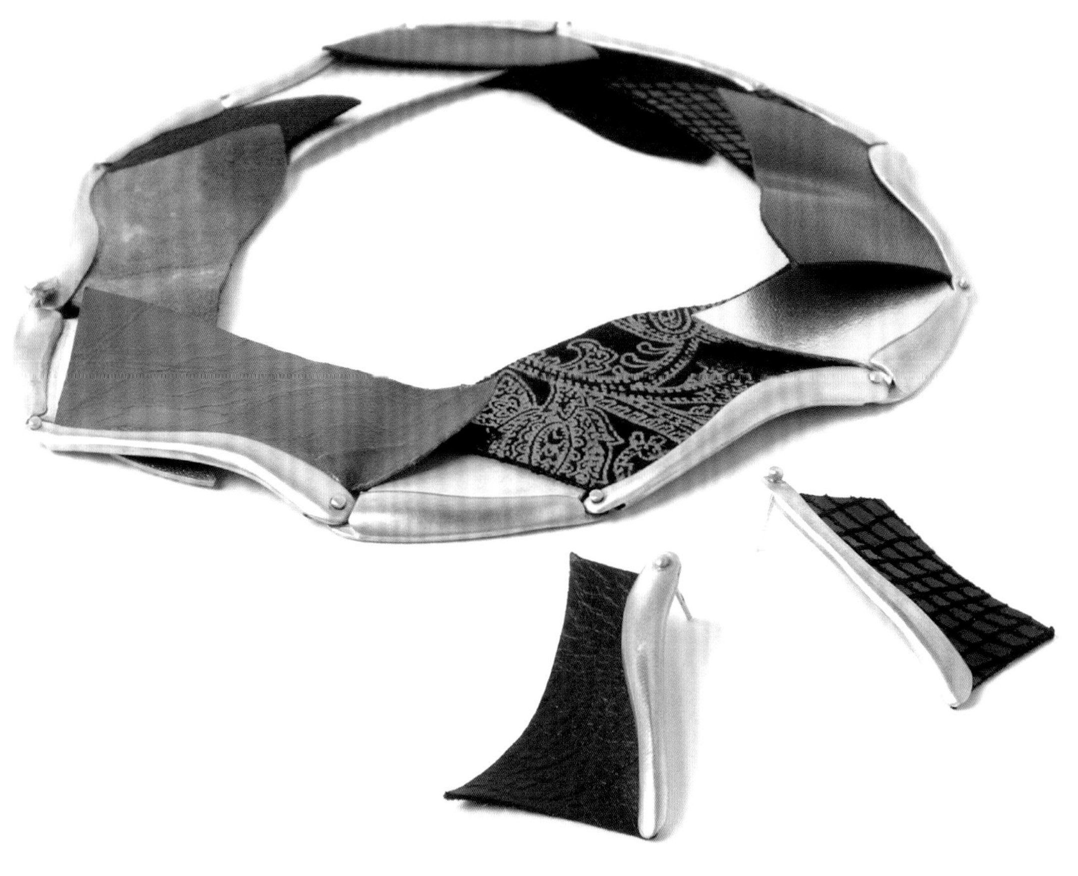

'GARGANTILLA Y AROS NEGROS' STERLING SILVER, LEATHER

ROBIN WERNICKE AUSTRALIA

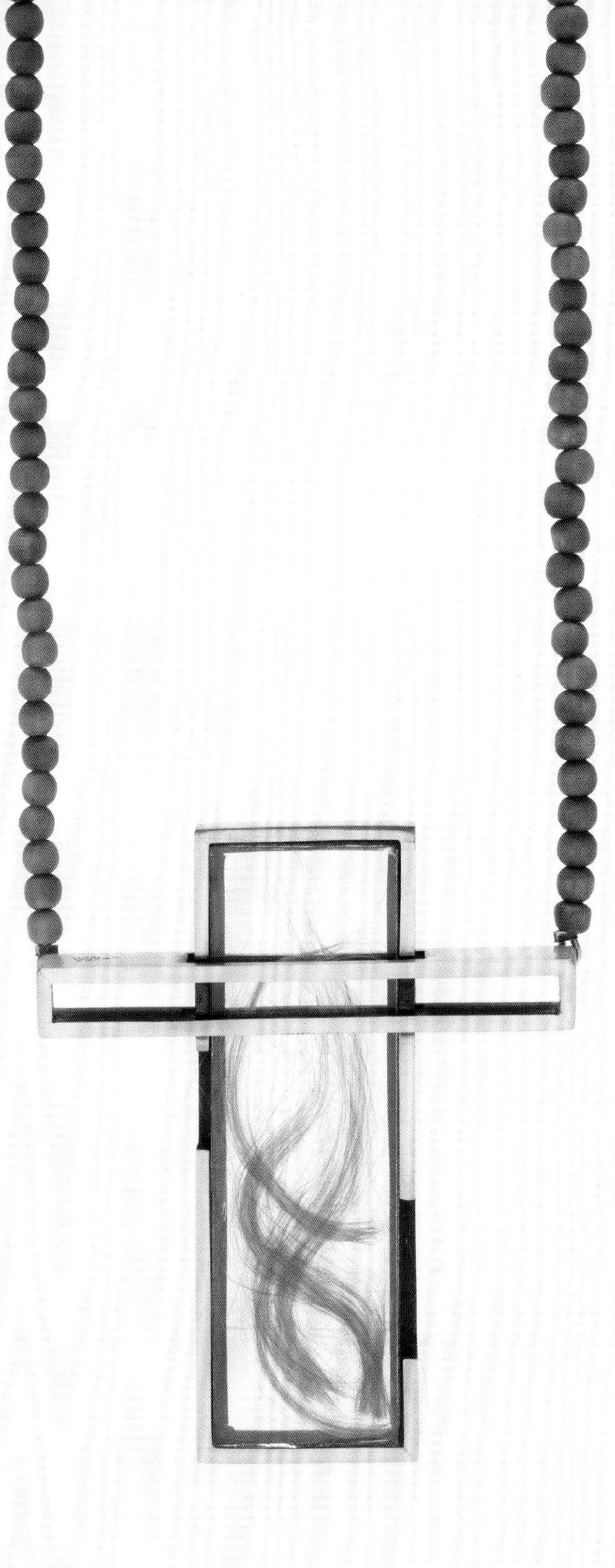

'IN MEMORY OF LIZZIE' HAIR, GLASS, STERLING SILVER

'THE VIEW' STERLING SILVER, RUBBER WHEELS

JASMIN WINTER GERMANY

UNTITLED SILVER, ENAMEL, RESIN, SILK

UNTITLED SILVER, ENAMEL, RESIN, SILK

CLAIRE WOLFSTIRN FRANCE

RING 'HERBES FOLLES' GOLD

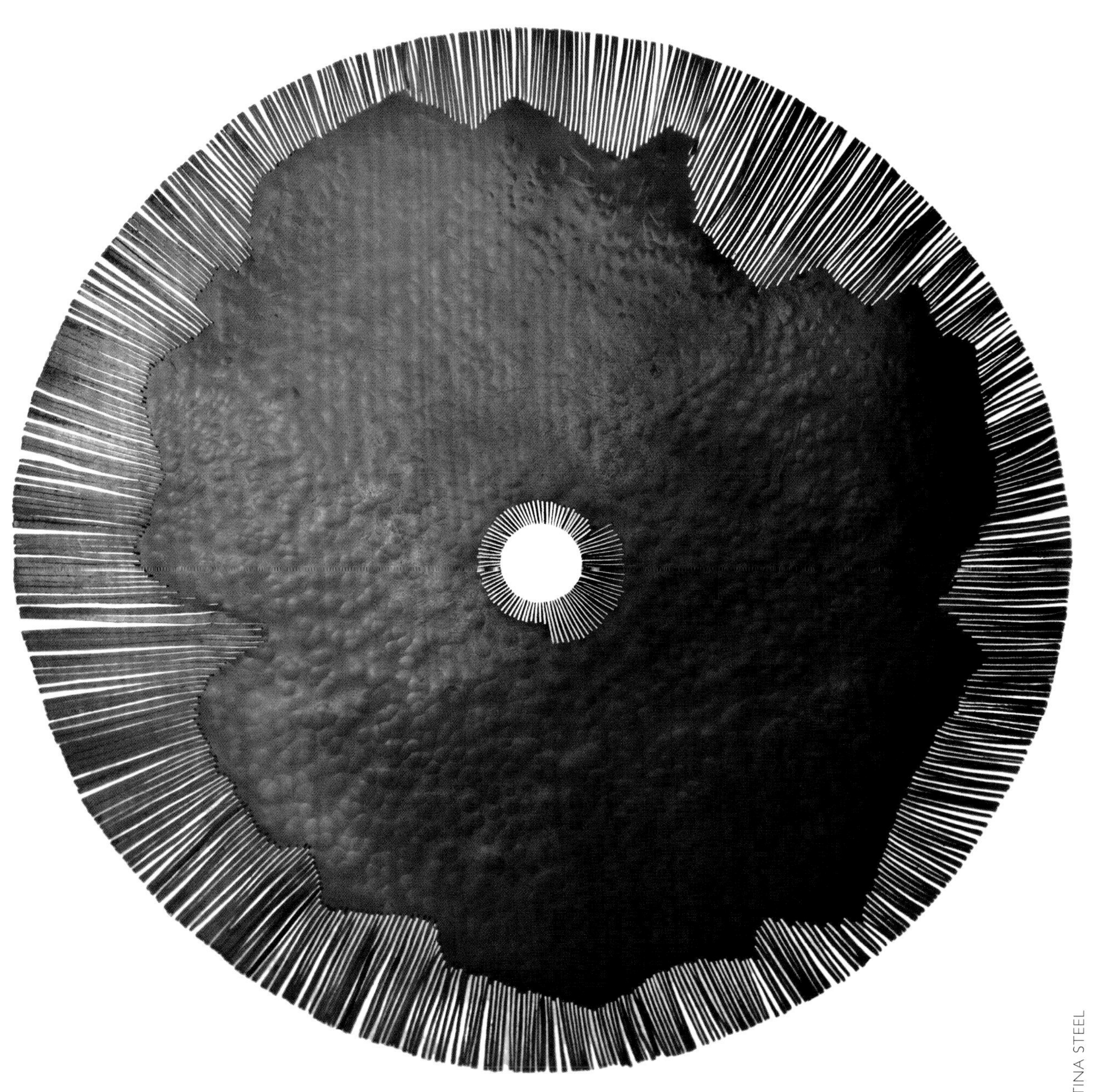

BROOCH 'RICOCHET' PATINA STEEL

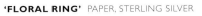

LI- CHU WU UK

'FLORAL RING' PAPER, STERLING SILVER

'FLORAL NECKLACE' PAPER, STERLING SILVER

SHU-LIN WU TAIWAN

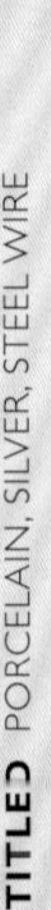

UNTITLED PORCELAIN, SILVER, STEEL WIRE

UNTITLED PORCELAIN, BAMBOO, SILVER, STAINLESS STEEL, RED THREAD

KAREN WUYTENS BELGIUM

'BALLOON' SLS 3D PRINTED, NYLON, CONCRETE COATING, BLUE COTTON THREAD

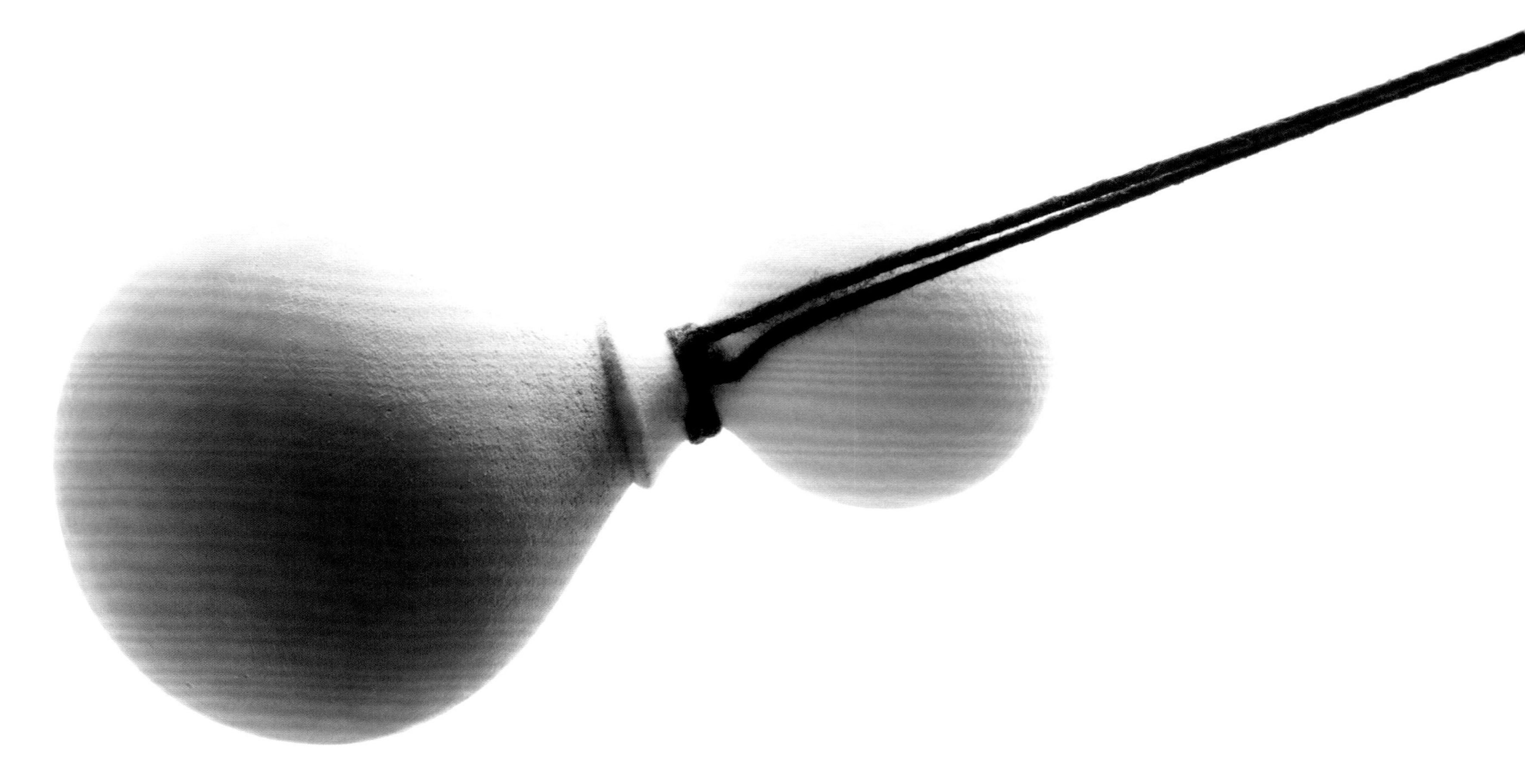

'NESTED' SLS 3D PRINTED, NYLON, SILVER

FRAUKE ZABEL GERMANY

PENDANT 'PORTRAIT OF THE CITY' BROWN COAL BIQUET, WAX, TEXTIL

MICHELLE XIANOU NI CHINA

'CAGE AND PLANTATION' SILVER, PEARL, BRASS, STEEL

UNTITLED IRON, SILVER, BRASS, COPPER

DAI XIANG NORWAY

ARTEMIS ZAFRANA GREECE

PENDANT WHITE THASSOS-MARBLE AND 750 GOLD

RING WHITE THASSOS-MARBLE AND 750 GOLD

ALEXIEVA ZWETELINA BULGARIA

COLLIER 'SENTINEL' SILVER, BLACK RHODINATED, HEMATITE BEADS

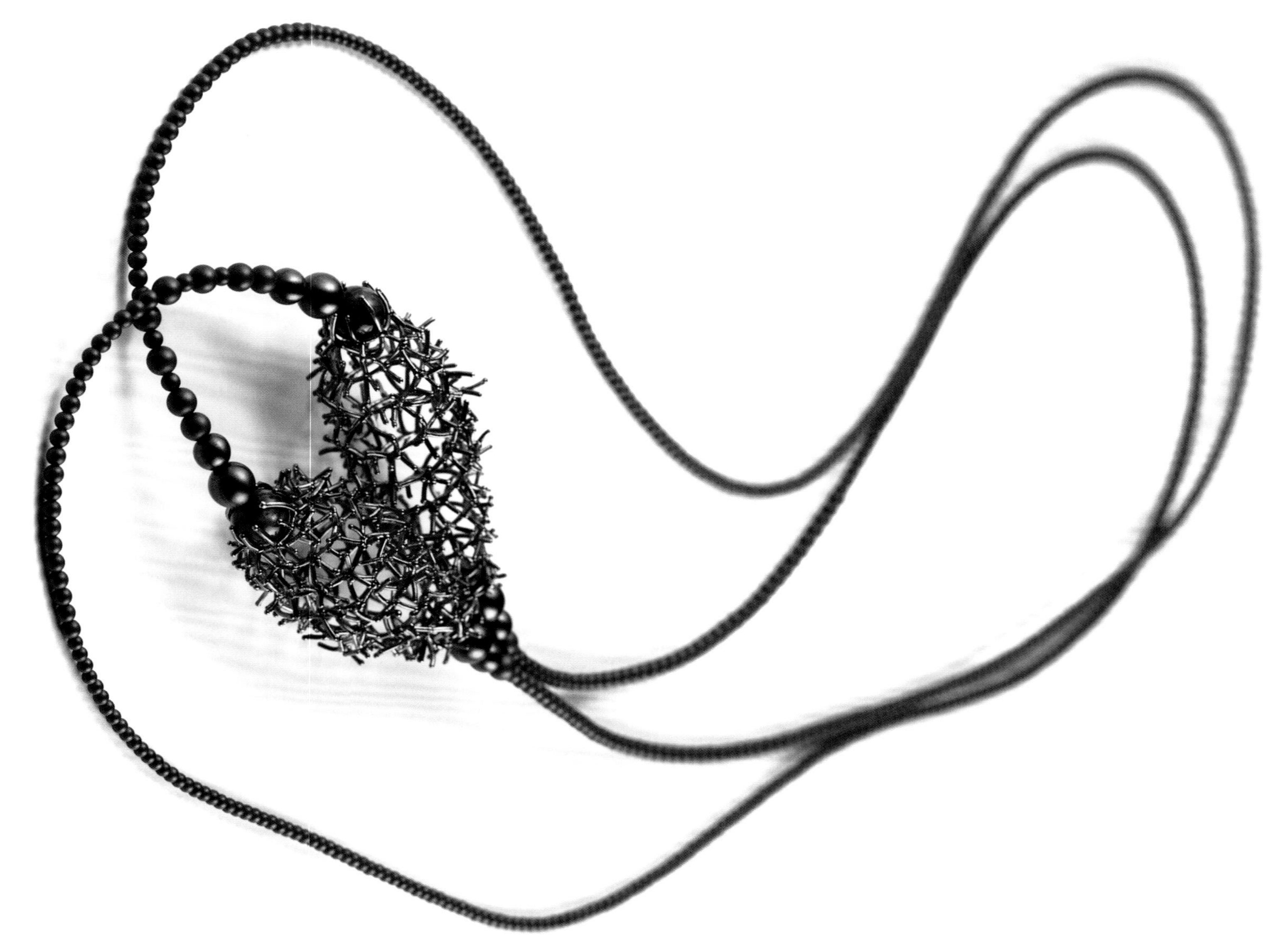

MARINA ZACHOU GREECE

UNTITLED BRONZE (OXIDIZED), SILVER, STEEL WIRE, QUARTZ, PAPER ROSES, SWAROWSKY CRYSTALS, LAMINATED OLD PHOTOGRAPH, LAMINATED COPY OF POEM

MI-MI MOSCOW
RUSSIA

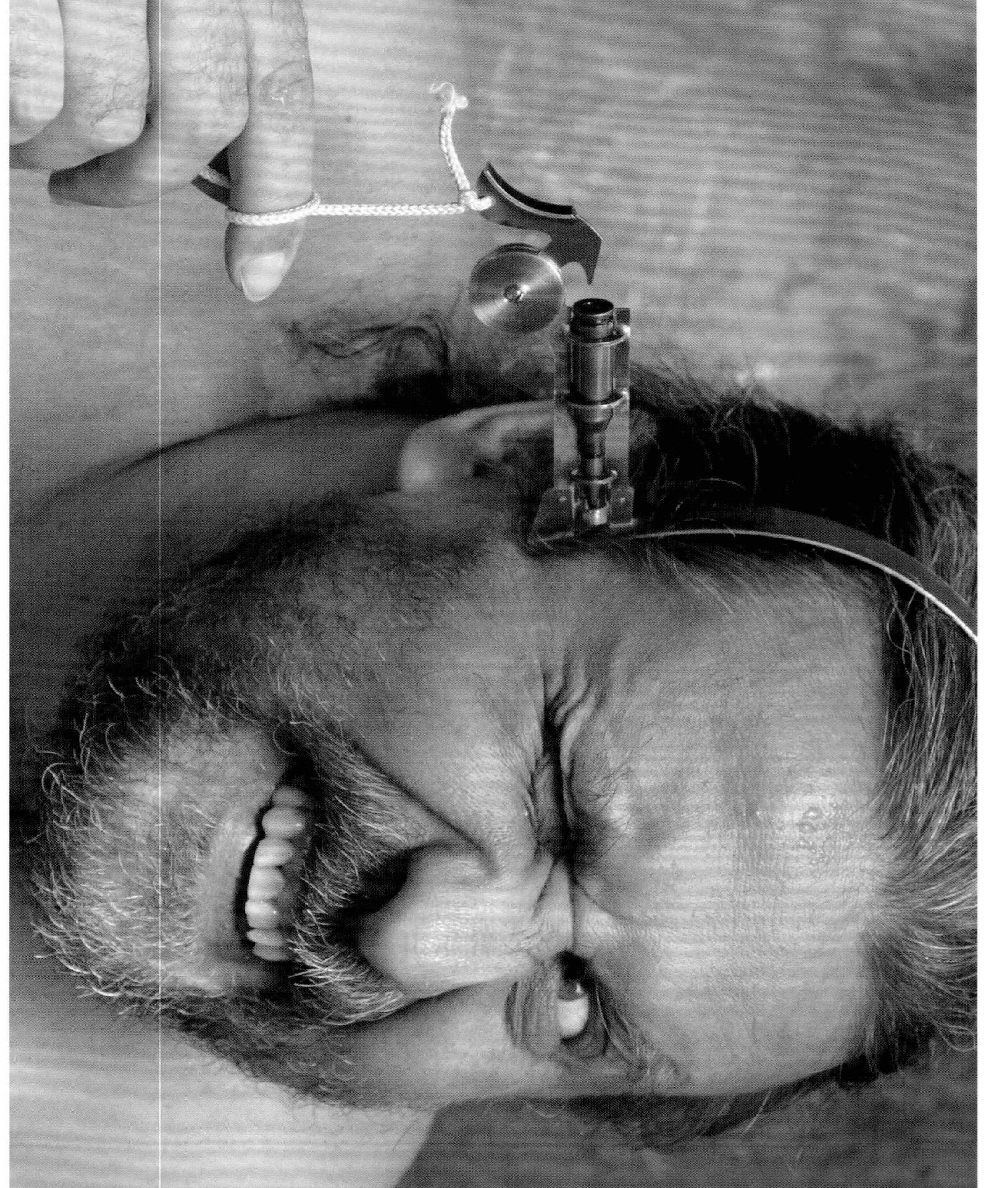

DIADEM 'DON'T MISS'
AK-CATRIDGE, MELHIOR, CORD

BROOCH 'FUCK THIS SOCKET AND BE BETTER' ELECTRIC-SOCKET, WOOD, GOOD MOOD

BROOCH 'SAINT SEBASTIAN' FORK, ART-COOKING EGGS

MI-MI MOSCOW RUSSIA

HANDBAG 'SALOMEA NON-STOP' EPOXY, MELHIOR, BRASS, STEEL, VELVET

PENDENT 'NEDVARVAN I' AMBOINA WOOD, SILVER

MARTINA DEMPF GERMANY

SELECTED ARTISTS

FARRAH AL-DUJAILI
UK

Photo p. 30-33: Farrah Al-Dujaili
Portrait photo: Farrah Al-Dujaili

LUIS ACOSTA
THE NETHERLANDS

Photo p. 34-35: Luis Acosta
Portrait photo: Luis Acosta

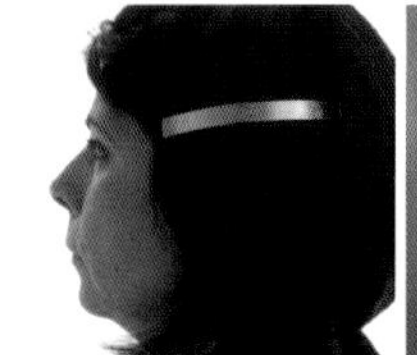

ANA ALBUQUERQUE
PORTUGAL

Photo p. 36: Gonçalo Villa Freitas
Portrait photo: Gonçalo Villa Freitas

NANCY AILLERY
BELGIUM

Photo p. 37: Nancy Aillery
Portrait photo: unknown

IRIS ALGOM
CANADA

Photo p. 38-39: Tanya King
Portrait photo: unknown

ESTEFANIA ALMEIDA
PORTUGAL

Photo p. 40: Hector Olguin
Portrait photo: Hector Olguin

ALIDRA ALIĆ
DENMARK

Photo p. 41: Dorte Krogh
Portrait photo: Katrine Rohberg

INÊS ALMEIDA
PORTUGAL

Photo p. 42-43: André Lima
Portrait photo: Inês Almeida

LAURA ALVARADO
VIVIAN MELLER GERMANY

Photo p. 28/44-45: Laura Alvarado
Portrait photo: Philipp Imlau

PATRICIA ALVAREZ
ARGENTINA

Photo p. 46-47: Patricia Pineyro
Portrait photo: unknown

RINALDO ALVAREZ
SPAIN

Photo p. 48-51: Fotojuanma Tapia
Portrait photo: Fotojuanma Tapia

KARIN ROY ANDERSON
SWEDEN

Photo p. 52-53: Karin Roy Anderson
Portrait photo: Pernilla Persson

MIRIAM ARENTZ
GERMANY

Photo p. 54-55: Juliane Halsinjer/Caphuatia
Portrait photo: Juliane Halsinjer/Caphuatia

NEVIN ARIG
BELGIUM

Photo p. 56-57: Nevin Arig
Portrait photo: Nevin Arig

YASAR AYDIN
SWEDEN

Photo p. 58-59: Tobias Alm
Portrait photo: Tobias Alm

IACOV AZUBEL
ARGENTINA

Photo p. 60-61: Iacov Azubel
Portrait photo: Valeria Budasoff

GIJS BAKKER
THE NETHERLANDS

Photo p. 62: Philippe Kafer
Photo p. 63-65: Rien Bazen
Portrait photo: Yoshiaki Tsutsui

SHIRLY BAR
ISRAËL

Photo p. 66-67: Boaz Nobelman
Portrait photo: Yaniv Kneller

GIAN LUCA
BARTELLONE ITALY

Photo p. 68: Waldemar Kerschbaumer
Portrait photo: Waldemar Kerschbaumer

BENJAMÍN BAZÁN
LOLA SOCAS SPAIN

Photo p. 69: Benjamín Bazán Garcia
Portrait photo: Benjamín Bazán Garcia

ROSALBA BALSAMO
ITALY

Photo p. 70: Riccardo de Antonis
Photo p. 71: Filippo Vinardi
Portrait photo: Francesca Romana Martino

ALINE BERDICHEVSKY
SPAIN

Photo p. 72-73: Aline Berdichevsky
Portrait photo: Oriol Miralles Castello

ANNE-MARIE BERNHARDT
SWEDEN

Photo p. 74-75: unknown
Portrait photo: unknown

CECILE BERTRAND
BELGUIM

Photo p. 76-77: Odile Joëssel
Portrait photo: Odile Joëssel

RAQUEL BESSUDO
MEXICO

Photo p. 78-79: Paolo Gori
Portrait photo: Renee Harari

CHRISTINA BIZZARRO
DENMARK

Photo p. 80-81: Fintan Damgaard
Portrait photo: Reno Bizzarro

TITTI BJERNÉR
SWEDEN

Photo p. 82-83: Titti Bjernér
Portrait photo: unknown

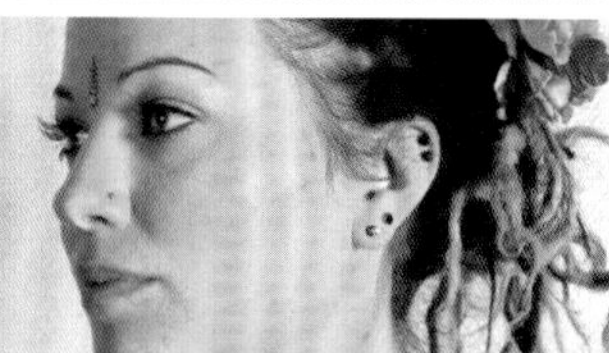

LISA BJÖRKE
SWEDEN

Photo p. 84-85: Lisa Björke
Portrait photo: Madelene Jonsson

ALEXANDER BLANK
GERMANY

Photo p. 86-87: Mirei Takeuchi
Portrait photo: Mirei Takeuchi

JUDITH BLOEDJES
THE NETHERLANDS

Photo p. 88: Geert Kerter
Photo p. 89: Tom Haartsen
Portrait photo: Geert Kerter

MARTA BOAN
SPAIN

Photo p. 90: Marta Boan
Portrait photo: Marta Boan

SOFIE BOONS
UK

Photo p. 91: Sofie Boons
Photo p. 92-93: Marie-José Van den Hout
Portrait photo: Kristof Vranken

ELEANOR BOLTON
UK

Photo p. 94-95: Alec McGhie
Portrait photo: Alec McGhie

FEMKE BOSCHKER
THE NETHERLANDS

Photo p. 96: Femke Boschker
Portrait photo: Femke Boschker

STEPHEN BOTTOMLEY
UK

Photo p. 97: Shannon Tofts
Portrait photo: Elizabeth Turrell

JONATHAN MATHEW BOYD
UK

Photo p. 98-99: unknown
Portrait photo: unknown

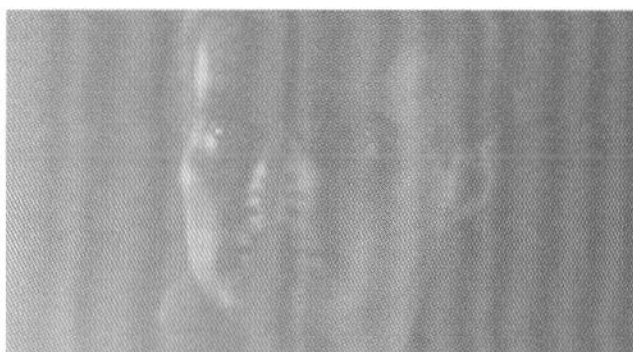

FRÉDÉRIC BRAHAM
FRANCE

Photo p. 100-101: Frédéric Braham
Portrait photo: Paul Duvochel

CATALINA BRENES
ITALY

Photo p. 102-103: Federico Cavicchioli
Portrait photo: Riccardo Rivello

LILIA BREYTER
ARGENTINA

Photo p. 104-105: Damian Wasser
Portrait photo: Paula Breyter

HELEN BRITTON
GERMANY

Photo p. 106-109: Dirk Eisel
Portrait photo: Dirk Eisel

SIGURD BRONGER
NORWAY

Photo p.110-111: Sigurd Bronger
Portrait photo: Hans Thorwid

BEATRICE BROVIA
SWEDEN

Photo p.112-113: Beatrice Brovia
Portrait photo: Nicolas Cheng

KIM BUCK
DENMARK

Photo p. 114-115: Kim Buck
Portrait photo: Camilla Hey

EVA BURTON
SPAIN

Photo p. 116-117: Silvia Walz
Portrait photo: Cecilia Tasso

YURY BYLKOV
RUSSIA

Photo p. 118-119: Yury Bylkov
Portrait photo: Karina Lebedeva

AMANDA CAINES
UK

Photo p. 120: Andra Nelki
Portrait photo: Andra Nelki

ROXANNE CASALE
ARGENTINA

Photo p. 121: Pablo Mehanna
Portrait photo: Pablo Mehanna

MELISSA CAMERON
USA

Photo p.122-123: Melissa Cameron
Portrait photo: Melissa Cameron

JOAQUIM CAPDEVILLA
SPAIN

Photo p. 124: Sergi Ballesté
Photo p. 125-126: Josep Casanova
Photo p. 127: Ramon Manent
Portrait photo: Roger Casas

JICHANG CHAI
UK

Photo p. 128-129: Richard Xu
Portrait photo: Jichang Chai/Richard Xu

JACQUI CHAN
AUSTRALIA

Photo p. 130: Jeremy Dillon
Photo p. 131: Jacqui Chan
Portrait photo: Ernesto Rios

DANIA CHELMINSKY
ISRAËL

Photo p. 132-133: Ran Erde
Portrait photo: Ran Erde

ATTAI CHEN
GERMANY

Photo p. 134: Attai Chen
Portrait photo: Carina Chitsaz-Shoshtary

NICOLAS CHENG
SWEDEN

Photo p. 135: Nicolas Cheng
Portrait photo: unknown

DAVID CHOI
USA

Photo p. 136: David Choi
Portrait photo: unknown

CARINA CHITSAZ-SHOSHTARY GERMANY

Photo p. 137: Mirei Takeuchi
Portrait photo: Michaela Harfst

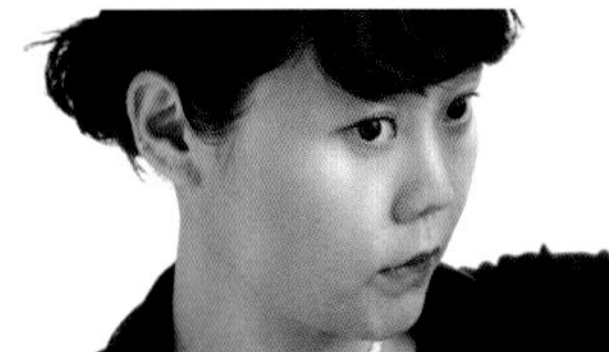

JEEHYUN CHUNG
UK

Photo p. 138-139: Kwang Choon Park
Portrait photo: Kwang Choon Park

THEA CLARK
USA

Photo p. 140: Steven Brian Samuels
Photo p. 141: Terry Greene
Portrait photo: Natalie Dix

EIMEAR CONYARD
IRELAND

Photo p. 142-143: Roy Moore
Portrait photo: Patrick Moore

ANA COUTO
PORTUGAL

Photo p.144: Rodrigo Cabral
Portrait photo: Gerardo Santos

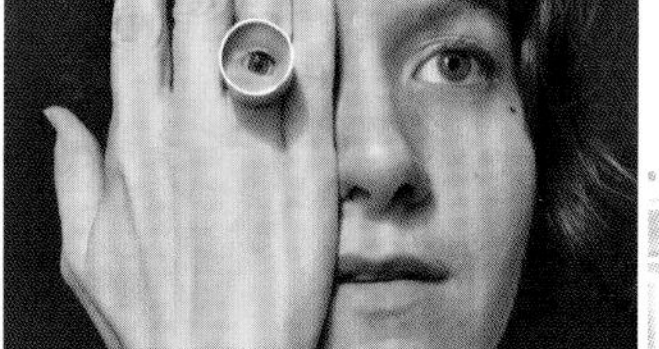

FRÉDÉRIQUE COOMANS
BELGIUM

Photo p. 145: Anne-Lyse Chopin
Portrait photo: Anne-Lyse Chopin

ELS CUVELIER
THE NETHERLANDS

Photo p. 146: Els Cuvelier
Portrait photo: unknown

RAMÓN PUIG CUYÀS
SPAIN

Photo p. 146-149: Ramón Puig Cuyàs
Portrait photo: Artur Puig Walz

JOHANNA DAHM
SWITZERLAND

Photo p. 150-151: Reinhard Zimmermann
Portrait photo: Ingrid Ferreira

ANNETTE DAM
DENMARK

Photo p. 152-153: Dorte Krogh
Portrait photo: Charlotte Due

TERESA DANTAS
PORTUGAL

Photo p. 154-155: Teresa Dantas
Portrait photo: Teresa Dantas

ALEXANDER DAUVIT
UK

Photo p. 156-157: Neilson Photography
Portrait photo: Simon Murphy

SYLVIA DE LA VEGA
SPAIN

Photo p. 158: Jesús Ángel Vega
Portrait photo: Jesús Ángel Vega

DAAN DE DECKER
BELGIUM

Photo p. 159: Paul Ielegems
Portrait photo: Paul Ielegems

TINE DE RUYSSER
UK

Photo p. 160-161: Tine De Ruysser
Portrait photo: Rik De Ruysser

JULIA DE VILLE
AUSTRALIA

Photo p. 162-163: Terence Bogue
Portrait photo: Luzena Adams

MARIELLE DEBETHUNE
FRANCE

Photo p. 164-165: Marielle Debethune
Portrait photo: Marielle Debethune

SIEGFRIED DEBUCK
BELGIUM

Photo p. 166: Michèle Francken
Photo p. 167: Didier Verriest
Portrait photo: Luc Gees

MARIE CLAIRE DESMEDT
BELGIUM

Photo p. 168: Marie Claire Desmedt
Portrait photo: Kari Decock

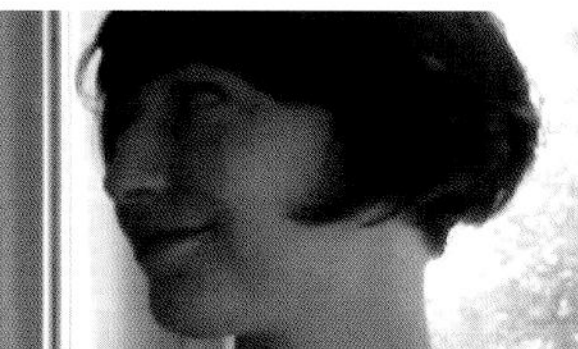

MARION DELARUE
FRANCE

Photo p. 169: Marion Delarue
Portrait photo: Marion Delarue

MARTINA DEMPF
GERMANY

Photo p. 170-173: Sebastian Ahlers
Photo p. 562-563: Sebastian Ahlers
Portrait photo: Axel Krause

IRIS MONDELAERS
BELGIUM

Photo p. 174: Koen Lemmens
Portrait photo: Denise Keris

CATARÌNA DIAS
PORTUGAL

Photo p. 175: João Dias
Portrait photo: João Dias

LAURENT DIOT
BELGIUM

Photo p. 176-177: Roland Cindy
Portrait photo: Jean-Marie Delcroix

JOUNGMEE DO
AUSTRALIA

Photo p. 178-179: Jeremy Dillen
Portrait photo: Sotha Bourn

JAN DONALDSON
AUSTRALIA

Photo p. 180-181: Jeremy Dillon
Portrait photo: Serana Hunt

JANEA DRESLER
GERMANY

Photo p. 182-183: Max Hofmann
Portrait photo: Max Hofmann

MARIE-ANGE DUMONT
BELGIUM

Photo p. 184-185: Dominique Demaseure
Portrait photo: Dominique Demaseure

SAM THO DUONG
GERMANY

Photo p. 186-187: Petra Jaschke
Portrait photo: Petra Jaschke

SUSANNE ELSTNER
GERMANY

Photo p. 188-189: Kai Schlender
Portrait photo: Uwe Klose

SINA EMRICH
GERMANY

Photo p. 190-191: Sina Emrich
Portrait photo: unknown

LINDA EZERMAN
THE NETHERLANDS

Photo p. 192: Linda Ezerman
Portrait photo: Willem Ezerman

LINNÉA ERIKSSON
SWEDEN

Photo p. 193: Linnéa Eriksson
Portrait photo: Linnéa Eriksson

TERESA FARIS
USA

Photo p. 194-195: Teresa Faris
Portrait photo: Unknown

RÉKA FEKETE
THE NETHERLANDS

Photo p. 196-197: Réka Fekete
Portrait photo: Sal Jua Bosman

MIRLA FERNANDES
BRAZIL

Photo p. 198-199: Bianca Viani
Portrait photo: Bianca Viani

JANTJE FLEISCHUT
THE NETHERLANDS

Photo p. 200-201: Wouter Stelwagen
Portrait photo: Unknown

ELINE FRANSEN
BELGIUM

Photo p. 202-203: Lieven Herreman
Portrait photo: Christophe Ketels

ARATA FUCHI
ITALY

Photo p. 204-205: Ichiro Usuda
Portrait photo: Yuki Kamiya

MOTOKO FURUHASHI
USA

Photo p. 206-207: Motoko Furuhashi
Portrait photo: Soyeon Kim

GISELE GANNE
UK

Photo p. 208: Gisele Ganne
Portrait photo: Unknown

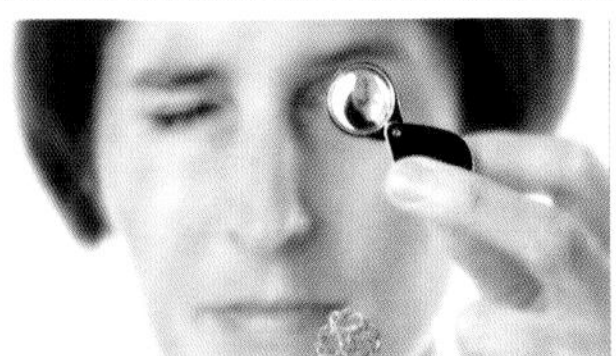

BETTINA GEISTLICH
SWITZERLAND

Photo p. 209: Roland Spring
Portrait photo: Sandra Stampfli

KAREN GILBERT
USA

Photo p. 210-211: Karen Gilbert
Portrait photo: Paul Pavlak

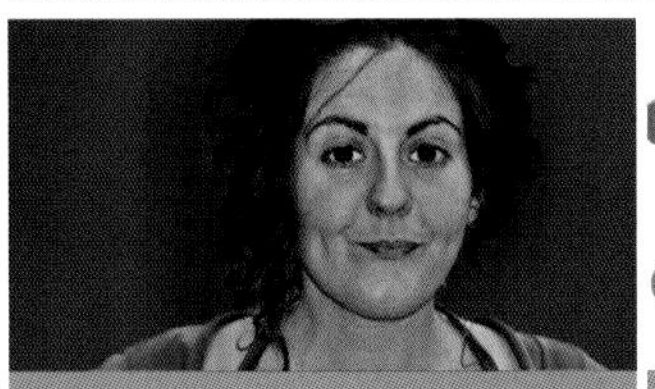

EVA GIRBES
SPAIN

Photo p. 18-21: Eva Girbes
Portrait photo: Albert Gil López

SUZANNE GOLDEN
USA

Photo p. 212-213: Robert Diamante
Portrait photo: Suzanne Golden

CAROLINE GORE
USA

Photo p. 214-215: Caroline Gore
Portrait photo: Mary Whalen

JED GREEN
UK

Photo p. 216-217: Russell Sadur
Portrait photo: M. Green

KATIE GRUBER
AUSTRIA

Photo p. 218-219: Federico Cavicchioli
Portrait photo: Stefan Liewehr

TAMARA GRÜNER
GERMANY

Photo p. 220: gallery for Art and Design Schmuckwelten Pforzheim,Germany
Photo p. 221: Tamara Grüner
Portrait photo: Thomas Nagel

MICHAEL GUERISSE
PHILIPPE HUMBEECK
BELGIUM

Photo p. 222-223: Ta Yang Hsu (WAH studio)/Javier Barcala/Ismael Moumin
Portrait photo: unknown

PREETI GUPTA
VIVEK PRASAD
INDIA

Photo p. 224-225: Preeti Gupta
Portrait photo: Amrita Gupta

GÉSINE HACKENBERG
THE NETHERLANDS

Photo p. 226-227: Gésine Hackenberg
Portrait photo: Thomas Heere

REBECCA HANNON
CANADA

Photo p. 228-229: Rebecca Hannon
Portrait photo: Anton Christianser

MARGIT HART
AUSTRIA

Photo p. 230: Atelier CJP, Vienna
Portrait photo: Fritz Maierhofer

ARIANE HARTMANN
GERMANY

Photo p. 231: Arianne Hartmann
Portrait photo: Ariane Hartmann

LIISA HASHIMOTO
JAPAN

Photo p. 232-233: Atsushi Hashimoto
Portrait photo: Atsushi Hashimoto

INEKE HEERKENS
THE NETHERLANDS

Photo p. 234-235: Eddo Hartmann
Portrait photo: Wendelien Daan

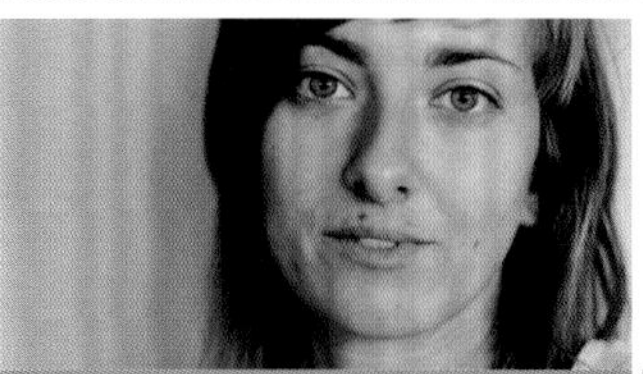

MIA HEBIB
USA

Photo p. 236: Joe Gold/Christina Tisi-Kramer
Portrait photo: Frank Ishman

HANNAH HEDMAN
SWEDEN

Photo p. 24-27: Sanna Lindberg
Portrait photo: Sanna Lindberg

MARIA HEES
THE NETHERLANDS

Photo p. 237: Maria Hees
Portrait photo: Peter Van Der Ham

ANNA HEINDL
AUSTRIA

Photo p. 238-239: Manfred Wakolbinger
Portrait photo: Manfred Wakolbinger

MARLEEN HENOT
BELGIUM

Photo p. 240-241: David Huycke
Portrait photo: unknown

HEIDEMARIE HERB
ITALY

Photo p. 242-243: Silvana Tili
Portrait photo: Silvana Tili

LOLA MOLINA
HERNANDEZ SPAIN

Photo p. 244-245: Mari Angeles 'Maki'
Portrait photo: Mari Angeles 'Maki'

PAVEL HERYNEK
CZECH REPUBLIC

Photo p. 246: Jan Herynek
Portrait photo: Tomas Herynek

SOPHIE HEYMANS
BELGIUM

Photo p. 247: Bert Vanderlinden
Portrait photo: Sabine Moulaert

LEONOR HIPOLITO
PORTUGAL

Photo p. 248-249: Arne Kaiser
Portrait photo: Arne Kaiser

LYDIA HIRTE
GERMANY

Photo p. 250-251: Jürgen Kossatz
Portrait photo: Jürgen Kossatz

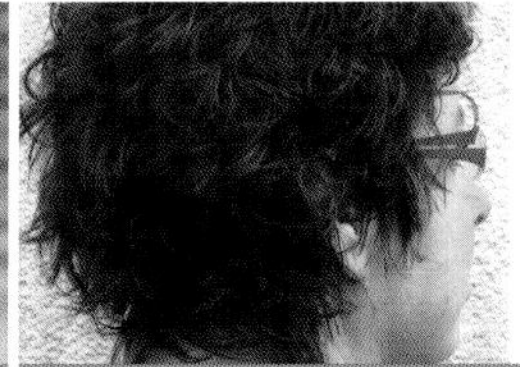

SUSANNE HOLZINGER
GERMANY

Photo p. 252-253: Suzanne Holzinger
Portrait photo: Suzanne Holzinger

PETER HOOGEBOOM
THE NETHERLANDS

Photo p. 254-257: Francis Willemstijn
Portrait photo: Peter Heij

KARINA HUNNERUP
DENMARK

Photo p. 258: James Bates
Portrait photo: Bjarke Broby

HEEJIN HWANG
USA

Photo p. 259: Jim Escalante
Portrait photo: Heejin Hwang

FRANCESC OLIVERAS I BALLUS SPAIN

Photo p. 260-261: David Campos Bel
Portrait photo: David Campos Bel

IRIS SAAR ISAACS
AUSTRALIA

Photo p. 262: David Higgs
Photo p. 263: Ben Hermans Product
Portrait photo: Paul Wesley Smith

REIKO ISHIYAMA
USA

Photo p. 264-265: David Katz
Portrait photo: Yasushi Nakamura

MELANIE ISVERDING
GERMANY

Photo p. 266: Melanie Isverding
Photo p. 267: Mirei Takeuchi
Portrait photo: Alexander Blank

MARGIT JAESCHKE
GERMANY

Photo p. 268-269: Uwe Koehn
Portrait photo: unknown

HELENA JOHANSSON
SWEDEN

Photo p. 270-271: Helena Johansson
Portrait photo: Jan EK

SVENJA JOHN
GERMANY

Photo p. 272: Tivador Nemesi
Photo p. 273: Svenja John
Portrait photo: Marion Schoenenberger

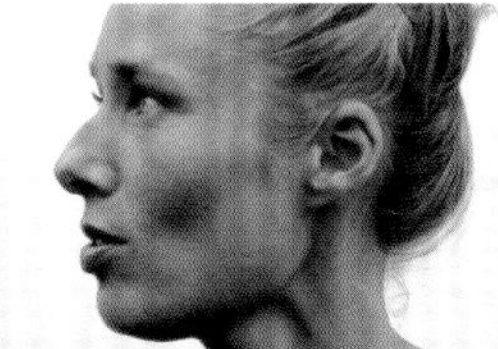

HILDUR YR JONSDOTTIR
ICELAND

Photo p. 274-275: Tamas Juhasz
Portrait photo: Brynhildur Palsdottir

HANNAH JORIS
BELGIUM

Photo p. 276: David Huycke
Photo p. 277: Hannah Joris
Portrait photo: Marleen Henot

KAORI JUZU
DENMARK

Photo p. 278-279: Anders Sune Berg
Portrait photo: Per Suntum

JIRO KAMATA
GERMANY

Photo p. 280-281: Gesa Simons
Portrait photo: Gesa Simons

DAEHOON KANG
AUSTRALIA

Photo p. 282-285: Jeremy Dillen
Portrait photo: Sotha Bourn

KEPA KARMONA
SPAIN

Photo p. 286-287: Kepa Karmona
Portrait photo: Kepa Karmona

MAKI KAWAWA
JAPAN

Photo p. 288-289: Seli
Portrait photo: Kimiaki Kageyama

BEPPE KESSLER
THE NETHERLANDS

Photo p. 290-291: Beppe Kessler
Portrait photo: Dolph Kessler

CHRISTINE KEYEUX
BELGIUM

Photo p. 292: Héloise Berns
Portrait photo: E. Maes

YONG JOO KIM
USA

Photo p. 293: Affandi Setiawan
Photo p. 294-295: Studio Munch
Portrait photo: Affandi Setiawan

INARI KIURU
AUSTRALIA

Photo p. 296-297: Inari Kiuru
Portrait photo: Marc Bennett

BEATE KLOCKMANN
THE NETHERLANDS

Photo p. 298-299: Beate Klockmann
Portrait photo: unknown

ANETTE KRAEN
DENMARK

Photo p. 300: Uffe Johansen
Portrait photo: unknown

YAEL KRAKOWSKI
CANADA

Photo p. 301: Yael Krakowski
Portrait photo: Yael Krakowski

JANTINE KROEZE
THE NETHERLANDS

Photo p. 302: Frank Penders
Portrait photo: Marie Cécile Thijs

DANIEL KRUGER
GERMANY

Photo p. 303: Udo W. Beier
Portrait photo: Matthias Ritzmann

JULIA MARIA KÜNNAP
ESTONIA

Photo p. 304-305: Ulvi Tiit
Portrait photo: Margus Johanson

AN-FEN KUO
TAIWAN

Photo p. 306-307: An-Fen Kuo
Portrait photo: An-Fen Kuo

DOMINIQUE LABORDERY
GERMANY

Photo p. 308-309: Dominique Labordery
Portrait photo: Markus Lienert

BIRGIT LAKEN
THE NETHERLANDS

Photo p. 310-311: Brigit Laken
Portrait photo: Iris Blancardi-De Jong

LORE LANGENDRIES
BELGIUM

Photo p. 312: Lore Langendries
Photo p. 313: Dimitri Lowette
Portrait photo: Dimitri Lowette

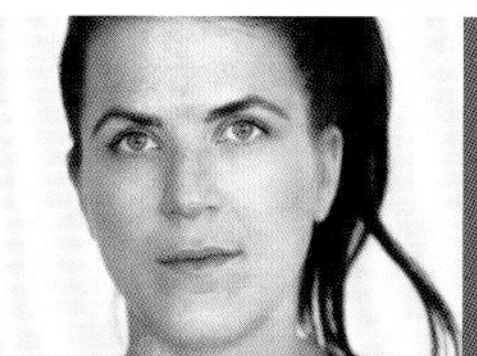

AGNES LARSSON
SWEDEN

Photo p. 314-315: Agnes Larsson
Portrait photo: Carl Dahlstedt

CLAIRE LAVENDHOMME
BELGIUM

Photo p. 316: Christophe Louergli
Portrait photo: Aurelia Declercq

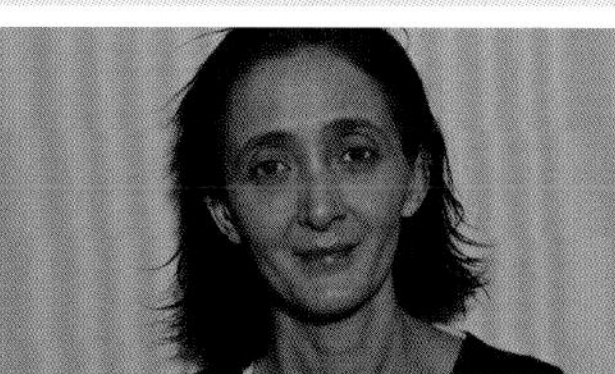

EINAT LEADER
ISRAEL

Photo p. 317: Einat Leader
Portrait photo: Ruti Goss

ELISABETH LEENKNEGT
BELGIUM

Photo p. 318-319: Stefanie Geerts
Portrait photo: Eddy Vangroenderbeek

ANNAMARIA LEISTE
GERMANY

Photo p. 320-321: Mirei Takeuchi
Portrait photo: Manu Theobald

GUANLAN LIANG
GERMANY

Photo p. 322: Udo Beier
Photo p. 323: Daniel Kruger
Portrait photo: Su Gao

PATRICIA LEMAIRE
FRANCE

Photo p. 324: Ecliptique
Portrait photo: Martine Denis

SARI LIIMATTA
FINLAND

Photo p. 325: Sari Liimata
Portrait photo: Sari Liimata

FELIX LINDER
GERMANY

Photo p. 326: Font-Sala Samantha
Portrait photo: Font-Sala Samantha

YU-PING LIN
UK

Photo p. 327: Yu-Ping Lin
Portrait photo: Carol Lin

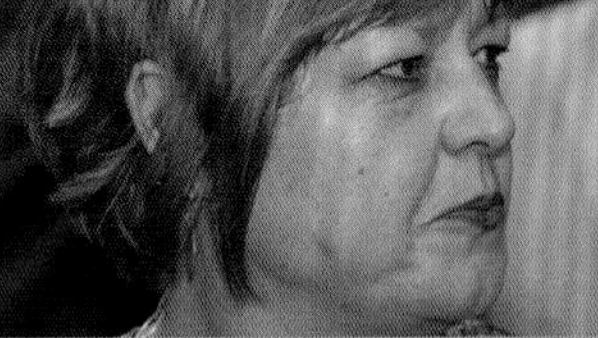

RIA LINS
BELGIUM

Photo p. 328-329: Dries Van den Brande
Portrait photo: Mark Lins

BLANDINE LUCE
FRANCE

Photo p. 330-331: Imagitrame
Portrait photo: unknown

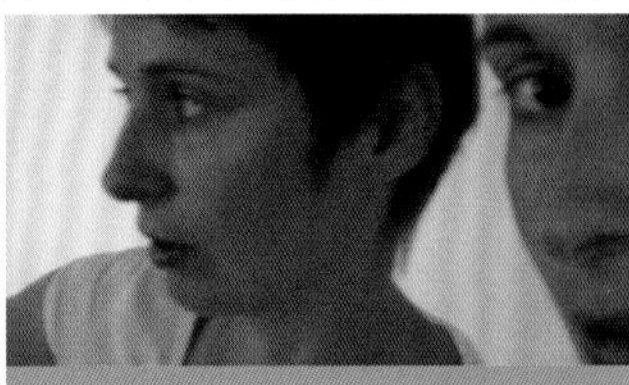

JANA MACHATOVA
SLOVAKIA

Photo p. 332-333: Peter Machata
Portrait photo: Jana Machatova

ALISON MACLEOD
UK

Photo p. 334: Colin Tennant
Portrait photo: Alison Macleod

MIRCA MAFFI
SWITZERLAND

Photo p. 335: Gian Marco Castelberg
Portrait photo: Gian Marco Castelberg

MIA MALJOJOKI
FINLAND

Photo p. 336-337: Mirei Takeuchi
Portrait photo: Conny Marshaus

PATRICK MARCHAL
BELGIUM

Photo p. 338/341: Patrick Marchal
Photo p. 339: J.P. Pfister
Portrait photo: Patrick Marchal

GIGI MARIANI
ITALY

Photo p. 342-343: Paolo Terzi
Portrait photo: Paolo Terzi

TUIJA HELENA MARKON-SALO FINLAND

Photo p. 344-345: Kalle Kataila
Portrait photo: Helena Markonsalo

CAROLINA MARTINEZ LIN-ARE GERMANY

Photo p. 346-347: Daniel Klimsch Photodesign
Portrait photo: Daniel Klimsch Photodesign

MÂRTA MATTSSON
SWEDEN

Photo p. 348-349: Märta Mattsson
Portrait photo: Anna Larsson

JUDY MCCAIG
SPAIN

Photo p. 350-351: Jose Coello
Portrait photo: Jose Coello

EMMA MCFARLINE
UK

Photo p. 352: Emma McFarline
Portrait photo: Danny McFarline

TIMOTHY MCMAHON
USA

Photo p. 353: Timothy McMahon
Portrait photo: Russell Denniston

TERESA MILHEIRO
PORTUGAL

Photo p. 354-355: Teresa Milheiro
Portrait photo: Luis Pais

MARILIA MARIA MIRA
PORTUGAL

Photo p. 356-359: Manuel Portugal
Portrait photo: Manuel Portugal

DARCY MIRO
USA

Photo p. 360-361: Elizabeth Waugh
Portrait photo: Glynis Selina Arban

KATHARINA MOCH
GERMANY

Photo p. 362-363: Elena Ruebel
Portrait photo: Gerhard Moch

IRENE MORET
ITALY

Photo p. 364: Irene Moret
Photo p. 365: Mario Piccaluga
Portrait photo: Irene Moret

EDGAR MOSA
USA

Photo p. 366: Edgard Mosa
Photo p. 367: Edgard Mosa & Ben Schonenberger
Portrait photo: Edgard Mosa

ROSA NOGUÉS FREIXAS
SPAIN

Photo p. 368/370: Paul Ruz
Photo p. 369/371: Rosa Nogués
Portrait photo: Paul Ruz

TED NOTEN
THE NETHERLANDS

Photo p. 2/12-15: Atelier Ted Noten
Portrait photo: Atelier Ted Noten

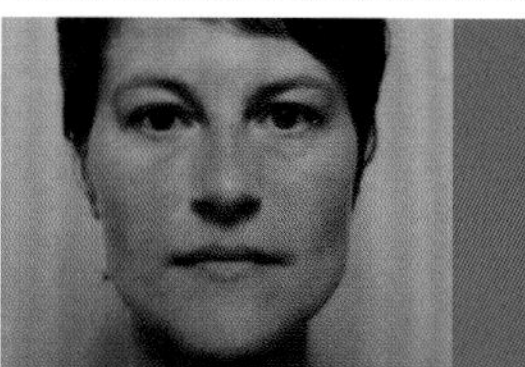

GITTE NYGAARD
THE NETHERLANDS

Photo p. 372-373: Gitte Nygaard
Portrait photo: unknown

KRISTI PAAP
ESTONIA

Photo p. 374-375: Kristi Paap
Portrait photo: Kulli Paap

TATIANA PAGES
USA

Photo p.376-377: unknown
Portrait photo: unknown

GUSTAVO PARADISO
ARGENTINA

Photo p.378-379: Gustavo Paradiso
Portrait photo: Gustavo Paradiso

FONT-SALA SAMANTHA PE/AH
GERMANY

Photo p. 380-381: Font-Sala Samantha
Portrait photo: Felix Linder

RUUDT PETERS
THE NETHERLANDS

Photo p. 382-385: Rob Versluys
Portrait photo: unknown

SUSAN PIETZSCH
JAPAN

Photo p. 386: Valentina Seidel
Portrait photo: Shintaro Imai

ANDREA PIÑEIRO
SPAIN

Photo p. 387: Antonio Alcobendas
Portrait photo: Antonio Alcobendas

ANDREA PINEROS
FRANCE

Photo p. 388: Caroline Hache
Photo p. 389: weweje
Portrait photo: unknown

ALICE POTTER
AUSTRALIA

Photo p. 390: Alice Potter
Portrait photo: Kate Potter

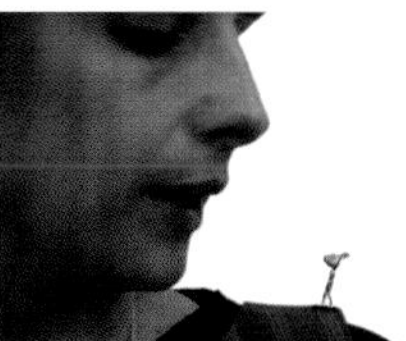

RENATA PORTO
BRAZIL

Photo p. 391: Ananda Campello
Portrait photo: Ananda Campello

BEVERLEY PRICE
SOUTH AFRICA

Photo p. 392: Des Tak
Photo p. 393: Beverly Price
Portrait photo: Hilton Price

KATJA PRINS
THE NETHERLANDS

Photo p. 394-397: Harold Strak
Portrait photo: Sanne Peper

WALKA STUDIO, NANO PULGAR / CLAUDIA BETANCOURT CHILI

Photo p. 398: Karen Clunes
Portrait photo: unknown

TIINA RAJAKALLIO
FINLAND

Photo p. 399: T. Rajakallio
Portrait photo: T. Rajakallio

KAIRE RANNIK
ESTONIA

Photo p. 400-401: Kaire Rannik
Portrait photo: Denes Farkas

ULI RAPP
THE NETHERLANDS

Photo p. 402: Uli Rapp
Portrait photo: Vincent de Waard

JORDAN REMBRANDT
BELGIUM

Photo p. 404-405: Johan Blommaert
Portrait photo: Johan Blommaert

DAVE RENPERMETER
NORWAY

Photo p. 403: Peter Vermandere
Portrait photo: Sigfrid Eggers

DENISE JULIA REYTAN
GERMANY

Photo p. 406-409: Denise J. Reytan
Portrait photo: Bodo Vitus

JOANA DA SILVA RIBEIRO PORTUGAL

Photo p. 410-411: Morento Lativo
Portrait photo: Max Laurent

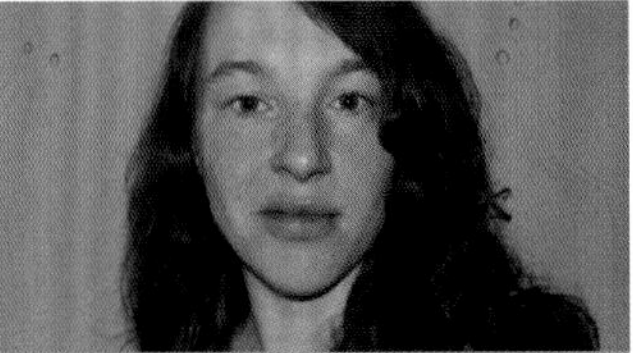

TERESA RICHTER
GERMANY

Photo p. 412-413: Stefan Melko
Portrait photo: Stefan Melko

CORINA RIETVELD
THE NETHERLANDS

Photo p. 414-415: unknown
Portrait photo: Irmgard Geelen

ZOE ROBERTSON
UK

Photo p. 416-417: Zoe Robertson
Portrait photo: Steve Snell

NORA ROCHEL
GERMANY

Photo p. 418: Nora Rochel
Portrait photo: Janusch Tschech

CRISTINA ROQUE
PORTUGAL

Photo p. 419: Tiago Reis
Portrait photo: Joaõ Roque dos Santos

REBECCA ROSE
SPAIN

Photo p. 420-421: Ann Guillermo, Orlando
Portrait photo: Riley Wilkinson, Los Angeles

DEBORAH RUDOLP
GERMANY

Photo p. 422-423: Deborah Rudolph
Portrait photo: Jenna janke

ELENA RUEBEL
GERMANY

Photo p. 424-425: Johanna Ruebel
Portrait photo: Johanna Ruebel

CARMEN AMADOR RUIZ
SPAIN

Photo p. 426: Alexander Steindorff
Photo p. 427: Gonzalo Caceres
Portrait photo: Alexander Steindorff

VANIA RUIZ
CHILI

Photo p. 428: Karen Clunes
Photo p. 429: Valeska Cirano
Portrait photo: Valeska Cirano

JILL RYCKAERT
BELGIUM

Photo p. 430: Jef Marcelis
Portrait photo: Jeroen Boeye

ESTELA SAEZ
THE NETHERLANDS

Photo p. 431: Jordi Puig
Portrait photo: David Castellano

PHILIP SAJET
THE NETHERLANDS

Photo p. 432-433: Beate Klockmann
Portrait photo: Beate Klockmann

GABRIELA SÀNCHEZ Y SANCHEZ DE LA BARQUERA
THE NETHERLANDS

Photo p. 434: Cynthia Salazar
Photo p. 435: Gabriel Monroy
Photo p. 436: Jimea Raminez
Photo p. 437-438: Gabriel Sanchez y SB
Portrait photo: Yorgos Bournousouzis

LUCY SARNEEL
THE NETHERLANDS

Photo p. 438-441: Eric Knoote
Portrait photo: Jelle Kampen

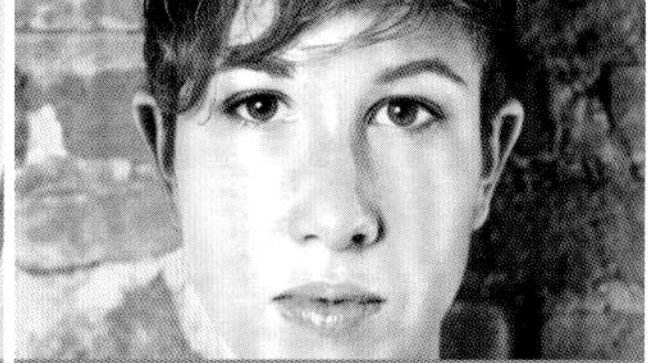

GIULIA SAVINO
ITALY

Photo p. 442-443: Ivan Cintura
Portrait photo: Ivan Cintura

FABRICE SCHAEFER
SWITZERLAND

Photo p. 444-445: Fabrice Schaeffer
Portrait photo: Annick Zufferey

NICOLE SCHUSTER
GERMANY

Photo p. 446-447: Nicole Schuster
Portrait photo: Angela Rauch

CLAUDE SCHMITZ
LUXEMBOURG

Photo p. 448-451: Patrick Muller
Portrait photo: unknown

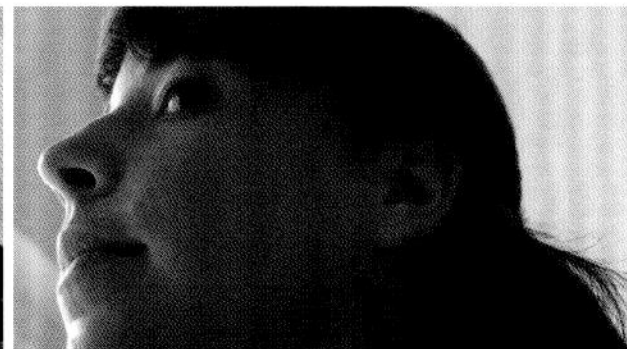

DANNI SCHWAAG
GERMANY

Photo p. 452-453: Danni Schwaag
Portrait photo: Danni Schwaag

PAOLO SCURA
UK

Photo p. 454: Paolo Scura
Portrait photo: Paolo Scura

REGINE SCHWARZER
AUSTRALIA

Photo p. 455: Grant Hancock
Portrait photo: Steve Smith

KARIN SEUFERT
GERMANY

Photo p. 456-457: Karin Seufert
Portrait photo: Tore Svensson

MARINA SHEETIKOFF
BRAZIL

Photo p. 458: Fernando Laszlo
Portrait photo: Renata Siqueira Bueno

ALEXANDRA SOLAR
LUXEMBOURG

Photo p. 459: Anita Dore
Portrait photo: Anita Dore

NATALIE SMITH
UK

Photo p. 460-461: Natalie Smith
Portrait photo: Sheena Smith

MANUELA SOUSA
PORTUGAL

Photo p. 462-463: Rodrigo Cabral
Portrait photo: Miguel Sales Lopes

KATRIN SPRANGER
GERMANY

Photo p. 464: Henning Spranger
Photo p. 465: Gerrit Meier
Portrait photo: Gerrit Meier

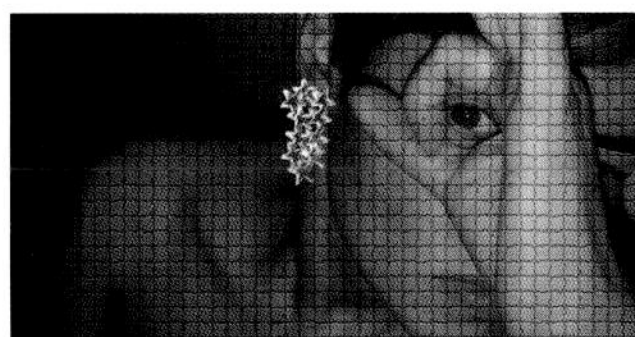

ALIKI MARGARITA STROUMPOULI GREECE

Photo p. 466-481: Aliki Stroumpouli
Portrait photo: Aliki Stroumpouli

GISBERT STACH GERMANY
RÉKA LÖRINCZ HUNGARY

Photo p. 467: Arion Kudasz Gabor
Portrait photo: unknown

NIKI STYLIANOU
GREECE

Photo p. 468-469: Niki Stylianou
Portrait photo: K. Biri

JIE SUN
CHINA

Photo p. 470-471: Jie Sun
Portrait photo: Li Wang

TORE SVENSSON
SWEDEN

Photo p. 472-473: Franz Karl
Portrait photo: Karin Seufert

NELLI TANNER
FINLAND

Photo p. 474-475: Kimmo Heikkilä
Portrait photo: Nelli Tanner

SALIMA THAKKER
BELGIUM

Photo p. 476: Salima Thakker
Portrait photo: Claude Smekens

SABINE THULER
SWITZERLAND

Photo p. 477: Sandra Stampfli
Portrait photo: Sandra Stampfli

KETLI TIITSAR
ESTONIA

Photo p. 478-481: Dénes Farkas
Portrait photo: Diana Didyk

RACHEL TIMMINS
USA

Photo p. 482-483: Joseph Hyde
Portrait photo: Rachel Timmins

JOHANNA TÖRNQVIST
SWEDEN

Photo p.484-485: Johanna Törnqvist
Portrait photo: Tomas Björkdal

FABRIZIO TRIDENTI
ITALY

Photo p. 486-487: Fabrizio Tridenti
Portrait photo: Paolo Tomassin

BARBARA UDERZO
ITALY

Photo p. 488-489: Studio Maraboli
Portrait photo: unknown

MARIA VALDMA
ESTONIA

Photo p. 490-491: Jaan Heinmaa
Portrait photo: Jaan Heinmaa

MERTE VAN DE PERRE
AUSTRALIA

Photo p. 492: Peter Vermandere
Portrait photo: Sigfrid Eggers

ANNA HELENA VAN DE POL DE DEUS ITALY

Photo p. 493: Federico Cavicchioli
Portrait photo: unknown

WILLY VAN DE VELDE
BELGIUM

Photo p. 494-495: Willy Van de Velde
Portrait photo: Willy Van de Velde

MECKY VAN DEN BRINK
THE NETHERLANDS

Photo p. 496-499: Mecky Van Den Brink
Portrait photo: Claartje Keur

CHRISTEL VAN DER LAAN
AUSTRALIA

Photo p. 500-501/503: Adrian Lambert
Photo p. 502: Robert Frith
Portrait photo: Alex Macdonald

FELIEKE VAN DER LEEST
NORWAY

Photo p. 504-507: Eddo Hartmann
Portrait photo: Kay Berg

NELLY VAN OOST
FRANCE

Photo p. 508-511: Carlos Monreal
Portrait photo: Carlos Monreal

ROOS VAN SOEST
THE NETHERLANDS

Photo p. 512-513: Roos van Soest
Portrait photo: Minka Medik

INGEBORG VANDAMME
THE NETHERLANDS

Photo p. 514-515: Peter Hoogeboom
Portrait photo: Ingeborg Vandamme

OCTAVE VANDEWEGHE
BELGIUM

Photo p. 516-519: Bart Vermaercke
Portrait photo: Bart Vermaercke

KAREN VANMOL
BELGIUM

Photo p. 520-521: Karen Vanmol
Portrait photo: Max Decock

TANEL VEENRE
ESTONIA

Photo p. 522-523: Tanel Veenre
Portrait photo: Tanel Veenre

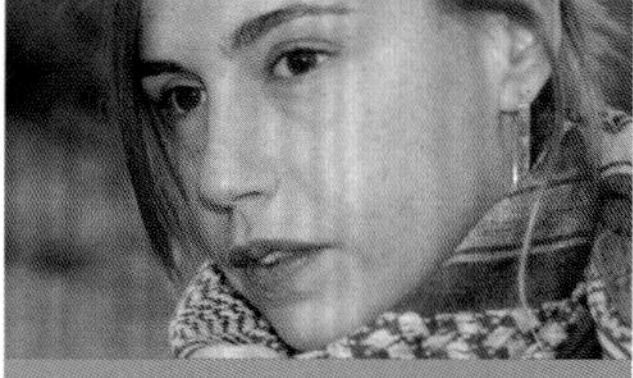

ROCIO VEGAS
SPAIN

Photo p. 524: Rocio Vegas O'Felan
Portrait photo: Rocio Vegas O'Felan

PETER VERMANDERE
BELGIUM

Photo p. 525: Peter Vermandere
Portrait photo: Sigfrid Eggers

BRECHJE VERMAAT
MAARTEN VERSTEEG
THE NETHERLANDS

Photo p. 526: Rob Glastra
Photo p. 527: Hugo Schuitemaker
Portrait photo: Firi den Hoedt

TINE VINDEVOGEL
BELGIUM

Photo p. 528-529: Johan Hespeel
Portrait photo: Tine Vindevogel

ANDREA WAGNER
THE NETHERLANDS

Photo p. 530-531: Andrea Wagner
Portrait photo: Julia Blaukopf

SILVIA WALZ
SPAIN

Photo p. 532-533: Ramón Puig Cuyàs
Portrait photo: Ramón Puig Cuyàs

NORMAN WEBER
GERMANY

Photo p.534-535: Norman Weber
Portrait photo: Christiane Forster

MARINA MOLINELLI WELLS
ARGENTINA

Photo p.536-537: Pablo Mehanna
Portrait photo: Marina Molinelli Wells

ROBIN WERNICKE
AUSTRALIA

Photo p. 538-539: Jeremy Dillon
Portrait photo: Susan Ewington

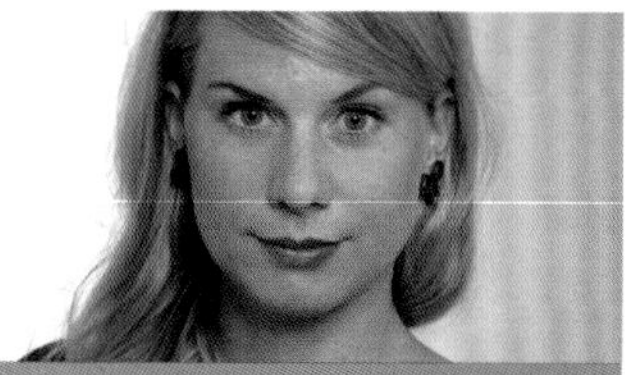

JASMIN WINTER
GERMANY

Photo p. 540-541: Carolin Müller
Portrait photo: Studioline photography

CLAIRE WOLFSTIRN
FRANCE

Photo p. 542: Gilles Cohen
Photo p. 543: Amelie Weirich
Portrait photo: Philippe Vermes

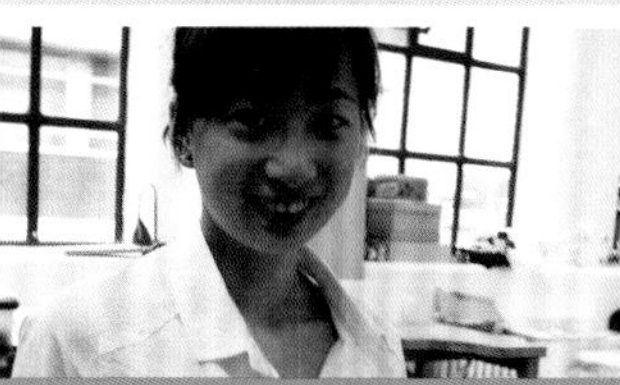

LI- CHU WU
UK

Photo p. 544-545: Mike Inch
Portrait photo: Jo Juan

SHU-LIN WU
TAIWAN

Photo p.546-547: Shu-Lin Wu
Portrait photo: Sophie Hanagarth

KAREN WUYTENS
BELGIUM

Photo p.548-549: Karen Wuytens
Portrait photo: unknown

DAI XIANG
NORWAY

Photo p. 552-553: Mats Ringqvist
Portrait photo: Karin Seufert

MICHELLE XIANOU NI
CHINA

Photo p. 551: Simon Armitt
Portrait photo: Cheng Feng Qing

FRAUKE ZABEL
GERMANY

Photo p. 550: Frauke Zabel
Portrait photo: Sophie Baugärtner

MARINA ZACHOU
GREECE

Photo p. 557: Sofia Papastrati
Portrait photo: Sofia Papastrati

ARTEMIS ZAFRANA
GREECE

Photo p. 554-555: Wolfgang Schotte
Portrait photo: Wolfgang Schotte

ALEXIEVA ZWETELINA
BULGARIA

Photo p. 556: Angel Penchev
Portrait photo: Angel Penchev

MI-MI MOSCOW
RUSSIA

Photo p. 558-561: Mi-Mi Moscow
Portrait photo: Vladimir Asmirko

COLOPHON

Concept and coverdesign
Jaak Van Damme

Jury
Ana Campos (PT)
Martine Dempf (DE)
Dorothy Hogg (UK)
Anne Leclercq (BE)
Jaak Van Damme (BE)

Co-ordination and final Editing
Nika Leys

Layout
www.groupvandamme.eu

Print
www.pureprint.be

Published by
Stichting Kunstboek bvba
Legeweg 165
B-8020 Oostkamp
Belgium
Tel. +32 50 46 19 10
Fax +32 50 46 19 18
info@stichtingkunstboek.com
www.stichtingkunstboek.com

ISBN 978-90-5856-395-8
D/2012/6407/3
NUR : 421